Shelf
Life

MICHAEL ROBB

Shelf
Life

A Journey Through the Past, Present & Future
of Bookselling and Publishing in Britain

For my parents, Joyce and Peter Robb,
for introducing me to books.

First published 2025

The History Press
97 St George's Place, Cheltenham,
Gloucestershire, GL50 3QB
www.thehistorypress.co.uk

British Library Cataloguing in Publication Data.
A catalogue record for this book is available from the British Library.

ISBN 978 1 80399 836 7

Typesetting and origination by The History Press
Printed and bound in Great Britain by TJ Books Limited, Padstow, Cornwall.

Trees for L🌱fe

Contents

Introduction

On Books
and Bookshops

Robbs Bookshop in Chelmsford, Essex, 1984. (Author's collection)

Discovering Books

Like many compulsive readers, I had often dreamed of opening a book-shop. I consider myself very lucky that my parents were booklovers, who read to my brothers and me regularly, sharing the *Just William* novels that my Dad had enjoyed as a child and a whole host of Enid Blyton volumes that my Mum had loved. Through doing this, they instilled in my broth-ers and me not just a love of books but an understanding of the delights to be discovered within their pages.

We all have our own memories of discovering books and each of us will have treasured titles from childhood that are uniquely significant to us – books that helped form our personal reading pathway. My par-ents took us to the library and the two local bookshops: a branch of W.H. Smith and an independent, Clarkes, which was really a stationery and art materials shop with books upstairs. I remember that within the latter there was a separate room for children's books, which had a table and chairs in the centre but was dominated by a big bookcase of Puffin books. I still fondly remember the wonderful feeling of being in that room, surrounded by shelves of interesting-looking books and often being left alone to browse at my leisure.

The first book I remember owning, one bought from Clarkes specifically for me and not just one I shared with my two older brothers, was *Ginger's Adventures*, a Ladybird story in simple verse about a dog called Ginger. Originally published in 1940, it was illustrated by Angusine Jeanne MacGregor, who illustrated many of the early Ladybirds. Memory can be unreliable at such a distance, but I recall reading this edition repeatedly as well as sometimes just looking through the pages at the illustrations.

This is my earliest memory of a direct relationship with a book, when I was probably around 5 or 6 years old. Already, though, I revelled in the ownership of the book and felt a strong attachment to the physical object itself, this treasured possession. From that point onwards, I grew to love books dearly. I also became increasingly obsessed with bookshops. I associated them with something magical, an Aladdin's Cave of riches, and always got excited when a bookshop visit was being planned. The door into a bookshop is the entrance into multiple other worlds and experiences.

As I grew older, I discovered more wonderful books from browsing in bookshops. For a while, I was entranced by the C.S. Lewis Narnia books with their iconic Pauline Baynes illustrations. I loved the experience of being lost in this fantastical other world and read all seven books at least twice. I still possess those original Puffin paperbacks to this day. *The Lion, the Witch and the Wardrobe*, and in particular its beginning, epitomises a very simple truth about reading. As Cathy Rentzenbrink says in *Dear Reader*, '*The Lion, the Witch and the Wardrobe* is not only a cracking story in its own right, but also represents the way every book offers an invitation to open a door and find a way to another world'. Lucy opens the door of a wardrobe, steps inside and finds herself walking from the normal world she knows into the magical world of Narnia, brushing through the snow-covered trees until she comes to the clearing with the lamppost.

The opening of that wardrobe door is, to me, a metaphor for opening the pages of a book. We read books for many reasons, but the most obvious is to be transported to other experiences. It doesn't have to be another world, such as Narnia, but all novels talk to us of experiences different to our own – what life was like for people who lived in earlier centuries or who live in other countries, or who go through experiences we have not.

Another thing that always appealed to me about the Narnia series was that, although the child protagonists entered Narnia and became involved in all sorts of adventures, when they returned to the real world no time had elapsed at all. To me, that seems to sum up the power of a good book – something we can lose ourselves in, detaching ourselves from the world around us, forgetting time and place, entranced only by the book and its alternative reality.

I formed the habit of looking for the next thing to read as soon as one book was finished, always wanting to have a 'book on the go'. In her memoir *Giving Up the Ghost*, Hilary Mantel summed this up perfectly: 'I wanted books like a vampire wants blood.' This habit started in earnest during those early years, moving from Enid Blyton to C.S. Lewis to Roald Dahl and many others, and then on towards more grown-up fare.

As a teenager, I trawled the bookshops to feed my science fiction obsession, seeking more books by Edgar Rice Burroughs, Michael Moorcock and Asimov. And then, when I hit 16, I discovered

George Orwell and bought a succession of the black Penguin paperbacks from Clarkes. Because the shop interestingly arranged books by publisher rather than author, I came to recognise the omnipresence of the Penguin logo. I had an assumption that if Penguin published it, a book came with a certain authority, and this in turn led me to the discovery of Evelyn Waugh, P.G. Wodehouse and Graham Greene. Other booklovers will have similar experiences of how they discovered books, each of us building our own reading pathway.

And of course, I discovered the personal magic of reading books. While a book is ultimately the work of the author, every reader also brings their own unique interpretation. As you read, your imagination creates pictures in your head, visualising the author's words, producing a completely personal experience. The author's voice is there, but it needs your input as reader to make the writing live. In an interview for *Marxism Today*, Angela Carter said, 'Reading a book is like re-writing it for yourself. You bring to a novel … all your experience of the world. You bring your history and you read it in your own terms.'

Every reader's experience of a particular book is unique to them. For example, my experience of reading *Great Expectations* is, in many ways, similar to yours. We will have Pip, Joe Gargery, Magwitch, Miss Havisham and the rest in common, along with the descriptions of places and events within the novel. But when I read Dickens' words, they conjure something unique in my imagination, my personal visualisation from Dickens' text. When you read the same words, it will be *your* imagination creating a separate unique experience. You will visualise the places, characters, scenes and conversations in your own fashion.

Wherever we went on holiday around Britain, we invariably ended up in a bookshop. These were mainly independent bookshops, and I grew to love the differences in what they stocked. I understood that the book selection and the way the volumes were displayed reflected the personalities of the booksellers. I appreciated the random and sometimes chaotic nature of this and benefitted from multiple serendipitous book discoveries. Still today, I prefer a small independent bookshop to a large, well-stocked chain store, drawn to the more personal curation of titles that the best independents offer.

At some point during my childhood, our family conceived a pipe dream of one day opening our *own* bookshop. For a long time, though, it was really nothing more than just a dream, a running family joke, something we really didn't expect would ever happen, the sort of thing I imagine many book-loving families talked about. But the joke persisted, going on for years and becoming part of our family myth. 'One day, when we open our bookshop ....' It was very much my personal dream too and, on numerous bookshop visits, I imagined how much fun it would be to work in such a place.

This fascination with books and bookshops finally paid off when, many years later, on a beautiful sunny Friday in early February 1984, my father and I opened our own bookshop. There was a wonderful buzz of excitement as we handed out glasses of wine to welcome our new customers. Friends and family dressed in T-shirts emblazoned with our logo were walking around the town handing out balloons and leaflets, touting for business. After months of planning, the dream had now become a reality, based on our belief that Chelmsford deserved its own independent bookshop.

The customers coming through the door seemed to agree. Time and again, we heard something along the lines of 'At last, the town has its own proper bookshop!' Never mind that our shop was quite small and our range was quite limited, but almost from that first weekend the town and its book buyers took us into their hearts. We had plenty to do to build our reputation, to earn customers' trust and let people know we existed, but it was a strong start.

After all the preparations, it was incredibly gratifying to see those first customers coming into our shop, smiles upon their faces, gleefully browsing among our shelves. It was hard not to smile in return as they started bringing their chosen books to the till and we rang up their purchases. That connection between customer and bookseller was truly magical, something I had hoped for and was now finally experiencing, recommending favourite titles to them and receiving recommendations in return. I delighted in this, the pure pleasure of bookselling, sharing a love for books with our customers.

Very quickly these customers also started moulding the shop to their needs and requirements, as they asked for things we didn't have in stock or where we held only a small selection. I soon noticed that our original vision of the shop was being daily changed by the customers. A bookshop certainly needs a vision of what sort of shop it will be, but the bookseller also has to take into account the customers' wishes and be prepared to be flexible. The bookseller and customers together, like a writer and their readers, give the shop its identity.

In this way, our bookshop started to develop a separate character of its own. It became almost like a living thing, grown from our original vision. We had created a public space, legally owned by us but in reality belonging to the whole town. It was gratifying to see the customers acting as if they were a part of the operation and having a stake in the business.

From that very small beginning the business grew, and over the next few years we became an established part of the town and part of our customers' lives. We sold thousands and thousands of books, built up a strong customer base, held regular events and created a wonderful space for people to discover and enjoy books. We ran a huge schools operation, supplying books to almost all primary and secondary schools within a 10-mile radius, as well as to the local further education college, the polytechnic, Essex County Council and many other businesses.

We were joining a lengthy tradition of bookselling in Britain that stretched back centuries. Our bookshop was very similar to hundreds of other independent bookshops around the country, many family-run like our own, all a much-loved part of their local communities.

The Changes

What we didn't realise at that time was that this very traditional world of British bookselling that we had just joined was about to experience a massive transformation. That transformation would ultimately kill off our bookshop, although not for another sixteen years. It would also revolutionise the way that books were bought and sold in Britain. In common with most retail sectors, the book trade had been constantly evolving and changing for centuries, but the next four decades would arguably see greater change than ever before and we would be caught in the middle of this tidal wave of revolution and development.

There were several major drivers of this change and upheaval, beginning with the huge growth of chain booksellers in the 1980s and 1990s, part of a national growth in retail chains and shopping malls across the UK. The new bookshop chains transformed British high streets into book utopias with fantastic large, new shops bursting with a much wider and more attractive stock range, creating a bigger market for publishers' books.

However, this rapid development of chain bookshops, while giving a massive shot in the arm to the book trade, inevitably led to the closure of hundreds of long-established independent bookshops that could not compete. This caused huge ructions throughout the trade, upending the accepted way of doing things and dramatically altering the nature of the UK book business.

During the same period, publishing, like so many industries, has had to completely change the way it works. Post-war publishing was predominantly enacted by family-run companies led by besuited white men, using production techniques little changed from the Victorian era. New computer technology, advances in printing techniques and more efficient distribution methods, many driven by more modern companies from Europe and beyond, forced massive change on the industry. Much of this has been realised in centralisation and the creation of larger publishing conglomerates, with huge media corporations swallowing up those smaller British businesses. These are better placed to face the challenges of a modern global market, but arguably lost some of the individuality and charm in the process. Alongside this, the industry has seen a huge overhaul in personnel, with more women taking over the reins of power and companies becoming more diverse to better reflect the modern world.

Then, the abolition of the Net Book Agreement (NBA) in 1997 meant the end of fixed pricing for books and the introduction of heavy discounting on best-selling titles. This resulted in supermarkets and other non-book retailers becoming more involved in bookselling and selling the top titles at very low prices, reducing margins for writers and publishers and, significantly, taking the bulk of these key bread-and-butter sales away from bookshops. It also made things easier for Amazon to establish itself and grow its business quickly when it entered the fray.

That dramatic growth in online selling and shoppers' general move away from physical retailers to the internet delivered another massive blow to the book trade. Amazon entered the UK market in the late 1990s, discounting heavily, delivering to the customer's door and leaving hundreds of competitor bookshops floundering in its wake. The abolition of the NBA provided the basis on which it could thrive.

The subsequent growth of digital publishing and the introduction of the e-book in the new century then seemed to threaten the very existence of books and bookshops, with many sales switching to Kindle and other devices. The prospect remains that the future of the book might well be in a digital format and physical books could disappear and, with them, physical bookshops.

Added to this is the recent massive growth in audiobook sales, another rival format to the printed book and a market mainly in the hands of Amazon through its company Audible, removing even more market share from bookshops. And, finally, the growth and rapid development of self-publishing online also threatens the businesses of traditional publishers and booksellers.

Each of these developments on their own would have resulted in dramatic change to the book trade. But, taken together, these changes occurring in rapid succession have resulted in the bookselling and publishing landscape today being almost unrecognisable from what it was four decades ago when I first started out as a bookseller. It is a fascinating story and yet it has still to reach its conclusion.

It is difficult to predict what else lies in store for booksellers and publishers in the coming decades, although the pandemic has in some ways added to retailers' difficulties, helping to speed up the changes in shopping habits and the move to online retail. Conversely, the pandemic did also stimulate a renewed regard for independent businesses, with lockdowns encouraging people to shop locally. Many businesses responded by offering home delivery or kerbside collections and had to improve their websites to offer postal deliveries. The pandemic demonstrated the resilience and ingenuity of independent bookshops, and the public responded favourably. The residual effect of this has continued even after Covid receded, with recent years seeing record growth of new independent bookshops in the UK with fifty-four new shops opening in 2021, forty-five in 2022 and fifty-one in 2023.

Where Do We Go From Here?

If we take a step back to look at the trade from a historical perspective, we see that previous crises in the book trade have been faced and dealt with by the passion and ingenuity of booksellers and publishers. Encouragingly, in the third decade of the new century, we see signs of a brilliant new generation bringing new ideas and new thinking to regenerate the book trade in light of these recent changes. A wave of new independent booksellers has been matched by vibrant growth in the independent publishing sector, bringing much-needed diversity and a fresh perspective to the trade.

As well as recounting the rich history of the book trade, this book will examine these wider changes to bookselling and publishing in recent decades and then ponder where it will go from here in the decades hence. In scrutinising the longer history of the book trade in Britain, we shall discover that there have indeed been peaks and troughs in the trade's fortunes on many previous occasions. During those centuries, booksellers and publishers have proved themselves to be resilient and adept at reacting to change.

I also want to look at the more existential idea of bookselling and publishing in the coming decades. Will we even read books in the future? Increasingly as a society, we access information digitally, through our phones and laptops, often in bite-sized chunks, selecting just the portion we want to read. There is no guarantee that we will always want to read long-form fiction or non-fiction in the future as a 'book', either physical or digital. Already, the digital revolution has meant that print reference books, dictionaries, encyclopaedias, textbooks, maps and guides have experienced declining sales, as the digital equivalent is easier to use, more accessible and constantly updated. The concept of the 'book' itself, the basis of the entire book trade, could be under threat and in the future could prove to be an irrelevance.

With the huge rise in self-publishing online in the past two decades, will we even need publishers in the future? Is this an old-fashioned model not fit for purpose in the modern era? Perhaps, as online publishing becomes even more ubiquitous and readers find easier ways to access content, the traditional route of a publisher or gatekeeper will be redundant?

And will we still need authors? We now have AI that can generate content and write articles, essays and stories. Will the human voice be redundant? Most pertinent to this narrative, will the physical book and, in turn, the physical bookshop, survive?

The history of bookselling and publishing demonstrates that new developments can take a long time to bed in, in some cases over decades or even centuries. When the codex format (essentially, the current book format that we know so well) was invented 2,000 years ago, it took centuries before people stopped producing the more cumbersome and less user-friendly scrolls, the predecessor format. And when printing was developed in Europe in the fifteenth century, again it was centuries before people stopped producing handwritten and hand-illustrated manuscripts.

On that evidence, it seems possible or even probable that the digital book will eventually replace the print version. At the moment, the print and digital versions exist side by side, along with audiobooks, as different options for how we consume books. But will the digital version ultimately win out, as more of our lives are determined by the digital medium? While this development wouldn't lead to fewer books being read, what would it mean for the future of our bricks-and-mortar bookshops?

We don't know the answers to any of these questions right now. But forty years ago, at what was a pivotal moment for the book trade in the early 1980s, we could barely envisage multiple huge bookshop chains across the land, while online bookselling and digital publishing were the stuff of science fiction. In similar fashion, from our present-day perspective, we cannot really envisage where the trade will be another forty years from now. One could ask, though, whether we are in danger of sleepwalking towards losing our physical books and bookshops in the decades ahead of us.

On the flipside, it is worth recognising in this discussion how much readers have valued the physical book throughout its several thousand-year history, whether as scroll, codex, manuscript, print, hardback or paperback. Likewise, readers have always revered bookshops, treating them, as I always have, as magical places where they can source more books to feed their addiction to the printed word. And we should emphasise the enthusiasm of publishers and booksellers for creating and promulgating books. Their excitement and enthusiasm have driven the popularity of books for hundreds of years.

There are around 84,000 people involved in the book trade in Britain today and there have been millions of others throughout its history, all bringing their own enthusiasm and ideas to the business. These professionals share a passion for books, an understanding of the power that books contain, and a recognition of what books can offer, alongside a desire to bring books to the widest possible audience, a theme we will see repeated throughout this book. The books we read exist because of them.

The history of the book trade is packed with fascinating personalities and their stories, and in this narrative we will endeavour to find out more about many of the personnel who have driven innovation and change across the centuries. We will discover the stories of booksellers and publishers from the early days of print, such as William Caxton and Wykin de Worde, innovative booksellers like John Hatchard, James Lackington and W.H. Smith, pioneering publishers such as John Murray, Allen Lane and Paul Hamlyn, as well as many others who transformed the book trade over the past few centuries, among them Charles Edward Mudie, William and Christina Foyle, Tim Waterstone, Terry Maher and Jeff Bezos. Over many centuries, the book trade has become a well-founded edifice, constructed upon the work of these great characters, their strengths underpinning the trade's success.

I will return to the story of our family bookshop and its demise later in this narrative. After the closure of our bookshop, I transferred to the publishing side of the business, where I have worked now for over two decades. Throughout these turbulent times, I have been very much working at the coalface, experiencing the changes first hand and being involved in adapting to them. Like many others, I have been caught up in the rollercoaster ride that the book trade has experienced in these decades, watching booksellers' and publishers' fortunes rise and fall.

I am someone who has always loved books and bookshops and cares deeply about the book trade, but I consider myself first and foremost a reader. As a reader, I am keen to explore whether physical books and bricks-and-mortar bookshops will still exist in another forty years. And, if we think their future is threatened, what can we do to ensure their survival?

This book aims to weave a path through these tempestuous waters and assess where the trade has washed up today and what stormy weather still awaits it in the years ahead. While I'm sure this book will be of interest to those working in bookselling and publishing, it is very much written for all readers and booklovers who care about the future of both books and bookshops.

The book is divided into three parts, each quite different in tone. Part One (The Past) recounts the history of bookselling and publishing over the past 2,000 years. The story is told through a series of smaller stories or vignettes, creating an overarching narrative that builds a picture of the trade's progression over the centuries.

Part Two (The Present) covers the last four decades of recent history, detailing the massive changes that the trade has undergone during this time. This period also covers my career in the book trade, so inevitably there is more personal reflection in this section.

Part Three (The Future) looks in detail at the state of the book trade today and examines where it might be heading in the years ahead. Again, this contains some personal reflection, along with a variety of other viewpoints to discuss the future of bookselling and publishing in Britain.

The history of the book trade is a huge subject and one that could fill a book many times the length of this one. So, this book is not a definitive, complete history but rather it is my personal version of that history.

PART ONE

Remembrance
of Things Past

1

William Caxton the Pioneer: Early Episodes in the History of Bookselling

William Caxton showing a specimen of his printing to King Edward IV; painting by Daniel Maclise. (Alamy)

The Codex

When did bookselling in Britain begin? If we wanted a neat and tidy narrative, we could say that the history of British bookselling began in 1476 when William Caxton set up the first printing press in England. But books had been created and sold long before that, with handwritten manuscripts dating back centuries and scrolls dating back thousands of years. So, to be completely thorough, we need to go right back to the ancient world when books were produced in the form of scrolls, to be unrolled and read either vertically or horizontally, sometimes in concertina fashion, more often just on a continuous roll. As different cultures had developed writing, knowledge and stories had been increasingly written down, inscribed on a variety of materials – whatever was at hand, including wood, stone, clay, tree bark, animal hide, papyrus, parchment and eventually on paper.

Once humans had learned to reproduce knowledge and stories as text, these ideas could be preserved for future generations. Those who created and sold scrolls, the early publishers and booksellers, would have recognised the importance of the texts they were reproducing, whether they consisted of factual knowledge, ideas or stories. They would probably have been lovers of the written word themselves and have possessed a desire, which was common to most people engaged in the book trade, to share this knowledge or retell these great stories. Humans have always wanted to know more and seem always – from the earliest times round the campfire – to have wanted to tell stories as a way of trying to understand the world and the lives they were living.

The scroll contained text written by hand by scribes, and in many cultures those scribes were slaves. Scrolls, made of papyrus, were still the dominant book format in Ancient Roman times, carried in handy scroll cases. The Romans had inherited the idea from the Greeks, who themselves had inherited it from the Egyptians or even earlier cultures. Scrolls could be up to 16m long and weren't easy to read, requiring two hands and very careful unwinding. Books of this fashion probably date back about 5,000 years, but we cannot be entirely certain.

The time of the Roman Empire also saw, around the first century CE, the very important development of the codex, in which folded leaves or pages of parchment were stacked and then pasted or sewn together at one end – an early version of the modern book. The word 'codex' derives from the Latin word '*caudex*', meaning 'trunk of a tree' or 'block of wood'.

The codex became a much easier way to read a work of literature and enabled the inclusion of page numbers, indices and tables of contents. It was a handier, compact format that could hold more content in less space, with writing on both sides, unlike scrolls. The codex offered the ability to easily go back to pages that had been read earlier, all of which made the book much more user-friendly.

There is research to suggest that the development of the codex was a natural transition from the use of the writing tablet, which had been common in Rome and across the Roman Empire for centuries. The writing tablet was generally two or more flat pieces of wood bound together by cords through pierced holes, either in modern book format or a concertina. These were used for writing messages, official letters, school exercises and for note taking. The tablet was sometimes coated in wax but, equally, users simply wrote in chalk or ink directly onto the wood. Notes taken for larger works could then be transcribed onto scrolls.

At the time of its introduction, the codex book format represented the most significant development in book publishing until the later invention of the printing press. It still took a few centuries for all booksellers and readers to adapt, but the scroll was gradually replaced by the codex.

Most scrolls were created using papyrus, made from the papyrus plant that grew in the wetlands of the Nile Delta. The codex was generally made from parchment, although both formats utilised both materials to some extent. Parchment, once made, was a longer lasting and more lightweight material, one of the best writing materials ever created. But parchment was made from animal skin and was much more difficult to produce, involving a complex simultaneous procedure of stretching and drying. It took centuries to perfect this technique and lead to the more widespread use of parchment. Consequently, the move from papyrus to parchment was slow and papyrus was still being used in Egypt up to the twelfth century CE. Paper only came to prominence as the material for creating books over 1,000 years later, with the dawn of printing.

Most early Christian Bibles adopted the new codex format, and the rapid spread of Christianity was aided by the Bible being available in this handy way. The introduction of the codex has also been said to be responsible for the fixed order of the books of the Bible, which was much more flexible before its introduction. A standard scroll would probably hold just one of the books of the Bible, while the codex format could contain several books. The word 'bible' derives, in fact, from the plural of the Greek word '*biblio*', meaning book, therefore 'books'. Until recent times, many of the key developments in book-trade history were driven by those wanting to distribute religious texts, most notably the Bible.

In the following centuries, the means of binding pages at one edge were refined and perfected to create a better product. Still today, pages are either glued or stitched together, albeit by more sophisticated methods. But here essentially was the birth of the book as we know it – a format that has remained relatively unchanged for two millennia and the basis of the huge book trade that thrives today in the twenty-first century.

I spoke of my affection for the physical object of the book earlier and, in my opinion, this basic format has yet to be bettered. The recent introduction of the digital book has not replaced the codex format, rather it has widened the different versions of a book available to the reading public. Books today can be read in print format (as hardback or paperback), digital e-book or audiobook – but the lead category by far is still that original paper format. It needs no power or batteries, its mechanisms don't get ruined if you drop it in the bath or get sand in its pages, it is portable, collectable and lovable. It will take something quite amazing to beat this perfect invention. Stephen King called books 'a uniquely portable magic' and, despite all the technical innovations on offer, that description still holds.

Atticus: Bookseller of Ancient Rome

Bookselling as a profession is as old as books. There is evidence of purveyors of books in Ancient Greek times, as well as during the days of the Roman Empire, but there would have been booksellers before this time too. The bookseller used scribes to make a copy of a book to order, often for a wealthy customer building a library. Both Aristotle and Plato acquired libraries in this way.

In Ancient Rome, there was a busy bookselling and publishing industry, with several booksellers setting up shops and reproducing texts by modern authors of the time as well as classic texts. These would have included books by Martial, Ovid, Virgil and Propertius.

A bookseller would advertise the texts for sale on a list outside his shop and, once a purchase was agreed, a copy would be made by the transcribers working for them, performing a sort of 'print-on-demand' business of the ancient world. In the twenty-first century, many books are printed on demand, although often today the end customer is unaware of this. As a result of improvements in printing processes and digital technology, some books (particularly more academic or specialist titles, but also a lot of online self-published books) are often printed in very low numbers or printed individually when a customer orders it. Most of these can be printed in a matter of minutes, thus saving the publisher committing to a print run until they actually have a firm order, which is almost a reversion to the Roman method of 2,000 years ago.

Titus Pomponius Atticus was a bookseller and publisher who lived in Rome from around 100–32 BC. He was famous for his friendship and correspondence with Cicero. Atticus seemingly was something of an entrepreneur, introducing new production techniques. He kept several slaves, who all copied the same text at the same time from one person's dictation, creating papyrus scroll books – an early form of mass production in publishing. This was less print on demand, but more a new development – a move towards speculative publishing, producing several copies of a book that he hoped would sell, rather than having firm pre-orders first. As well as publishing works by his friend Cicero, he also published famous works by many Greek writers, including Plato.

Atticus' success bred imitators utilising similar methods, including Tryphon and Dorus, who were all part of a bustling early publishing and bookselling industry. Other booksellers at this time distributed different parts of the text to different slaves, so that each inscriber was copying out the same text over and over. These methods were the early and more laborious precursors of the printing press.

In civilised Rome, literacy was quite widespread but restricted to wealthier citizens. And this was true throughout the Roman Empire, including in Britain, benefitting from the strong literary culture at the heart of the empire, and it seems that there were booksellers in Roman Britain, too. There is no way now of knowing for certain, but these were probably the earliest booksellers in Britain – the first evidence of the British book trade and the early beginnings of our story.

Copies of works by the likes of the poet Martial were distributed and sold throughout the Roman Empire, carried by those serving in the army to the outer reaches, including Gaul and Britain. Martial, who was most famous for his books of *Epigrams*, refers to several of his works being published in the handy new codex format: 'You who long for my little books to be with you everywhere and want to have companions for a long journey, buy these ones which parchment confines within small pages. Give your scroll-cases to the great authors, one hand can hold me.'

The codex could be said to be the paperback of its day: it was so much easier to take to read on a journey. It is fascinating to consider that reading, for some at least, was available in this fashion in Britain at such an early date.

The introduction of the new codex, a pivotal moment in book-trade history, can indeed be compared to the upheaval and furore created when Allen Lane introduced the cheap Penguin paperback editions in the 1930s or when e-books were first developed early in the twenty-first century. Change is often viewed initially with suspicion before it becomes absorbed into the mainstream.

The Middle Ages

Although Britain was undoubtedly more disorganised, less efficiently run and less civilised after the Romans' departure, booksellers in Britain continued to supply literature to the select few, predominantly to religious communities and the wealthy. Most of the population were not literate and would have had very little need for such things.

Book production in the early Middle Ages was mainly conducted by a monastic monopoly, with monks creating beautiful tomes, mostly of religious or educational texts, with distribution to a very limited number of people, often for use within the monastery itself.

The Middle Ages were not, however, a cultural desert. Hundreds of beautiful and significant books were created at this time, including such works as *The Book of Kells*, the *Lindisfarne Gospels* and *The Anglo-Saxon Chronicle*. These manuscripts required a great deal of skill from the scribes and illustrators who produced them and were also beautiful works of art. *The Anglo-Saxon Chronicle* is, in fact, a collection of several books that were separately created, but together they provide future generations with a record of Anglo-Saxon rule, demonstrating how important books have become over the centuries.

It was also during this time that we see the strong beginnings of an English literary tradition. The fourteenth century witnessed the writing of *Sir Gawain and the Green Knight* and *Piers Plowman*. But of most significance were the writings of Geoffrey Chaucer, a diplomat and royal official who went on to write some of the most influential poetic works of English literature.

Chaucer was well travelled and grew to love French poetry after journeying across the Channel. But it was his trips to Genoa and Florence that introduced him to Italian poetry, specifically Boccaccio, which had the most influence on him. Chaucer's most important early work, *Troilus and Criseyde*, often referred to by critics as the first modern novel, owes a great deal to Boccaccio's *Il Filostrato*. *The Canterbury Tales*, which he wrote in retirement, echoes the storytelling structure of the Italian poet's *Decameron*, but has a construction and style of its own.

Chaucer was one of the first poets to write in the emerging English language, setting a precedent for those who followed. His works would probably have been read or recited initially to a courtly audience, and only after his death did they become available as books. However, particularly following the introduction of print, Chaucer quickly became an established part of the English literary canon, to be followed by Shakespeare, Donne, Milton, Wordsworth, Dickens, Austen, et al.

The foundation of the universities also created a growing demand for instructional texts for education, such as law books. Oxford University dates from as early as 1096, and Cambridge from 1209. In addition, the universities built extensive libraries, which created further demand for relevant texts. These works, copied out by hand, were known as 'manuscripts', which means 'written by hand' in Latin.

Universities also needed to provide reliable textbooks for their students, so they began to license '*stationarii*' (stationers), an early form of bookshop. Each stationer was licensed to create master copies of textbooks. These master copies were then broken down into '*peciae*', which were essentially four-page excerpts from the manuscript that the student would borrow and then make their own copy of, for a small fee. This has some similarities to how universities today, in the digital age, pay a subscription or rental fee to publishers for the use of their texts, which enables the university to supply relevant excerpts to individual students for a subscription fee. This reduces the cost to students and removes the necessity for them to each own and carry around weighty tomes, when they might only need to study a certain chapter or section of the relevant book. Like many things in this narrative, publishing has come full circle and found contemporary solutions to age-old problems.

After the Norman invasion, the country gradually became more civilised, and various book producers (including scriveners, limners and binders) began operating in London, already gathering in an early publishing community around St Paul's Churchyard. As demand for other types of secular texts grew, the *stationarii* were no longer just supplying educational texts to students. More English noblemen were becoming book collectors, imitating their counterparts in France and elsewhere in Europe and driving this demand for more books. The Company of Stationers (taking its name from the *stationarii*) was incorporated in 1404, with its headquarters at Station Hall.

These developments reflected an ongoing growth in the number of bookshops in the early fifteenth century, supplying secular manuscripts to their customers and importing from the continent. A skeleton book trade existed before the age of print, ready for growth when print was introduced and in a good position to exploit its potential.

William Caxton and the Introduction
of the Printing Press

Mass printing of texts had first been developed in China, Korea and Japan as early as the tenth and eleventh centuries, mainly through woodcut printing. In Europe, it wasn't until the 1450s that Johannes Gutenberg developed the first printing press in Mainz, Germany.

There had been several difficulties in developing printing in Europe. Printers in the Far East had used carved wood blocks to print but their alphabets were composed mainly of symbols and images and wood blocks were perfect for this. However, wood was not good enough to achieve decent legibility with the letters of the European alphabet. These had to be small enough to fit many words in a line but big enough to be read clearly; the letters had to be moved around repeatedly and then reused after frequent inking. Only metal would give the required definition and reliability.

Gutenberg was trained as a goldsmith, so he already understood the techniques required to forge small objects from metal and this helped him develop the movable type as a solution. To make a success of printing, Gutenberg not only had to create the moulded type itself, he also had to develop a workable printing press and then source a good enough ink to achieve the required results.

Once he had eventually developed a viable printing process using movable metal type, many other printers set up in the same area, using his methods. Many of these worked for Gutenberg first before setting up on their own and, in those early years, book printing was mainly associated with Germans. As well as those in Mainz, Johan Mentelin had a print workshop in Strasburg, Berthold Ruppel in Basle, Heinrich Kepfer in Nuremberg and Ulrich Zell in Cologne, among others. Gradually, printing spread across mainland Europe, with printers established in Venice and Paris by 1470.

As a result of Gutenberg's breakthrough, books would gradually become available to a wider audience. Gutenberg's most famous work was the first printed version of the Bible, and its availability to a wider audience was of huge significance. The initial buyers of printed books were still the aristocracy or the ecclesiastical market, but the new process eventually opened the door to the mass distribution of different types of books and pamphlets. In addition to Bibles, psalters, books of indulgences and other religious material, printers also started to publish grammars, almanacks and educational texts.

William Caxton was the first person to introduce a printing press into England and, as the first known English printer and retailer of books, he has been called 'the father of English bookselling'. Caxton was born in Kent sometime between 1415 and 1424, although there is no definitive confirmation of his place of birth. That hasn't stopped some claiming that he was born in Tenterden and, indeed, the town still has a pub called the Print House, which boasts a Caxton Lounge.

William was originally apprenticed to Robert Large, a mercer dealing in silks, importing and exporting from the Low Countries. Caxton's parents would have had to be relatively well off to be able to place him in such an apprenticeship.

Caxton seems to have done well in this profession and, after Large's death in 1441, he set up in business for himself and lived in fashionable Bruges, where he became a successful and influential merchant, diplomat and writer. Bruges was a major business and cultural centre, and Caxton would have been exposed to many wider influences there, including literature and the arts. He may well have started trading in books during these years, alongside his mercers' business, and have developed a passion for books himself. He spent time in Bruges, Antwerp and Ghent, areas that had many workshops producing highly sought-after manuscripts.

Caxton's success as a mercer is significant. He had learned how to raise capital to finance projects, he understood the import and export business between England and mainland Europe and he recognised the importance of connections with influential men. Caxton came to printing as a businessman, not as an artisan, and this experience would enable him to start a professional publishing and bookselling business in England. Many of the early printers across Europe went bankrupt but Caxton's experience stood him in good stead. Eventually, he would run down the rest of his business and concentrate solely on being a merchant of books.

In 1471 Caxton began translating the *Recuyell of the Historyes of Troye*, heroic tales inspired by Homer, which would become the first book ever printed in the English language. He began this translation with a view to printing it, so he had already decided that he wanted to be a printer, supported by his early patron, Margaret of Burgundy.

Caxton travelled to Cologne in 1471 with the specific aim of learning about printing, Cologne being the nearest city with a printing press. For the next couple of years, he learned the essentials of printing and the various processes involved, and at this time he took Wynkyn de Worde into his employ as his assistant. De Worde would work with Caxton for the rest of Caxton's life. During his time in Cologne, Caxton also acquired a printing press and the necessary metal type, probably from the printer Johan Veldener, from whom he had learned about printing.

Caxton set up this press in Bruges and printed the first copies of the *History of Troy* there in 1473. He then returned to England and set up his printing press in Westminster in 1476. Among the works he subsequently printed was *The Canterbury Tales*, not only the first printed edition of this work but the first book to be printed in England. Caxton also printed *Aesop's Fables*, various histories and chivalric romances and, in 1484, Thomas Malory's *Morte D'Arthur*. He printed over 100 titles, mostly in English, and a large number of these were translated by him.

Although Caxton was the first to set up business as a printer in England, printed books were already flooding into the English market from mainland Europe. Most of these, however, were in Latin or French, so printing books in English was exploiting a gap in the market – an inspired part of his business plan, and probably his main reason for moving his business to England.

To make the business as cost-effective as possible, Caxton printed a variety of works, including smaller pamphlets alongside larger works. He also imported and distributed books from the Continent, both printed books and manuscripts, using his existing knowledge of this market.

Although his business was based in the precincts of Westminster Abbey, he did not specialise in religious works, but instead sold predominantly secular works to the many important businessmen, courtiers and merchants who frequented Westminster. Caxton had swapped silks for books but remained a businessman working to turn a profit. Printing was not a hobby adopted for retirement; this was hard work. To facilitate and grow the business, he employed assistants and apprentices, including the aforementioned Wynkyn de Worde, who managed the print workshop.

Initially, like manuscripts before them, the first printed books were aimed at the wealthy and were often printed to order in small quantities. But the invention of the printing press would eventually lead to cheaper books and make them available to a wider market. This, in turn, created more demand and underpinned the growth of the book trade as others followed Caxton's example in the ensuing decades.

The Caxton printing press, following the Gutenberg model, used movable metal type arranged on a wooden plate, called the lower platen. The type (the letters) was always arranged in the same order in trays, so that the typesetter could easily access it. Capital letters were kept in the top tray, or case – hence 'upper case' and 'lower case'. The type was arranged on the plate in the order of the text, but back to front and upside down to create the page. Ink was applied to the type by use of a leather inking ball or 'dabber', a sheet of paper placed onto it and an upper platen was brought down to press the plate and paper together, imprinting type onto the page. The platen would then be removed, the printed sheet taken out and hung to dry, while the next sheet of paper was inserted and the press cranked into place again.

The print shop was not spacious and would have been very loud and busy. This was a slow and laborious printing method, but it was quicker than books being copied out by hand. It was also easier to read, as the type was uniform and multiple copies could be made repeatedly. Up to 250 sheets could be produced in an hour by the speediest printers, although most did not achieve that number. A new plate would be introduced when the next page was to be printed.

Early printers had no model to follow except manuscripts, so the first printed books looked very like manuscripts, including the design of a page and the type itself, which initially imitated the calligraphic style of handwritten manuscripts. Caxton printed his books in folio; that is, one sheet of paper folded once to provide four sides of printed text. For binding, sheets were gathered into bundles of different sizes. Caxton favoured the '*quaternion*', whereby four folded sheets were bundled together to form sixteen pages of text. So, the outer sheet of the four would hold pages 1, 2, 15 and 16 of the book, the next 3, 4, 13 and 14 and so on. The *quaternion* would then be bound to the next bundle of four and so on.

Setting up as a printer was an expensive business and a much bigger initial outlay than producing manuscripts. The printer had to invest in the printing press itself, the metal movable type, ink and supplies of paper, and staff to handle all these different elements of the process. Printing multiple copies was also more of a gamble than just creating one handwritten copy. If the printer printed too many copies, any profits would be wiped out. Equally, once printed books became the norm, if a print book proved a success and the initial print run was sold out, it was a lengthy and laborious task to reprint, as each page would have to be typeset anew to print once more.

All of this meant heavy investment, with a long wait for a return on that investment. Printing several hundred copies of one book could take months and no revenue would be received until the whole book was printed, so publishing as a business was not without its risks. Nonetheless, the introduction of the printing press was a hugely significant development – the next pivotal moment in bookselling history – and it can be argued that this marked the true beginning of the book trade as an industry in England.

William Caxton was a pioneer: one of the key figures in the British book trade who significantly transformed it. By introducing the printing press into England and making a successful business of publishing, he instigated a revolution and brought change, with others swiftly following his lead. Caxton demonstrated the two key attributes of a successful publisher and bookseller, creating a template that thousands would follow in the ensuing centuries.

First, he possessed a passion for books and an awareness of what they could do in spreading knowledge, stories and ideas. Caxton was obviously a booklover, and he held a strong desire to share this passion with others. We can see this love of literature in his translation of those stories from the Trojan War and his publishing of Chaucer's great poetic masterpiece, *The Canterbury Tales*.

Second, Caxton had good business sense, not only understanding the key tenets of income versus costs, but also demonstrating a talent for identifying what to publish and how to publish something he believed in. That ability to know what to publish – to sniff out a bestseller – these were attributes that would be vital to bookselling and publishing for ever after. Caxton was the template, the starting point. Those who came after took up his example and expanded upon it, honed the required skills and developed the professions of bookselling and publishing.

We can draw a direct line from Caxton's time to our own and chart the growth of the trade from then onwards. The increasingly widespread availability of the printed word in the coming centuries, whether through books, journals or newspapers, revolutionised Britain, enabling the spread of knowledge and the sharing of thought and ideas among the public at large. In her memoir *Stet*, the editor Diana Athill says that books 'have taken me so far beyond the narrow limits of my own experience and have so greatly enlarged my sense of the complexity of life'.

The wider availability of books post-Caxton helped transform society and our view of the world. We can argue that books can be seen as an aide to understanding reality better – a tool to make us better human beings. Penelope Lively describes this in her memoir *Ammonites & Leaping Fish*, 'What we have read makes us what we are – quite as much as what we have experienced and where we have been and who we have known. To read is to experience.'

What keeps all of us reading is the eternal quest to know or understand more about life and the world. In her recent book *Transcendent Kingdom*, Yaa Gyasi writes, 'The truth is we don't know what we don't know. We don't even know the questions we need to ask in order to find out, but when we learn one little thing, a dim light comes on in a dark hallway, and suddenly a new question appears.' This explains why we turn to books time and again. Books don't necessarily provide us with all the answers, but they aid our exploration of life and of ideas, they force us to ask more questions and to explore further. Books make us humble, make us accept that we don't know everything and that we have much to learn from others, that we all start from a position of ignorance and can always learn more. As Philip Larkin wrote in *Innocence*, 'Strange to know nothing, never to be sure/Of what is true or right or real.'

For the next few centuries, the professions of printer, publisher and bookseller were very much intertwined and generally the same person or company performed all these functions. It was only much later, as we get into the seventeenth and eighteenth centuries, that these roles became separate functions and more specialised roles became the norm. At that point, the role of bookseller started to be different to the publishing and printing side.

It is worth noting that, despite the development of the printing press, manuscript production continued for the next couple of centuries alongside the printed book. Gradually, the printed book became the more usual version for libraries and collectors, but this process took a long time. Likewise, in the twenty-first century, the introduction of the digital book and audiobook has not replaced the printed book, rather the various media exist alongside each other. It may well be some time before we know if the digital book will eventually replace the printed version or if some other version appears that we can't currently envisage.

Initially, the black-and-white printed book was a poor substitute for a beautifully produced and coloured manuscript. In many instances, printed books had handwritten headers or coloured decoration added afterwards, alongside the letterpress printing, to make a more elaborate production. In this way, printers were still somewhat reliant on manuscript techniques. To add pictures to a book, a separate device would be needed to create a woodblock illustration, although later engraved illustrations, known as intaglio printing, became the norm. This might be carried out by another craftsman, not necessarily within the printer's establishment, and the page containing the illustration would then have to be bound within the printed pages. It took some time for the printed book to match its manuscript predecessor in beauty.

2

Wynkyn de Worde and the Development of the Publishing Business

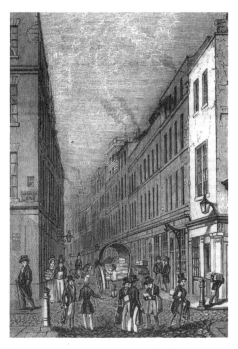

Paternoster Row near St Paul's, for centuries
the centre of the British book trade. (Alamy)

Wynkyn de Worde

William Caxton died sometime around 1492, leaving behind a wife, whose name we don't know, and a daughter called Elizabeth. His assistant, Wynkyn de Worde took over his Westminster premises and the business. De Worde, a German immigrant, had been born in Worth in Alsace and lived a long life until 1535. As with Caxton, we know little of his personal life beyond his achievements as a printer, publisher and bookseller. He was Caxton's workshop foreman, supervising the running of the printing presses, and was much more involved with the day-to-day operation of the process than his boss. De Worde carried on the business successfully for forty years after Caxton's death – a very capable and efficient operator.

By the time de Worde took over, the book market in England was growing and other printers had already set up shop in London, including Richard Pynson and Johannes Lettou. It was an exciting time, the trade growing as more people joined the profession and more books were being published.

In 1500, de Worde moved from Caxton's shop at the sign of the Red Pale in Westminster to the sign of the Sun in Fleet Street, in a house opposite Shoe Lane. De Worde was the first printer to set up in Fleet Street, which subsequently became the centre of the English printing trade. In addition, de Worde set up a book stall in St Paul's Churchyard, an area that has great importance in our story and became the centre of publishing and bookselling in London for the next few centuries, right through to the middle of the twentieth century.

Like Caxton, de Worde initially relied on rich patrons for sales but gradually moved towards a more commercial business model, producing cheaper books for a wider market and significantly expanding his sales. He also saved on costs by not importing paper from mainland Europe, instead buying from John Tate, the first English papermaker, whose paper mill was based near Hertford.

Wynkyn de Worde published over 400 titles, including plenty of books for the religious market; but his greatest success was Robert Whittington's Latin grammar for schools. De Worde recognised the wide market for cheaper publications and so began printing early romances in affordable editions – titles that had previously only been available in manuscript – such as *Bevis of Hampton, Sir Degare* and *Ipomydon*. He also published basic histories for a mass market, children's books, books of manners, books on household management, ballads and almanacks. De Worde introduced more use of woodcut illustrations into books, something that Caxton had only dabbled in, and often included an illustration at the start and end of each book.

If we are forced to compare the two, we should say that Caxton was more the scholar, whereas de Worde was more the craftsman. Publishing and bookselling have always been professions that reflect the taste and world view of their proprietor. Caxton and de Worde were very different in their approach. Caxton was very familiar with the book-buying tastes of the upper echelons of European society, and he published books targeted at that audience. De Worde didn't work for a patron in the way Caxton did; rather, he relied on his own judgement as to what to publish and learned from the market, developing a template that future publishers would follow. This is why he is important to our story – in the way he enlarged the book-buying market by expanding the types of books being published and, in so doing, reached a wider popular audience.

St Paul's Churchyard and Paternoster Row

As mentioned above, Richard Pynson was another bookseller–publisher to follow in Caxton's wake and a key rival to de Worde, although seemingly producing books of a higher standard. Pynson, originally from Normandy, produced the first English cookbook in 1500, *The Boke of Cokery*, as well as works from the Roman poet Terence, numerous legal and religious texts and the beautifully produced *Morton Missal*, which included stunning hand illustrations, added after the printing of the text in a throwback to manuscript production techniques.

The Boke of Cokery was the forerunner of Mrs Beeton, Elizabeth David, Delia Smith, Jamie Oliver and a multitude of other cookery writers in the succeeding centuries. From that moment on, cookery has grown to become one of the strongest categories in publishing and there are generally several cookery titles in the top twenty bestsellers list to this day – the number increasing in the pre-Christmas season. *The Boke of Cokery* focussed on grand medieval feasts, with recipes for game and various other meats, including peacock served splendidly with its tail fully spread, as well as many dishes we no longer cook, such as *charmerchande,* a mutton stew, and *jusselle*, a sort of meat broth.

Between them, Pynson and de Worde were responsible for the bulk of publications produced in the early sixteenth century, but many other bookseller–publishers soon edged into this expanding market. These included Richard Grafton, who printed the Matthew Bible in 1537, based on William Tyndale's translation, and John Daye, who mainly produced religious books of sermons and psalms, but is most famous now for publishing *Actes and Monuments* by John Foxe in 1563 – better known as *Foxe's Book of Martyrs*. This key book, which recounts the suffering endured by Protestants during the reign of Queen Mary, influenced English negative attitudes towards Catholicism for generations and is credited more widely with developing English notions of nationhood and xenophobia and a lingering distrust of the foreign or the different.

A typical bookseller's shop at this time wasn't large and would include a printing press in one room and a retail office at the front – very different to the look of a modern bookshop. The printing workshop was often rather cramped, containing the printing press itself alongside space for drying pages (on lines strung across the room), space to store supplies such as paper and cases of type, as well as some room for those operating the press and those preparing the next plate of text. Many booksellers also had movable stalls that could display their wares outside their shops.

For the next few hundred years, the bulk of the booksellers and publishers worked cheek by jowl in crowded conditions such as these in small shops in Paternoster Row, alongside St Paul's Churchyard – two streets that rapidly became the centre of the English book trade. Many other related tradesmen were handily located nearby. Books, booksellers and publishers proliferated in Paternoster Row throughout the sixteenth and seventeenth centuries. It should also be noted that most of these operators in the business at this time belonged to the Company of Stationers, a guild which held sway over much of the bookselling business until the eighteenth century.

The Stationers' Company

As we have discovered, the area around St Paul's Churchyard and neighbouring Paternoster Row had become the centre of the British trade as early as the 1300s. At that time, the various professions involved in producing books included scriveners (scribes), text writers, limners (illustrators) and binders. Eventually, with the introduction of the printing press, some of these roles would become redundant or would adapt due to the new processes required.

Following this growth in the numbers of those setting up businesses to produce books, the Stationers' Company was formed in 1404 to regulate these associated businesses and to help them work together more effectively. At this time, there were already some thirty shops in this area of London associated with book production. During the 100 years after the introduction of the printing press, the numbers of shops in the Churchyard and Paternoster Row more than trebled.

As mentioned earlier, booksellers were originally called *stationarii*, named for their post or station, from which they sold. Following the introduction of print, the Stationers' Company received its first charter in 1557 from Queen Mary and, with this, their control of the early book trade came into effect. The Company managed the trade on behalf of the Crown, authorising what was printed and who could print what. The Stationers' Company also had the power to seize and destroy any books printed outside this agreement.

Bookseller–publishers had to navigate the tight restrictions and censorship practised by the Stationers' Company. These limited the growth of the book trade for the first couple of hundred years after the printing press was introduced, although it should be recognised that the company did also support and work for the benefit of its members.

During the English Civil War, however, the restrictive laws became relaxed amid the upheaval and there followed a riot of publishing for the next decade or so. Thousands of books, pamphlets, news sheets and ballads were released, reflecting the multiple issues and opinions that were rife throughout the land. However, with the Restoration of the monarchy, the laws were tightened once more, and so things remained until towards the end of the century.

Following the Glorious Revolution of 1688–89 and the enthronement of William and Mary, an Act of Toleration was passed in 1689. In the same spirit, the Licensing Act was allowed to lapse finally in 1696, enabling an explosion of publishing in the eighteenth century. The Stationers' Company lost its monopoly, though not its influence and, from that point, more bookseller–publishers entered the market, and the sorts of books published widened enormously.

The Stationers' Company's power may have been reduced but its importance continued with most bookseller–publishers in London and associated tradesmen still belonging to the Company. In 1603, the Company founded the English Stock, a joint publishing venture which successfully bid for several patents, including *Old Moore's Almanack*. As well as proving profitable to its members, the English Stock had a charitable element, giving jobs to out-of-work artisans within the trade and donating some of the profits to the poor. The present-day Book Trade Benevolent Society shares some of these values.

Stagecoach to the Provinces

From the time of Caxton through to the mid-seventeenth century, years marked by political upheaval and irregular bouts of plague, the population of England and Wales grew from approximately 3 million to 5 million. England was still an agriculture-based economy, with most of the population lacking the time, money or opportunity for leisure pursuits such as reading. But throughout this period, there was also a very gradual increase in wealth and literacy among the middling classes. It was these people, as well as the very wealthy, who were not only the buyers of the increasing number of available books, pamphlets and periodicals, but who also started to keep libraries and collections of books in their houses as a symbol of their wealth and status.

In *The Origin and Growth of Printing* published in 1664, Richard Atkyns estimated that there were more than 600 booksellers in London by that time, most living above their shops. Although the majority of these were still based around St Paul's Churchyard and Paternoster Row, booksellers were also starting to spread across London, including some shops on old London Bridge, and to the towns beyond the capital.

With a book trade now firmly established, booksellers were naturally looking to grow their businesses. In *Shadows of the Old Booksellers*, Charles Knight describes them as 'carrying forward the great work of national enlightenment, sometimes indeed in a narrow and mercenary spirit, but not unfrequently in a spirit far above that of mere money-getting'. Many of those involved in bookselling and publishing today are similarly driven – primarily by a belief in the importance of books with profit only a secondary motive.

Booksellers printed and sold all manner of materials to make their businesses profitable. As well as books, this could include maps and charts, engraved prints, ballad sheets, news sheets, pocket books and other forms of stationery. A ballad sheet contained a poem printed on one side of a sheet of paper, set to a suggested well-known tune and often of a topical or political nature. These were produced and distributed quickly and were sold in the streets for a penny.

To attract custom, booksellers advertised their titles in the newly available newspapers and periodicals, built up customer mailing lists and sent out catalogues of new and backlist publications. Shops were no longer just content to open their doors and wait for customers to find them; instead, they would go out and seek business. Using new transport networks, wholesalers and regional sales representatives called 'chap-men', booksellers began to sell their books beyond London in provincial towns.

Distribution to the provinces of books, newspapers and periodicals was via the various stagecoach routes spreading out from the great coaching inns in London, a network that continued to grow in significance during the next two centuries, until the introduction of the steam train in the mid-nineteenth century. The Goose and Gridiron, near St Paul's Churchyard, and the Bell Savage, in nearby Ludgate Inn, were of particular significance due to the presence of so many booksellers in that area. The Bell Savage, or Belle Sauvage, which dates back to at least 1420, has an illustrious history and is featured in Dickens' *The Pickwick Papers*, Samuel Richardson's *Clarissa* and Walter Scott's *Kenilworth*. Distribution of books to some areas of the country was also achieved by boat, either up the coast or via the Thames to major destinations such as Oxford.

Booksellers expanded their trade by selling at regional book fairs in various towns outside of London, including at Stourbridge and St Frideswide's Fair in Oxford. And some bookseller–publishers were selling internationally, particularly to the colonies in New England and Virginia. This market developed as the colonies expanded from the 1640s onwards.

But much closer to home, Europe was vital too. One English book-seller, John Bill, issued a catalogue for the Frankfurt Book Fair in the early 1600s, demonstrating even at this early stage the international nature of bookselling. The Frankfurt Book Fair, which dates from the late fifteenth century, is still in existence today and is the largest book fair in the world, regularly attended by UK publishers and booksellers every October, including me. It is one of the key events of the pub-lishing calendar and now hosts over 7,000 exhibitors from over 100 countries. I love the buzz at Frankfurt Book Fair, and it is a great place to see the diverse range of books that make up the modern world of bookselling and publishing, as well as an opportunity to catch up with friends and clients from around the world.

The Early Years of the Book Trade

The book trade initially grew very slowly. During the sixteenth and seventeenth centuries, growth in the numbers of publications created in Britain was very gradual. The trade was initially dominated by imports from mainland Europe, and it is only towards the end of this period that homegrown production really increased.

It took several hundred years for books to move from a luxury item purchased by a select few to something that was readily used by a sizable percentage of the population. Publishers often pooled their resources, joining together to print certain books – particularly bigger projects or multi-volume works. In this way, they shared the costs and, if successful, the profits too.

For most of this time, London remained the centre of Britain's publishing industry, assisted by the restrictive practices of the various guilds and the Stationers' Company, as we have seen. The Stationers' Company worked to protect publishers' rights, introducing a copyright law, which predated the printing press and was based on the 'right to copy' a text although, until the eighteenth century, this only protected the publisher of a text, not its author.

One of the most momentous publications of the seventeenth century was the King James Bible, published in 1611 by Robert Barker, printer to King James I. Although there had been a couple of other English translations prior to this edition, this was very much the 'authorised' version, after James had charged the translators with sticking closely to Church of England doctrine. The impact of this publication reverberated down the centuries and with the Church enjoying such dominance at this time, it was a hugely significant publication.

But among the other strong new publishing genres in the sixteenth and seventeenth centuries were poetry and plays. Both John Donne and Shakespeare came to prominence in the late 1500s and the following century witnessed a flowering of the theatre in England, with many other brilliant and prolific playwrights, including John Webster, Aphra Behn and Ben Jonson. The period also produced a swathe of important poets – none more so than John Milton, whose major work *Paradise Lost* was first published in 1667 by the bookseller Samuel Simmons.

As bookselling and publishing expanded, booksellers quickly learned that books could be used to spread the latest ideas and theories and could sell in large quantities if published on a current hot topic. A classic example of this would be the 'pamphlet wars' during the time of the English Civil War. With Parliament and Charles I at loggerheads and the unstable political situation changing almost daily, small pamphlets or tracts were an easy way to get views and opinions out into the open to form part of ongoing arguments and disagreements. Over 20,000 pamphlets were issued during the Civil War, most of which were incredibly biased towards their own opinion as the nation divided. This rapid exchange of ideas was only possible because of the development of the printing press.

Print encouraged the democratisation of books, with less emphasis on books for the religious or wealthy customers. Cheaper and shorter books and books on topical current issues encouraged a different class of reader to start buying and reading them. Once encouraged in this way, these new readers became regular customers for bookshops, further growing the book market.

Some of the most significant books of ideas published during this period not only created a huge stir at the time but resonated for centuries afterwards. These included Hobbes' *Leviathan* (1651), Newton's *Principia* (1687) and John Locke's *Essay Concerning Human Understanding* (1689). Politicians, scientists and philosophers became used to spreading their ideas through the medium of print, whether in news sheet, pamphlet or book form. In this way, new and radical ideas could reach a wider audience.

Publishing Shakespeare

Shakespeare's reputation had certainly grown during his lifetime, but at his death he was still considered just one of several key playwrights of his generation. His reputation as the greatest English playwright was only established after his death, thanks in no small part to the ongoing publication of his works alongside the regular theatrical production of his plays. Repeated publication of Shakespeare's works, scholarly re-examination in the ensuing centuries and then the idolatry afforded to him in the eighteenth century all played their part in this.

The first definitive collected edition of Shakespeare's plays was published in 1623. *Mr William Shakespeare's Comedies, Histories & Tragedies* (known as the *First Folio*), was published by William and Isaac Jaggard and Edward Blount and contained thirty-six Shakespeare plays. This mighty tome was edited by the actors John Heminges and Henry Condell, who had worked alongside Shakespeare in The King's Men and are directly responsible for preserving Shakespeare's plays for posterity.

There had been numerous small editions of some of Shakespeare's plays prior to this and individual editions of the plays, but the *First Folio* is the text that scholars and publishers now refer to. Only 750 copies of the *First Folio* were printed, of which 233 still survive – several are in the British Library.

Nicholas Rowe's six-volume edition of 1709 (published by Jacob Tonson) was also hugely important, and he is considered Shakespeare's first editor and biographer. Not only did he add biographical details to the volumes, but he divided the plays into scenes and added stage directions, creating the editions that we know today.

Then Samuel Johnson, a lover of Shakespeare since childhood, produced an edition of the plays which was finally published in 1765 after extensive research. His Preface to the works helped to cement Shakespeare's reputation at the pinnacle of English literature. He states that Shakespeare's works 'through variation of taste and changes of manners, and, as they devolved from one generation to another, have received new honours at every transmission'. Through these books, and countless other editions, publishing has been hugely influential in building and maintaining Shakespeare's reputation.

Later, we see, from 1894 onwards, that J.M. Dent began to publish inexpensive individual volumes of the plays in the *Temple Shakespeare* series. These helped popularise the plays even further and got them into the hands of a much wider public. The series lasted for almost forty years and was only exceeded in popularity by Allen Lane launching the *Penguin Shakespeare* paperbacks in the 1930s – a series that is still going strong almost a century later.

3

James Lackington's
Temple of the Muses:
Bookselling in the Age
of the Enlightenment

James Lackington's Temple of the Muses bookshop. (Alamy)

The Arrival of the Modern Bookshop

How would we define a good bookshop? Today's best bookshops are wonderful spaces, packed full of a brilliant range of books across many subject areas, enticing the customer to explore new directions and expand their thinking. They are places where people can meet, browse freely, receive recommendations from knowledgeable and passionate booksellers, listen to authors talk about their latest book and discuss books with other readers in book groups or over coffee.

Bookshops like this are an accepted part of our modern culture, but they have their origins in the eighteenth century. Prior to that, a bookshop had been a jumbled mix of office, print workshop and storeroom, crammed next to a small sales area in which to transact business. With the increased numbers living in towns and cities, the development of a cultured society and with many more women becoming readers, bookshops were transformed into more attractive and appealing outlets. The introduction of the novel and a much wider range of subjects being printed, combined with the growth in literacy, meant that books gained in importance and popularity during this time. A bookshop became a destination – an essential part of this exciting new literate culture – and a place to be seen, not to mention where readers could discover thousands of brilliant new books. And there were countless great new books being published.

The eighteenth century witnessed a huge cultural shift. With growing prosperity on the back of an expanding empire, the population in towns and cities increased across the country. Approximately half of the population worked in agriculture at the start of the century, but this had dropped to a third by the century's end. The shift to towns and cities led to the establishment of a more civilised society, a growth in literacy, an increasingly strong literary culture and a huge growth in the number of books published.

With the growth of professions in towns, as opposed to the rural, the middle classes were swelling with an increase in the numbers of shopkeepers, tradesmen, clerks and administrative staff. Spare money to spend on books was still limited, though, leading to the development and growth of circulation libraries in the early part of the century, which helped the less well-off to access books regularly for a small annual subscription fee. And, although most libraries stocked a range of literature, it was the novel that became the main attraction.

As James Raven demonstrates in *The Business of Books*, during the century the number of books published annually in Britain rose from 1,800 to over 6,000 – the biggest leap forward for the book trade thus far. To facilitate this, there was a dramatic rise in the number of printing presses in London.

Literacy was increasing in tandem with this, with 40 per cent of women and 60 per cent of men able to read by 1800. This was to rise massively in the following centuries as a result of better education.

This was the exciting era of the Enlightenment: a time of new thinking and discovery, with developments in philosophy, history, science, invention, the arts and political thought. Books were a key way of sharing and exchanging such ideas.

As we have seen, throughout the seventeenth century there had been ongoing restrictions on what could be printed. It was only after 1695, when the Licensing Act lapsed, that those restrictions were lifted, and we see the explosion of printed works that characterised the eighteenth century. A wealth of newspapers, magazines and books followed. These societal and political changes all enabled a significant growth in the trades of publishing and bookselling.

The publication of magazines and journals became much more widespread and integral to eighteenth-century culture. Magazines gave budding writers a place to cut their teeth with articles, essays or stories. For much of his career, Samuel Johnson was a jobbing writer, and the magazines gave him a much-needed income. He wrote most of the articles in *The Rambler* magazine as well as writing his *Idler* essays for various other magazines. Oliver Goldsmith similarly survived initially by writing for magazines and Laurence Sterne was first published in the popular *Gentleman's Magazine*.

Poetry was also incredibly important and heavily featured in such magazines. Sales of poetry books were proportionately much stronger than today. For example, Dryden made a fortune with his translations of Virgil.

Alongside a flurry of new literature, existing works continued to be popular and were staple publications for bookseller–publishers selling to the growing new readership. Classical Greek and Roman literature were still much printed and read, often now in English translations for the first time, reaching those who hadn't studied Greek or Latin. The Bible continued to be a mainstay of households across the classes. In poorer households, often the only books they possessed were the Bible and a copy of *The Pilgrim's Progress*.

Another fascinating development at this time is the change in how people read books or periodicals. We see the increased development of silent reading because many readers had more leisure time to read to themselves, being able to shut themselves off from the world and lose themselves in a book. But the establishment of a literary society also provided platforms for reading aloud or shared reading. For some, this would have been among the family at home, with one person reading aloud to the others, many of whom probably could not read. We also see shared reading in literary clubs and societies. And we see the new phenomenon of home entertaining with extracts from different books read aloud to guests.

The home was changing, particularly for those in towns and cities, becoming a place for leisure and for receiving guests, many of whom would be entertained by this shared reading. Consequently, these new social occasions inspired a great age of elocution and rhetoric. A flurry of books was published teaching people how to speak in public. Reading at a domestic social occasion became a performance of sorts and these instruction manuals would include tips on how to read clearly and with confidence, and how to express emotion using the eyes, facial expressions and hand gestures, such as the demonstrative clutching of one's heart.

The Whig politician James Burgh published *The Art of Speaking* in 1761, a guide to oratory aimed at those reading at home. The book, which included extracts from Milton, Aristotle and other classic works, emphasised the importance of emotion and passion when reading, and gave tips on how to transmit these to your audience.

There was a boom in the publication of miscellanies, collections of extracts from larger works such as novels, plays, poems and biblical readings that could be utilised when reading to an audience. Many households also had their own 'Commonplace Book' containing personal selections that could be read alone but were more often used when reading to others. Many people didn't necessarily read a whole novel but nonetheless enjoyed and were made aware of books in this way, often repeatedly hearing or reading key extracts from the books of the day. This led to a wider general awareness of literature, even if whole works weren't always consumed. Those reading silently were perhaps more likely to read a whole book from start to finish and, likewise, some families gathered each evening to hear the next instalment of whichever book they were collectively reading.

It is worth remembering that, at this time, light to read by in the evenings was very limited. Until the introduction of an effective domestic oil lamp in the early nineteenth century, lighting was provided by candles. The poorer households would have used homemade tallow candles, whereas wax candles, the best form of lighting at the time, were only available to the better-off sectors of society. To compound this, spectacles were not yet widely available and effective pairs would not be introduced until later in the eighteenth century. This increased the importance of one family member reading aloud to the others, perhaps those who either could not read or might have had poor eyesight.

The Dawn of the Novel

One of the most important developments in the eighteenth century for our story was the rise of the novel, from Daniel Defoe's *Robinson Crusoe* onwards. The dramatic development and growth of the novel in the eighteenth and nineteenth centuries coincided with and was partly facilitated by the massive upsurge in literacy. This created increased demand for the printed word, which in turn, led to significant growth of the industry that we now know as the book trade.

Adult fiction is undoubtedly one of the key elements in today's book trade and currently accounts for almost 30 per cent of all book sales annually. The development of the novel and its consequent importance hugely benefitted the book trade, further increased the status of books in the public's consciousness and significantly aided the growth in book sales.

The novel represented a new way of writing, a more realistic form of fiction that was attempting to portray all varieties of the individual human experience. Characterisation and more detailed and realistic backgrounds became important, enabling the new readers of novels to identify with the characters and their stories, often seeing themselves reflected in these narratives. It created a more personal experience for the reader and forged a unique bond between the reader and the author, as I discussed in the Introduction.

The novel was essentially formless, full of infinite possibilities, and could veer off in any direction, marking a profound shift from the narrative forms of classical tradition. In *Pamela*, for example, Samuel Richardson very much fixes the book in a specific real time and place, providing detailed descriptions of locations and interiors, even noting exact times of day on the letters that formed the novel. Contemporary readers could imagine themselves being Robinson Crusoe or Pamela and could identify with the decisions they made.

The Life and Adventures of Robinson Crusoe of York, Mariner was first published in 1719. 'I was born in the Year 1632, in the City of York, of a good Family, tho' not of that Country, my Father being a Foreigner of Bremen, who settled first at Hull.' Thus begins this famous novel, epitomising the attraction of books in their ability to help us explore other lives and lands that we know nothing about, coupled with a heavy dose of escapism, peril and adventure to grip the reader.

Defoe, a journalist and a spy, had grown up among political insurrection and intrigue, as well as living through the Plague and the Great Fire of London. He was renowned for his pamphleteering in the late seventeenth and early eighteenth centuries, in an era when hundreds of pamphlets were being published to echo every political viewpoint of the day. Then, in his fifties, he transformed himself into a novelist. The success of *Robinson Crusoe* was followed by *Journal of the Plague Year* (1722), *Moll Flanders* (also 1722) and *Roxana* (1724), among others.

Books and literature were available in increasingly varied ways, not only through bookshops, but also from more general retailers, a thriving second-hand market and the new circulating libraries. The printed word seemed to be everywhere. Books, magazines and newspapers were read aloud, shared and borrowed, available in part-works, monthly instalments or abridged versions. *Robinson Crusoe* seems to have mainly been read in abridged form and many children's versions were also produced. There were chapbooks (cheap abridged versions) of many other popular books, including *Pilgrim's Progress, Gulliver's Travels, Tom Jones* and *Moll Flanders*.

Print runs for books were still very low, however, often only 500 to 750 copies. Price was clearly deterring many potential readers, so we see circulation libraries starting to become important, offering a range of books to borrow for a small fee or subscription. Other readers accessed literature through the many monthly magazines, such as the *Monthly Review* or the *Literary Journal*, which were more affordable and consequently had much higher sales, several selling over 3,000 copies each. There is much evidence, too, of multiple readings of a magazine, book or newspaper, shared between households and read by many people, which suggests an even higher readership.

Samuel Richardson's *Pamela*, about a wealthy man's relationship with a young maidservant, is often cited as the first true English novel as we define the term today and was certainly the first bestselling English novel. It was published by one of the big name bookseller–publishers of the eighteenth century, Charles Rivington, based in Paternoster Row. *Pamela's* success influenced much of the fiction that followed and confirmed the arrival of the novel as a cultural phenomenon. Novels became highly fashionable and certain key titles were the talk of the town. Ladies at the Ranelagh Pleasure Gardens in Chelsea would ensure that they were seen brandishing copies of *Pamela* to demonstrate just how fashionable they were.

Samuel Richardson had started his working life as a printer and publisher, although always harbouring ambitions to be a writer himself. He was apprenticed to the printer John Wilde in 1706 and several years later set up on his own, printing hundreds of titles from his shop near Fleet Street. In 1733, he won the contract to print *The Journals of the House* (of Commons) which helped grow his business. He also went on to print two newspapers, *The Daily Journal* and *The Daily Gazetteer*, and became a very successful businessman and a good friend of Charles Rivington. However, his personal life was beset by tragedy, as his first wife Martha and all six of their children died. He married again to Elizabeth and had another six children with her, with four daughters surviving into adulthood. Like Defoe, he was a latecomer to the novel and only at the age of 51 did Richardson turn to fiction and the writing of *Pamela*.

The most marked increase in readers in the eighteenth century was among women. In consequence, women became the prime readers of the novel at this time and could be said to have underpinned its success. Women from the middle and upper classes were unable to participate in most of the work undertaken by men, including business, politics and estate management, or leisure activities such as hunting. At the same time, many of the tasks that had traditionally occupied women in towns in previous generations were no longer necessary. Spinning, weaving, the creation of food and drink were now provided for by the increased number of shops, markets and factories. This gave women more leisure time than men and, for some, reading filled this time. Many women became voracious and enthusiastic readers. Books enriched their day-to-day lives and offered them a new dimension, a form of escape from the daily grind.

Another new category of reader were household servants, who either had access to decent libraries or perhaps had money for a circulation library subscription, and who also often had time on their hands. A book like *Pamela* would appeal to both middle-class women readers and the household servant, which helps to explain its massive success. Pamela herself can be seen as a heroine to that new readership of female domestic servants.

With this vast new readership available, booksellers probably favoured producing books of easy entertainment for strong sales rather than more critically acclaimed but difficult work, hence the rise of the novel. There is no doubt that the huge success of *Pamela* was due in no small part to this new female readership, but the male readership was also showing greater sensibility, emotion and 'sentimentalism' – the latter very much in vogue in the eighteenth century – and the better novels certainly appealed to them, too. Richardson himself was very much of this type, interested in character and emotion, as well as in the domestic detail of city or town life.

The success of *Pamela* and the excitement and buzz it generated was something that would become a regular occurrence in publishing over the following centuries. Other titles that became big bestsellers for bookseller–publishers in the eighteenth century were *A Sentimental Journey* by Laurence Sterne (a mixture of fiction and travel writing), *Tom Jones* by Henry Fielding, *The Adventures of Roderick Random* by Tobias Smollett and *The Vicar of Wakefield* by Oliver Goldsmith, a book that would influence Dickens. Among this wealth of great novels and novelists of the eighteenth century, it's important to also note the rise of women writers, including Ann Radcliffe, Maria Edgeworth, Mary Wollstonecraft, Charlotte Lennox and Frances Burney.

Frances Burney's debut, *Evelina* (1778), an epistolary novel like *Pamela*, was an instant success and quickly sold through its original 800-copy print run. Three more printings of *Evelina* followed in swift succession (of 500, another 500 and then 1,000 respectively), proving that book sales could escalate with the right book that captured the current mood. Her novels, dealing with social issues and the lives of the upper middle class, predated Jane Austen's novels in their themes and subject matter and broke new ground at the time. The success of *Evelina* led to three more strong sellers, *Cecilia* (1782), *Camilla* (1796) and *The Wanderer* (1814). Burney also wrote plays and published several volumes of her journals. She was paid just £20 for her first novel by bookseller–publisher Thomas Lowndes. However, following the success of *Evelina*, she was paid £250 for her next novel *Cecilia* and its first printing was 2,000 copies. Very quickly, translated editions of *Evelina* began to appear in Germany and Holland.

Burney was the daughter of music historian Dr Charles Burney, and originally wanted to remain anonymous. However, this proved to be impossible, and she was soon celebrated in London literary circles, becoming friend to the big names of the day including Hester Thrale, Samuel Johnson and James Boswell. She feared the reaction of the critics, but *Evelina* was almost universally well received, with the *Monthly Review* declaring it 'one of the most sprightly, entertaining and agreeable productions of this kind'. Johnson told her that the book was 'full of merit, it is really extraordinary'. Burney had to quickly get used to acquaintances praising her novel in this way.

Following the revolution instigated by Defoe, Richardson, Burney and others, the number of novels being printed dramatically increased, from about seven per annum in the early decades of the century up to about forty per annum by 1800. The nineteenth century would witness even greater growth. Many of these early novels were of little merit, including a wave of Gothic novels. But a few key writers do stand out, creating more exceptional work that has stood the test of time, names such as Fielding, Smollett, Sterne, Frances Burney and then, at the start of the new century, Jane Austen.

John Newbery

It was also during the eighteenth century that the first books for children specifically aimed for their enjoyment were published. At the start of the century, children certainly read general adult books such as collections of fables, fairy tales and assorted miscellanies, but books published for children tended to be mainly instructional books, such as spelling books, history books or books of a religious nature. The first known children's educational instruction title *Orbis Sensualium Pictus*, published in 1658 and available in English translation from 1659, aimed to help children learn letters and sounds through pictures.

In the 1740s, however, the public mood began to shift, possibly because of societal changes and a revision in attitudes about family life, and several London-based publishers capitalised on this by releasing books that youngsters could enjoy – books that were published just for them.

A Little Pretty Pocket Book by John Newbery was published in 1744, spearheading this new movement. It is considered to be the first book that was aimed specifically at children and unusual for its time as it was published with a colourful, attractive cover. It also came with a free gift – either a rubber ball for a boy ('Little Master Tommy') or a pincushion for a girl ('Pretty Miss Polly'), both of which were divided into a red side and a black side. Children were encouraged to monitor their own behaviour and stick a pin in the red side if they had been good or into the black side if they had been naughty. Newbery believed that children could be encouraged to good behaviour through play. It was this book, containing poems, songs and proverbs, that started the new trend of publishing for children.

John Newbery is still remembered today as an author of several children's books but, more significantly, as a children's book publisher, and he is often called 'the father of children's literature'. He demonstrated that entertaining children's books could sell, thereby launching an industry that would eventually lead to the million-copy sales of Enid Blyton, Roald Dahl, J.K. Rowling, Shirley Hughes, Judith Kerr, Julia Donaldson and so many other authors who sell today in the twenty-first century.

Newbery led an exciting transformation in book publishing and bookselling. He published *The Lilliputian Magazine*, the first periodical for children, and his book *The History of Little Goody Two-Shoes* (1765) is regarded as the first children's novel. He wrote several other books for children himself but also published almost 100 children's books by other authors, including titles by such famous names as Samuel Johnson and Oliver Goldsmith. As a tribute to his significant achievements, the American Library Association still awards the annual John Newbery Medal to 'the most distinguished contributions to American literature for children'.

Among other children's books first issued in the 1740s were *Description of Three Hundred Animals* by Thomas Boreman and *Tommy Thumb's Pretty Song Book* by Mary Cooper of 1744, the first known collection of nursery rhymes. Sarah Trimmer's book, *Fabulous Histories*, published in 1786, about a family of robins, was one of the first children's books to tell a story through animal characters, paving the way for future writers such as Beatrix Potter, Dick King-Smith and Julia Donaldson.

Another pioneering children's writer was Anna Letitia Barbauld, author of *Lessons for Children* and *Hymns in Prose for Children*, who wanted to make her books accessible to children and encouraged parents to read the books with their child (something organisations like the Book Trust are still championing today). She insisted on large type and a limited number of words per page to facilitate easier reading.

From these beginnings in the eighteenth century, children's literature mushroomed and grew as a separate category with more books appearing every year, including specially abridged versions of adult classic titles aimed at youngsters, explaining their enduring popularity. *Robinson Crusoe* and *Gulliver's Travels* became staples of this genre. I first read *Robinson Crusoe* as a child in an abridgement from Dean & Son, a publisher set up in the 1800s that was still producing cheap children's classics in the mid-twentieth century.

Above all, Newbery introduced to children the idea of reading for pleasure and for fun – what I and millions of others would enjoy through Ladybird and Puffin books and multiple others in our own childhoods. We take all this for granted today, but we owe a massive debt to John Newbery. The modern children's publishing industry provides education, enjoyment, inspiration and stimulation to successive generations.

Hatchards

As mentioned, the eighteenth century is significant for our narrative as we start to see bookshops that looked less like printing workshops and more like the shops we know today. The growth of these was underpinned by the century's increase in the numbers of books published, the widening subject areas covered and the success of the novel.

Much of this business was still focussed on London but bookshops were springing up across the country, too. Cambridge now boasted William Thurlbourn's bookshop in Trinity Street and Thomas Merrill in Regent Walk, and from the 1740s Robert Watts opened Cambridge's first circulating library. In Oxford, Daniel Prince had a bookshop in Broad Street, as did Fletcher & Hanwells from 1731, a shop that was later taken over by Joseph Parker in the nineteenth century and then bought by Blackwell's in the late twentieth century.

Samuel Hazard started a successful bookselling business in fashionable Bath in 1772, and John Smith opened his bookshop in Glasgow in 1751, the oldest surviving bookshop business in Britain today, although it is now in a different location in the city. The century also saw multiple new bookshops opening across London itself – Andrew Millar in the Strand, John Bell, with his 'British Library' bookshop and circulating library near the Strand, and Charles Rivington, mentioned above, based in St Paul's Churchyard.

Charles Rivington was one of the key booksellers of the eighteenth century. Having taken over Richard Chiswell's business in Paternoster Row in 1711, Rivington erected the sign of 'The Bible and the Crown' over his doorway, which also appeared on his many publications released in subsequent decades. Rivington specialised in theological and educational books, issuing books of sermons as well as publishing Thomas a Kempis' *Imitation of Christ* and many early Methodist tracts by George Whitefield, one of the movement's leaders.

When Charles Rivington died in 1742, his son John carried on the business, producing theological texts in conjunction with the Church of England and severing the connection with the Methodists. Rivington's other son, James, emigrated to America in 1760 where he set up as a journalist and publisher, particularly of newspapers, including *The New York Gazetteer*. He backed the British during the Revolutionary War, was lucky not to be killed and was certainly never as successful after the revolution. Rivington Street in New York is named after him.

The eighteenth century also saw the earliest iteration of W.H. Smith, although only as a vendor of newspapers at this stage (W.H. Smith would become a key bookseller that we will learn more about in future chapters). But probably the two greatest bookshops of the eighteenth century were Hatchards in Piccadilly, still thriving to this day, and James Lackington's book megastore, The Temple of the Muses.

John Hatchard was born in 1769 and had worked for several different parts of the book trade before setting up on his own. He started out at printer Thomas Bensley, then became apprentice to John Ginger in Westminster, before becoming an assistant to Thomas Payne at his shop in Mews Gate, which was also a popular coffee house, sited roughly where today's National Gallery stands.

Hatchard opened his own bookshop in Piccadilly in 1797, moving to its current site next to Fortnum & Mason in 1801. Hatchards is the oldest bookshop still existing in London, has always been associated with the rich and the famous, and is the holder of three royal warrants. Since its inception, it has played a key role in London bookselling as one of the best and most-loved bookshops in the capital and has long been associated with the most high-profile authors. It was Oscar Wilde's favourite bookshop and today 'Oscar's Table', where he used to sit and sign his books, is still situated on the ground floor of the bookshop. A painting of John Hatchard can be also seen as you ascend the staircase in the centre of the shop.

Hatchards was acquired by the publisher William Collins in 1956, then purchased by the Pentos group (owners of Dillons) in 1990. The whole Dillons chain was subsequently acquired by Waterstones and Hatchards continues as part of the Waterstones group today, although still retaining its name and unique flavour.

Throughout its history, Hatchards has been renowned for its authoritative and knowledgeable staff, the backbone of the successful bookseller. It was a bookshop that I called on as a publisher's sales rep after the closure of our bookshop. Today, despite being part of a larger chain, Hatchards remains a treasure trove of wonderful discoveries and is a true destination bookshop, a visit to which never disappoints.

The Temple of the Muses

James Lackington revolutionised the book trade and created the first modern bookshop. He was a great self-promoter and innovative businessman who loved books and believed strongly in their ability to spread knowledge. But Lackington, who subsequently wrote two volumes of autobiography, came from lowly beginnings. He was the son of a shoemaker in Somerset and only learned to read and write in his early twenties. With this late-discovered passion for books, he moved to London with barely a penny to his name and eventually managed to open his first small bookshop in Featherstone Street in 1774 at the age of 28.

Lackington may have come to books late, but that discovery had transformed his life. It meant so much to him that he wanted to enable others who were less fortunate to share the pleasures of books too, a theme that is repeated time and again among bookselling and publishing entrepreneurs.

The shop had a circulating library but, most significantly, it sold cheap or remaindered books as part of its overall offer. This part of the business expanded rapidly and was one of the foundations upon which Lackington's success was built. He was unusual for his time in that he bought up huge volumes of unsold books and whole libraries of second-hand books. Many publishers would previously have just dumped these books, but Lackington sold them cheaply, thus enabling more people to have access to books, particularly those who normally could not afford them. This brought more customers into his shop, helping to grow his business.

Another key foundation to Lackington's success was his refusal to supply customers on credit and to only accept cash. This was a new approach at the time and upset others in the trade, but giving credit had been the downfall of many booksellers and continued to be so well into the twentieth century, particularly for those retailers supplying to the 'carriage trade', the extremely wealthy who were heavy book buyers but often did not pay their bills, thus affecting a bookseller's profitability.

In 1793, buoyed by his early success, James Lackington opened his crowning glory in Finsbury Square, a huge new bookshop called The Temple of the Muses. This beautiful establishment had a sign over the door proclaiming it as 'The Cheapest Bookseller in the World'. The Temple of the Muses was spacious and inviting, with a shop front 140ft long and displaying over one million books inside. In *Shadows of the Old Booksellers*, Charles Knight stated that The Temple of the Muses' 'dimensions are to be measured by the assertion that a coach and six might be driven round it'. He went on, 'In the centre is an enormous circular counter, within which stand the dispensers of knowledge.' A grand, wide staircase led to more rooms of books upstairs, displayed and accessible to the customer and conducive to easy browsing. The higher you climbed in the shop, the cheaper the books became.

The shop became a popular place to meet, exchange gossip and browse the new and old publications displayed within, and it was soon at the hub of Georgian society. The Temple of the Muses had a similar impact to when Tim Waterstone started his bookshop chain in the 1980s, introducing the British public to larger shops with a much deeper stock.

Lackington was famed for stocking a huge range of titles and producing a catalogue reflecting this, which started at about 12,000 titles but eventually grew to list around 200,000 by 1796. In his memoirs, he says, 'I loved books, and that if I could but be a bookseller, I should then have plenty of books to read, which was the greatest motive I could conceive to induce me to make the attempt'. He believed that books were the key to knowledge and thought that everyone, regardless of class or background, deserved access to books.

Lackington was certainly a formidable businessman, but one with altruistic motives too. He was a celebrity in his day and, in his ambition to sell cheaply and in volume, he could be compared to Allen Lane in the 1930s, Paul Hamlyn in the 1960s, Terry Maher of Dillons in the 1990s or Jeff Bezos of Amazon in the twenty-first century, all of whom we shall meet later in this narrative.

As well as introducing reading areas and space to browse and making books affordable to the everyman, Lackington was a great publicist and marketeer, travelling the streets of London in a carriage inscribed with his motto, 'Small profits do great things'. He also issued tokens which could be exchanged for books, an obvious forerunner of today's book tokens, which were not introduced nationally until 1932.

Lackington retired to his estate in Gloucestershire in 1798, passing the business to his cousin, George Lackington. But, by then, he had established the very modern concept of the large welcoming bookshop at the hub of cultural and literary society.

4

Charles Edward Mudie and W.H. Smith: Literary Culture in the Nineteenth Century

A circulating library. (Alamy)

Developments in Printing Techniques

In addition to examining how publishers and booksellers developed, it's important to look at changes in how books were created. While production techniques had improved and become much speedier since Caxton first introduced the wooden printing press to England in 1476, printers were still essentially using the same methods at the dawn of the nineteenth century. However, several inventors were working on improvements.

Charles Stanhope produced a cast-iron press in 1800, which doubled the size of the printed area and could print up to 480 sheets per hour. Then, on 28 November 1814, *The Times* newspaper was produced for the first time by a steam-driven printing press, an important innovation.

In 1810, London-based German inventor Frederick Koenig, working with Andreas Bauer, had patented a steam-powered, double-cylinder printing press, following decades of attempts to improve upon the manual printing press. His model replaced manual labour with steam power, with a rotating cylinder introduced into the process in what became known as rotary printing. As with previous key developments, it took at least a couple of decades before all printers switched over to the new model. Printers could now print up to 1,000 sheets per hour, which was a dramatic increase. Koenig and Bauer still exist today as a German company making printing presses.

Richard Hoe's further development of the rotary printing press in 1843 improved techniques and led to even higher quantities being printed. Hoe's machine revolved 2,000 times per hour, producing four pages each time and enabling the printing of 8,000 sheets per hour. These improvements increased the production of books, magazines and newspapers, facilitating the further growth of these industries.

The development of 'linotype' printing in the late nineteenth century was also hugely significant. The linotype method was developed by Ottmar Mergenthaler in 1884. The machine assembles type onto a cast, based upon the operator typing words. Instead of assembling type by hand, each press of a key delivers a letter to the cast at the same speed as the typing, creating lines of type. This was transformative and dramatically sped up the typesetting process.

The first commercial use of the linotype machine was by the *New York Tribune* in 1886 but, very soon, most printers were using similar methods. Newspapers and book publishers would operate multiple linotype machines to speed up the process even further. Linotype and steam printers helped drive the huge growth of book and newspaper publishing throughout the twentieth century. The linotype was so efficient that only towards the end of the century were these processes replaced by digital typesetting and digital printing, which is the norm today. Advances in the past two or three decades have further progressed the capabilities of the printing and publishing industries.

Throughout the nineteenth century, the bigger publishers (such as Murray, Longman and Blackwood) expanded their range of subjects printed, increased the number of titles on their lists and the size of their print runs, sometimes printing as many as 10,000 copies of a title. Improved printing techniques led to larger machines in bigger premises or factories, now employing hundreds of workers at each establishment – all a far cry from the small hand-driven printing presses in cramped bookshops in Paternoster Row that had been the norm in the immediate post-Caxton period of the late fifteenth century.

These improvements facilitated a massive growth in readership throughout the nineteenth century, alongside a golden age of fiction publishing from many authors who are still widely read today – Dickens, Austen, the Brontës, George Eliot, Elizabeth Gaskell, Thomas Hardy and Anthony Trollope among them.

The Inimitable Charles Dickens
and *The Pickwick Papers*

Dickens arrived on the literary scene in the 1830s with bombastic impact, akin to a debut novelist today hitting the No. 1 spot in the bestsellers list and staying there for weeks. His success boosted sales of monthly or weekly serialised fiction – all of his novels were originally published in this fashion and then later issued in book form.

Serial publication in magazines or journals had continued to grow. It made reading more affordable and accessible for the consumer, involved less initial outlay and was a key route for those on lower incomes to access literature. Monthly journals were in great demand in the early nineteenth century and were generally published on the last weekday of the month, on what became known as Magazine Day. A good serial writer's job was to leave the reader wanting more at the end of an instalment, guaranteeing a readership for the next issue.

Until the 1830s, serial fiction had been rather looked down upon by the literary establishment, but Dickens' success changed that, and serials became an important part of the novel publishing process for the rest of the century and beyond. They were generally profitable for publishers and booksellers, who benefitted from the sale of the monthly editions but were remunerated again when the completed novel was published in two or three volumes once the serialisation had finished and often selling to a different readership. The flip side of this was that serialisations that failed to attract sufficient readership would be cancelled after just a few issues, which was bad luck for the author but more financially sensible for the publisher.

The success of writers like Dickens and Thackeray depended on attracting and retaining readers and thereby increasing circulation. Famously, Dickens' first serialised novel, *The Pickwick Papers* only hit its stride in Issue 4, even though Dickens was not a complete unknown on publication. Writing under the pen name 'Boz', he had achieved considerable success already with a series of stories and observations published in various magazines, collected as *Sketches by Boz*. But it was *The Pickwick Papers* that really launched his career, after which his fame continued to grow right up to his death in 1870.

Following the success of *Sketches by Boz*, Dickens had been approached by the publisher William Chapman of Chapman & Hall to write short, descriptive texts to accompany a series of sporting prints by the successful and prolific artist Robert Seymour. The prints would depict the humorous adventures of a club of Cockney sportsmen in a new magazine series. This was very much in the tradition of similar successful series such as *Dr Syntax*, illustrated by Thomas Rowlandson, and *Life in London*, illustrated by George Cruikshank.

Dickens, although a novice writer, was already brimming with such confidence in his own abilities that he persuaded Chapman & Hall that he should develop the story, and Seymour should supply illustrations based upon Dickens' ideas. And this was what happened.

Seymour, a troubled soul with various problems in his personal life, committed suicide after illustrating just two issues. The publisher brought in Robert William Buss as illustrator for the third issue, but Dickens was not convinced. Instead, the 19-year-old Hablot Knight Browne took over on the fourth issue and adopted the pen name 'Phiz'. He subsequently became Dickens' illustrator for the next twenty-four years.

The first monthly issue of *The Pickwick Papers* was published in March 1836 and sold 1,000 copies, but sales dropped to fewer than 500 for the next two issues. Like many serialised stories, it looked like *The Pickwick Papers* wasn't going to attract sufficient interest to continue. It lacked that certain something to turn it into a bestseller. However, everything changed with the introduction of the lovable humorous cockney, Sam Weller, as Mr Pickwick's valet in the fourth issue – and the book's fortunes were turned around. Very quickly, the magazine became the talk of the town and, through word-of-mouth, book sales took off. Soon there were people recounting 'Wellerisms' to one another and laughing together over the Pickwick Club's antics. The magazine was quickly selling over 20,000 copies per month, reaching 40,000 at its peak. Dickens' success was born and, already the workaholic that he was to be for the rest of his life, he followed it up promptly with two more serialised hits, *Oliver Twist* and *Nicholas Nickleby*, which he wrote concurrently for different publishers and established his reputation as the hottest-selling writer in Britain.

Dickens' success reflects the huge excitement generated by certain books, the same that had greeted Richardson's *Pamela* and would greet thousands more titles in the years to follow – that wonderful buzz that fuels the publishing and bookselling industry to this day. With Dickens, the phenomenon of the bestselling writer was born – his was a name that would bring joy to millions, not just in Britain but around the world, and for generations to come.

The Difficulties of Getting
Published as a Woman

However, despite this being a golden age of fiction writing, it remained much more difficult for a female author to get published than for her male counterpart. And this was still the case right through to the second half of the twentieth century. Only in very recent decades have we seen women writers come to dominate the bestseller lists, just as it is now more normal to see women working in positions of power in both bookselling and publishing. Throughout the nineteenth century, many of whom we would now class as major writers initially struggled to get their works taken seriously, let alone achieve publishing success.

Jane Austen could be said to be the heir of Frances Burney but, in truth, she took influences from Richardson and Fielding as well, combining elements of each of them to create a more accomplished narrative of daily life, with wit and criticism built into the prose. Austen didn't use the first-person narrative but told stories as an assured author leading her readers deftly through the plots, characters and relationships within the novel, at the same time commenting on events and giving readers a real closeness to the characters. In her books, Austen reflected many of the key eighteenth-century issues, particularly the role of women in modern society, alongside the middle-class quest for status and the debate about the concept of marriage. The influence of women both as writers and readers is reflected in her work, challenging the previous male dominance.

Jane Austen achieved early success when her first novel, *Sense and Sensibility*, was published in 1811 by Egerton's of Whitehall, albeit at the author's expense. As was the case for many female novelists at this time, the book was published anonymously. Despite it being a poor printing, the book sold out and the publisher arranged a reprint. *Pride and Prejudice* followed in 1813 and was much a much bigger seller, but *Mansfield Park* (1814) was not a success.

Jane and her brother, the banker Henry Austen, who acted almost as her agent, sent the manuscript of her next novel, *Emma*, to John Murray. Murray was a much more prestigious publisher and was currently the talk of the town due to its success as the publisher of Byron.

The company had been inundated with manuscripts as a result but, luckily, Jane Austen's reputation forced John Murray to take notice and his reader, William Gifford, reported, 'Of *Emma*, I have nothing but good to say.'

Jane and Henry proved tough negotiators, rejecting Murray's initial offers. Indeed, with her growing reputation and confidence, Jane requested that Murray call on her to try to find some agreement – an unusual way of doing things for any writer, let alone a woman. But they did reach agreement, albeit with Jane still paying the initial costs of publication, but she was to benefit from the increased sales afforded by such a major publisher taking her on. *Emma* was still not the huge bestseller either author or publisher had hoped, despite a positive review from Walter Scott in the *Quarterly Review*.

Sadly, Jane died in 1817 from Addison's disease before her reputation was really established. Murray went on to publish all of her backlist, but it wasn't until the 1860s, with the publication of James Edward Austen-Leigh's *A Memoir of Jane Austen*, that her modern popularity really began. Sales of her novels grew and helped establish her reputation as the major writer we know her today.

The three Brontë sisters from Haworth in Yorkshire also feared publishing under their real names. Their initial joint collection of poems was published under the pseudonyms of Acton, Currer and Ellis Bell, not only hiding their identities but their sex. Anne and Emily then reached an agreement to publish their novels *Agnes Grey* and *Wuthering Heights* in a joint edition, but Charlotte's first novel, *The Professor*, struggled to find a publisher.

Charlotte's breakthrough, however, came about when she sent the manuscript to the publisher Smith, Elder & Co. Although the company rejected *The Professor*, William Smith Williams wrote from the publisher to praise the 'great literary power' evidenced in the text. He was convinced that 'Currer Bell' 'could produce a book which would command success'. Charlotte had nearly completed another novel and, encouraged by the publisher's interest, she promptly finished that and sent it off. Williams was so impressed with the new manuscript that he insisted his boss George Smith read it immediately. Smith himself was then so consumed by it that, having started reading it at breakfast, he cancelled all engagements that day to complete the book by evening. The next morning, he had made an offer to publish *Jane Eyre* under the pseudonym of Currer Bell as well as options on two further novels.

Jane Eyre was met with huge acclaim, including from Thackeray, who said he had 'lost (or won if you like) a whole day in reading it'. In time, William Smith Williams would become a close friend of Brontë and a champion of her work, publishing both *Shirley* and *Villette* in her lifetime. And, as more people within the London literary establishment became aware of her true identity, Brontë also became friends with Thackeray and G.H. Lewes. But the path to success for women writers still wasn't easy.

A few decades later, Mary Anne Evans was editing the *Westminster Review* and contributing essays to that journal before she turned her hand to fiction. Her partner, George Henry Lewes persuaded her to submit her stories to the publisher John Blackwood, who then published *The Sad Fortunes of the Reverend Amos Barton* in the popular *Blackwood's Magazine*. Launched in Edinburgh in 1817 by publisher William Blackwood, the best-selling literary journal for much of the nineteenth century subsequently published *Amos Barton* as one of three stories in *Scenes from Clerical Life*, released in book form in 1858.

Mary Anne Evans chose to publish under the pen name George Eliot, probably for a variety of reasons. As with Jane Austen and Charlotte Brontë, she may have felt that her work would be taken more seriously if readers thought she was a man. Indeed, initially, many believed that 'George Eliot' was a country parson. But Mary Anne Evans was also concerned about public perception of her relationship with Lewes, who she lived with although he was a married man. Soon after the publication of *Adam Bede*, George Eliot's second novel, the secret of her identity became public knowledge, but she stuck with the pseudonym for her entire publishing career. She also continued to be published by Blackwood, including many bestsellers such as *The Mill on the Floss*, *Silas Marner* and *Middlemarch*.

Today, we revere Austen, Brontë and Eliot as three of the major writers in the English literary canon but, for all three, initially publishing as a woman was a challenge. Even in the twentieth century, publishing as a woman was never as easy as it was for men. Books by women were less likely to get published, less likely to be shortlisted for prizes and less likely to attract reviews. Publishers like Virago and The Women's Press were set up specifically to challenge and change this in the latter half of the twentieth century and, even as late as the 1990s, it was deemed necessary to set up the Women's Prize in response to other awards such as the Booker Prize being so male-dominated.

Circulation Libraries

Although literacy was increasing in the nineteenth century and with it this great thirst for new books, the price of books was still expensive, making them prohibitive for a large proportion of the potential readership. Circulation libraries, so-called because the books circulated among readers, were introduced by many bookshops and quickly became a popular way to access books, bringing literature to a mass readership.

The first commercial circulation libraries had opened in the 1740s, offering the latest titles to readers who, by paying a small subscription, could access a wide range of books. The libraries would buy up multiple copies of key titles and, as this market grew, these provided the basis for print runs for many publishers. The success of the libraries broadened the types of people reading books, including more from the lower classes.

Some of the pioneers of the circulating library in London were Thomas Lowndes (publisher of Frances Burney), John Noble (publisher of Daniel Defoe), William Lane in Leadenhall Street, Thomas Hookham in Bond Street (whose library was eventually taken over by Mudie's in the 1870s) and John Bell (who owned the British Library bookshop in the Strand). Some estimates suggest that there were up to 1,000 libraries throughout Britain in the eighteenth century.

Circulation libraries were of huge social importance in widening readership and played a significant role in the sales of popular novelists throughout the eighteenth century, such as Frances Burney, Samuel Richardson and Henry Fielding. The phenomenon continued into the nineteenth century, particularly after the establishment of Mudie's Subscription Library.

Charles Edward Mudie was born in 1818 and originally worked in the family newspaper business before opening his first bookshop in Bloomsbury in 1840. He then decided to devote over a third of his shop to the lending library. While he was by no means the first to open such a library, by charging his customers a 1 guinea annual fee to borrow one book at a time, he dramatically undercut the competition, who charged anything up to 10 guineas. Mudie's cheaper subscription meant that he had a much bigger audience than his rivals and could then afford to buy more copies of the most in-demand books and offer a much wider range of books, which, in turn, made his libraries more attractive than its competitors, thus increasing his subscription base even more.

Mudie personally selected books that he thought were decent and proper for the desired middle-class readership. Due to the growth of his business, he soon moved his 'Select Library' to larger premises in New Oxford Street, close to the British Museum, followed by branches elsewhere in London, as well as Manchester and Birmingham. W.H. Smith had offered Mudie the opportunity to open libraries at their station bookstalls in 1858. Mudie didn't take them up on this offer, so W.H. Smith opted to open their own libraries and became Mudie's biggest competitor, although focussing more on single-volume reprints, which were much easier for the travelling passenger.

Mudie had really wanted to distribute quality non-fiction and continued to do so throughout his career; but it was primarily the popularity of the novel that drove the company's growth. He would buy hundreds of copies of new novels and barter for a high discount because of his large purchases. He held massive power over what was selected and, in consequence, over what was published and what most of the population were reading. Because of his prudish values, he made enemies of those publishers and authors he didn't select, who were then disadvantaged in their access to this huge market. He was a hugely influential figure, very much the Allen Lane or Jeff Bezos of his day, making books accessible to a wider section of the populace.

The lending libraries boomed throughout the second half of the nineteenth century and continued as a crucial part of the book trade right through to the 1960s, only declining then because of the availability of cheaper paperback books and the growth of public libraries. Mudie's became such an important part of Victorian society that it is mentioned in many of the most popular novels of the era, including frequently in the works of Anthony Trollope and George Gissing, and even in Virginia Woolf's later *Jacob's Room* from 1922. In George Gissing's *The Odd Women* (1893), the controlling husband buys his wife, Monica, a subscription to Mudie's as a sop instead of letting her go out and socialise, knowing that books from Mudie's were relatively unthreatening.

Mudie was responsible for the dominance of the 'triple-decker' Victorian novel. Creating a novel in three volumes forced the publisher to put the price up and therefore made books too expensive for most readers to buy at 31*s* 6*d*. This created a generation of readers who could not afford to buy novels, driving them towards the libraries.

The triple-decker novel had first been introduced by the publisher Archibald Constable with Walter Scott's weighty novels earlier in the nineteenth century, and the format and length became very popular for the next sixty years or so, with many authors copying Scott in the hope of similar success. George Gissing's *New Grub Street* is a brilliant satire on the writers who were forced to produce such lengthy works. Its main character, Edwin Reardon, after some early success, is struggling to write his next novel for this market and is stuck after just two chapters. 'The three-volumes lie before me like an interminable desert,' he says. 'Impossible to get through them.' However, by the end of the novel, towards the end of the nineteenth century, the love of the huge triple-decker novel had started to wane and slimmer novels, with arguably less excess padding, started to appear.

W.H. Smith

The dawn of the railways in the mid-nineteenth century was hugely significant for book distribution, as for so many businesses. The greatest beneficiary of this transport revolution was W.H. Smith, who owed their dramatic growth to the rapid expansion across Britain of the railway network. And the growth of W.H. Smith in the nineteenth century directly assisted the increase in book sales.

W.H. Smith has always been adept at adapting to the retail environment and its changing trends throughout its history, and its longevity is in part due to this agility. Henry Walton Smith had started the business as a news vendor in 1792. The business then grew significantly under the management of Henry's son, William Henry Smith. He expanded the business's reach and bought out other companies, dominating the sale and distribution of newspapers and journals, initially in London, then throughout the UK, cleverly utilising and expanding the existing coach network. Increased literacy and a demand for news helped feed this growth.

He renamed the business W.H. Smith & Son in 1846, with his son, another William Henry, as partner. The development and expansion of the railways presented the company with a great opportunity beyond just selling newspapers. The company opened its first book stall at Euston Station in 1848, with many more opening in subsequent years. As the rail network grew, so did W.H. Smith. Within two decades, they had several hundred book stalls at stations across the country, selling newspapers, journals, books and stationery to the travelling public.

With the development of the railway network and increased travel came the new habit of reading on journeys, which was so much easier on a train than in a bumpy horse-drawn carriage. This increased the market for mass-produced books, newspapers and magazines. Cheap books, including 'yellow backs', were sold for 1s or 2s 6d in this way. 'Yellow backs', sometimes called 'mustard-plaster novels', were cheap, entertaining reads created specifically for the new genre of 'railway reader'. They were reprints of older titles, including the likes of Robert Louis Stevenson, and were generally romances, adventure novels and more popular non-fiction, such as travel books.

W.H. Smith also controlled the advertising at railway stations, adding another revenue stream to its business model. In 1860, W.H. Smith added a circulation library to many of its station book stalls. This was a successful operation that further expanded their importance as a business and continued until 1961.

In 1905, yet again demonstrating its success at adapting to the market, W.H. Smith began opening retail shops in town centres. This was initially a response to losing book stall contracts with two key railway companies, but it proved to be a game-changer, and this part of the business was to grow rapidly. The new shops proclaimed 'W.H. Smith & Son – Booksellers, Librarians, Newsagents, Stationers' in classic signage designed by Eric Gill. Stationery was booming with the growth of offices and the consequent requirements for paper, pens and so on, and likewise book sales and readership continued to flourish. In addition, a nationwide newspaper circulation business was further developed as well as a printing business, all continuing the company's growth.

John Murray

Another significant name during the eighteenth and nineteenth centuries was John Murray, who set up as bookseller–publisher in 1768 and whose company went on to become one of the most successful and richest publishers of the nineteenth century, surviving into the twenty-first century.

Murray's original bookshop was open twelve hours a day, six days a week, but the company became more famous as a publisher, dating from when the second John Murray managed the business in the nineteenth century, publishing Jane Austen and Byron, among many other illustrious names. The Murray family is an amazing dynasty, with seven different John Murrays running the company between 1768 and the early twenty-first century, almost like Doctor Who regenerating for each new era.

The third John Murray published Darwin and Arthur Conan Doyle. Early in the twentieth century, Murray bought Smith, Elder – the publishers of Charlotte Brontë, Thackeray and Thomas Hardy – adding these great names to their roster. Later in the century, the sixth John Murray ('Jock' Murray), a great book-trade character, continued the success of the company, publishing John Betjeman and an impressive selection of great travel writers, including Freya Stark and Patrick Leigh Fermor. He also published Beryl Cook and Ruth Prawer Jhabvala, who went on to win the Booker Prize with *Heat and Dust*, which was later made into a film in 1983 by Merchant Ivory.

However, things had got much tougher for small publishers in the late twentieth century, with agents demanding bigger advances for authors, making it more difficult to compete. After much discussion, a difficult decision was taken and the John Murray list was sold to Hodder Headline in 2002, and absorbed into the global giant Hachette a couple of years later. As a sales rep at the start of the new century, I represented the John Murray list for two short years before its sale. I got to know the seventh John Murray, a lively and enthusiastic presence at the sale conferences held in the historic offices in Albemarle Street.

For over 200 years, John Murray had been one of the most successful publishers in Britain, alongside other long-established businesses such as Longman, which dates back even earlier than John Murray, having been founded by Thomas Longman in 1724. Longman was another family firm, with generations involved, until the company was eventually swallowed up by the Pearson Longman conglomerate in the late twentieth century. Longman published many big names in its early life, including Wordsworth, Coleridge and Walter Scott, but increasingly came to focus on educational and academic titles, which underpinned its huge success, both at home and internationally. It was well known as a publisher of textbooks, dictionaries, reference books and the iconic *Roget's Thesaurus*.

Mrs Beeton

We featured *The Boke of Cokery* earlier in this narrative as the first known cookery title and discussed the ongoing importance of cookery as a publishing genre. The major cookery bestseller of the nineteenth century was *Mrs Beeton's Book of Household Management*. First published in 1861, it had originally been serialised in twenty-four monthly parts in *The Englishwoman's Domestic Magazine*, published by Samuel Orchart Beeton, husband of Isabella Beeton. Isabella had started writing a regular cookery column in the magazine before beginning the serialisation, which seems to have relied on quite liberal plagiarism from other contemporary cookery writers.

The book was wide in scope, offering incredibly detailed advice to Victorian housewives on all aspects of English cookery, from fish and game to dairy, fruit and vegetables, as well as pies, cakes and breads. The recipes gave very thorough and meticulous instructions to first-time cooks and, as a result, *Mrs Beeton's Book of Household Management* was an immediate success, selling an amazing 60,000 copies in its first year and reaching almost two million by the end of the decade. These were phenomenal sales for the time and a publishing triumph. The book became a staple of the Victorian home, and a must-have reference book.

Mrs Beeton herself has a very traditional, matronly reputation, and the book is full of advice on how to conduct yourself in Victorian society. In fact, Isabella Beeton was only 25 when she wrote the book, so not the matronly figure of our imagination, and she tragically died aged 28. Her book remains her legacy.

Today, rather encouragingly for lovers of the physical book, cookery seems to be one of those categories where people still want to have an actual copy on the kitchen shelf, rather than just researching recipes on the internet or reading them on a tablet. Perhaps that is just from habit picked up over the years, so it will be interesting to see if cookery books remain bestsellers in physical form for future generations.

Following Mrs Beeton's success, the twentieth century has given us an incredibly rich and wide selection of cookery writers, one of the most important of whom was Elizabeth David, who couldn't have been more different from Mrs Beeton. Elizabeth David rebelled against convention throughout her life and revolutionised the English attitude to cooking by introducing influences from her travels in Europe.

She had studied art in Paris in the 1930s and ran away to Italy and Greece with a married man, before ending up in Egypt, where she worked for the British Government. She returned to Britain after the war and was quite disgusted by the state of English cuisine. Her first title, *A Book of Mediterranean Food*, introduced the English to ingredients such as olive oil, basil and aubergines, and was followed in 1951 by *French Provincial Cooking* – books that had a huge influence on subsequent generations of chefs and cookery writers and helped to change how the

English ate. Those influenced by her include Jamie Oliver, Prue Leith, Nigel Slater and Rick Stein.

Julian Barnes is also a big fan and has written about her in *The Pedant in the Kitchen*, a collection of his writings on cookery. One of the main things that shines through in this book is Barnes' love of cookery books, most particularly those by Marcella Hazan and Jane Grigson. Interestingly, he also references Mrs Beeton, a copy of which was given pride of place by his mother when he was growing up, although more as a status symbol than a regularly used reference book. 'There were, for instance, seventeen pages illustrating how to fold napkins,' he writes. 'Had people ever lived like this?' he asks. 'Perhaps there really were houses with a butler's pantry.'

5

Allen Lane and the Paperback Revolution: The Quest for a Wider Book Market in the Twentieth Century

Early Penguin paperbacks. (Alamy)

Several hundred years after the time of Caxton, the book trade was now a fully functioning professional business. There had been continuous advances in printing techniques, an ever-growing number of publishers and an increasing number of fantastic books. Britain now had hundreds of bookshops in its major cities and smaller towns, a comprehensive distribution network and, most importantly, a public who were eager to read more books. During the twentieth century to come, this book trade would be transformed from an industry of small family businesses into a global operation run by huge international conglomerates. It would also develop into a mass-market operation selling millions of copies of books. At heart, though, however big the trade would become, its core strength would still be the people involved in it, whether they be pioneering booksellers, brilliant writers or publishers passionate about the books they published, all sharing the desire to create great books and expand the book market.

At the beginning of the century, however, the book trade was stuck in a bit of a rut. Book sales were not as buoyant as many believed they could be. The importance of the libraries had kept retail book prices unreasonably inflated and beyond the reach of most consumers, creating a generation of readers more used to borrowing books than buying them. Change was now needed to drive growth in book sales.

Efforts to grow the books market dominated the book trade throughout the twentieth century. There were several publishers who wanted to make books more affordable to increase sales, and they also wanted to sell through outlets other than bookshops to reach those who would rarely enter a bookshop, either put off by the perceived stuffiness of the book trade or simply not considering themselves as book buyers. We saw this in James Lackington's Temple of the Muses bookshop, selling books cheaply to make books available to everyone; in the advent of serial fiction in magazines, which were more affordable than books; and in the growth of circulation libraries, making books accessible to a much wider readership for a minimal rental fee.

Throughout the first half of the twentieth century, several new and innovative publishers would define the new era for the book trade. This contingent of bold, independent publishers would be the driving force in the trade. Only later in the century would larger businesses come to the fore.

Upcoming publishers such as Heinemann and Dent, influenced by the success of lower-priced European editions of English classics, introduced cheaper books from the 1890s onwards and were instrumental in this process of change. William Heinemann, born in 1863 to a Jewish family of German heritage, had travelled extensively in Europe and been impressed by inexpensive paperback editions of classics published by Tauchnitz in Germany. He worked first for the publisher Nicholas Trubner before setting up his own company with a loan from his father.

Heinemann achieved early success in 1890 with his first published novel from the historical novelist Hall Caine. Heinemann made the revolutionary decision to release Caine's latest book *The Bondsman* in a cheap edition priced at only 3s 6d just six months after the triple-decker edition had been released for the libraries. This practice was unheard of and could have very easily upset the powerful libraries, but *The Bondsman* became a mass-market bestseller, shifting 450,000 copies and setting a precedent for the years ahead. In a further challenge to the stranglehold of the libraries, Heinemann then issued Caine's follow-up, *The Manxman*, direct into a single-volume edition at 6s, with no triple-decker edition at all.

The Manxman sold over 400,000 copies, proving that keenly priced books could achieve huge sales. Other publishers swiftly followed suit, and the triple-decker's days were numbered. Libraries continued to thrive but were forced to switch to single-volume editions, while book sales to the public began to grow, facilitating the further growth of bookshops throughout the century.

In 1901, another young publisher, Grant Richards, having started his eponymous publishing company at the age of 24, introduced a range of cheap hardback reprints of classic fiction and non-fiction called 'World's Classics', featuring the likes of George Bernard Shaw, A.E. Housman and Samuel Butler. A few years later, when Richards' company faced liquidation, this series was sold to Oxford University Press, which still publishes the series today.

Another rising star in the publishing firmament at this time was Joseph Malaby Dent, who had only developed a love of literature at the age of 15 when reading Boswell's *Life of Johnson* through his local Mutual Improvement Society. A latecomer to books, much like the eighteenth-century bookseller James Lackington, Dent said that books 'have been the great solace and help of my life, and it has been my supreme happiness to have been associated with literature all my days, even though only as a door-keeper of the Temple'. Like Lackington, he was keen to share his discovery and make books accessible to all levels of society.

Dent had previously produced the Temple Shakespeare series, pocket editions of the plays priced at 1*s* 6*d*, and then went on to launch the Everyman's Library in 1905. His aim was to create a vast series of affordable world literature that was accessible to all classes and covering all interests. The first title issued in the series was his much-loved Boswell's *Life of Johnson*, and the series eventually exceeded 1,000 volumes.

The Net Book Agreement, 1900

One factor working against the book trade's growth was the uneasy co-operation between booksellers and publishers at the start of the century. Publishers knew they needed booksellers, but they were still reluctant to give them better terms. Booksellers complained that they couldn't make money on existing very low discounts.

Book pricing had caused ongoing disagreements during the Victorian era. By the mid-nineteenth century, there existed a Booksellers Association, an organisation whose key function was to bind its members to not selling books below the published price. However, in 1852, a group of booksellers led by Bickers & Bush decided that they could increase sales by offering books to the public at cheaper prices than their competitors and they broke ranks by discounting many of the books they sold. They were willing to take a hit on margin to increase book sales and, inevitably, other booksellers followed their lead.

As the controversy grew, two publishers, John Chapman and John W. Parker, called a meeting of concerned individuals, including publishers and writers, among whom was one Charles Dickens, and those gathered agreed various resolutions deploring the Booksellers Association as being anti-competitive and against the principles of 'free trade'. After various subsequent meetings of authors, booksellers and publishers, the Booksellers Association was scrapped and, during the following decades, underselling or discounting became the norm in Britain.

It was usual for new books to be sold at 25 per cent discount, sometimes more. Publishers increased prices accordingly to allow themselves and booksellers to make sufficient profit. Those who experienced the book-trade price wars of the 1990s and early 2000s will recognise the cyclical nature of all of this and, towards the end of the century, several voices were beginning to suggest that this situation was not sustainable. They argued that if the trade returned to fixed pricing, books would remain affordable to the public, while booksellers and publishers could both turn a profit.

The trade journal *The Bookseller* had been launched in January 1858 by Joseph Whitaker. The Whitaker family became hugely important to bookselling and publishing, with Joseph's descendant, David Whitaker, being instrumental in the introduction of the Standard Book Number in the 1960s, which developed into the International Standard Book Number (ISBN) that uniquely identifies each book to this day – the ISBN is the thirteen-digit number you will find on the copyright page and the back cover of a book.

The Bookseller pre-dates many other famous trade journals and celebrated its 6,000th weekly issue in 2022. Joseph Whitaker was a pioneer and a key figure for development within the business. He campaigned for better-educated booksellers, warned of the dangers of publishers becoming too big and was instrumental in the creation of associations within the book trade. Whitaker disliked discounting and used the pages of *The Bookseller* to campaign against it.

In 1890, the publisher Frederick Macmillan set out the arguments for fixed pricing and standard discounts for booksellers in a letter to *The Bookseller*. Macmillan began setting fixed (net) prices for its books, refused to supply booksellers who would not conform to this standard and worked hard to get other publishers on his side. The idea was to create a level playing field that gave all booksellers an equal chance to sell books, with a fixed retail price and a reasonable discount from the publishers. Discussions continued throughout the 1890s until the newly formed Associated Booksellers of Great Britain and Ireland (later renamed as the

Booksellers Association, BA) and the Publishers Association (PA – itself only inaugurated in 1896) reached agreement on decent terms to supply net books to bookshops.

The Net Book Agreement (NBA) came into force on 1 January 1900. From that point onwards, and for most of the twentieth century, all booksellers had to sell books at the fixed retail price. The key principles of the NBA were that all booksellers would sell net books at prices specified by the publisher, regardless of discount. If prices were fixed, the reading public would benefit from cheaper books overall, which did in fact happen. The NBA consequently underpinned the stability and the success of the book business for the rest of the century.

It took time for this to transform the industry, and it was several years before all publishers and booksellers were fully on board. The NBA faced its first real test in 1905 when *The Times* newspaper tried to remedy lagging sales by introducing *The Times* Book Club. It initially offered discounted books to the paper's subscribers in co-operation with several publishers, but this caused a furore in the trade and much acrimony.

It took a few years to sort out, but eventually the PA agreed on a united front and the book club finally carried on without discounting. From this point onward, the NBA became the industry standard and remained so for almost 100 years. This, alongside better co-operation due to the existence of the BA and the PA, formed a more coherent and co-operative basis upon which the trade grew, with both sides recognising the important role the other played in the business.

Faber

Faber & Faber, founded in 1929 by Geoffrey Faber, is a great example of a small publishing house that has remained independent and has been a leader in the British publishing firmament throughout its existence. Geoffrey Faber had first worked for several years in Faber & Gwyer, a joint publishing effort with Sir Maurice Gwyer (a friend from his days at All Souls College, Oxford) and his wife, Alsina, building on their inheritance of the already successful Scientific Press. Splitting from the Gwyers and setting up on his own, Faber began the growth of the publisher into one of the most renowned and successful independent publishing companies in Britain.

Faber as a company became very good at employing great editors who would help drive the company's growth. T.S. Eliot worked for them from the beginning and stayed there throughout his working life. Faber very successfully published his works, but Eliot was also responsible for establishing the company as the premier poetry publisher, discovering the likes of Siegfried Sassoon, Ted Hughes, Seamus Heaney and Philip Larkin.

Faber had many big successes over the years, starting from its first bestseller, *Memoirs of a Fox Hunting Man* by Siegfried Sassoon. One of the books that continues to support the company is *Old Possum's Book of Practical Cats* by T.S. Eliot, a more whimsical and humorous collection than Eliot was usually known for. This book not only earns revenue from its book sales, but also the ongoing royalty as the text for Andrew Lloyd Webber's musical *Cats*.

Faber also published playwrights including Tom Stoppard, Harold Pinter, Samuel Beckett and John Osborne, and has been a home to some of literary fiction's most-renowned authors, including William Golding, Alan Bennett, Lawrence Durrell and James Joyce. In more modern times, Faber published Peter Carey and Kazuo Ishiguro, both of whom were brought to the firm by Robert McCrum and both of whom won the Booker Prize during our bookshop's life – Carey for *Oscar and Lucinda* and Ishiguro for *The Remains of the Day*. Carey would go on to win the prize for a second time with *The True History of the Kelly Gang* in 2001.

Faber has remained a much-admired independent literary list to this day and an antidote to the trend towards conglomeration from the 1970s onwards, as the bigger publishers swallowed up many of the outstanding independent publishers that had played such an important part not only in the growth but also the direction of publishing throughout the century. Geoffrey Faber summed up the independent attitude in 1939 in *The Publishers' Circular and Booksellers' Record*:

The big firms say that they intend to retain the imprints of the small publishers they absorb. But I doubt if that ever works for long. You might retain the imprint, but you must inevitably lose the elusive character of the individual firm, compounded by its proprietor's personality and taste.

Penguin and the Paperback Revolution

The big story of the twentieth century is the introduction of Penguin Books by Allen Lane. It was the single most significant event in bookselling and publishing in that period and a development that had immense impact on the book trade. It is something that still affects the way we buy and read books to this day.

Bookselling and publishing had hit a slump in the 1920s and 1930s, affected by the Depression, as many other trades were. Paperback and cheaper editions of books had existed before Penguin came along. There had been many attempts to offer lower-priced books to attract a wider readership earlier in the century, but there had been nothing of significant scale and certainly nothing that came close to what Penguin achieved.

There are many apocryphal stories about how Allen Lane, then working at The Bodley Head, came up with the idea of Penguin Books. The legend is that, travelling back from visiting his author and friend Agatha Christie in Devon, he could find nothing decent to read at the Exeter Station book stall. He decided that a range of interesting and affordable books for just such an eventuality was needed. Whatever the truth of that story, Lane had been musing on the idea of cheaper editions for some time before this.

Born in Bristol in 1902, Lane had been given a job at The Bodley Head in 1919 by his uncle, John Lane. He started at the bottom, learning the nuts and bolts of the publishing business, working first as a packer and then doing other lowly jobs before later joining the editorial department. This understanding of the whole business, including the production department and its costings, stood him in good stead later.

Like many British publishers, Lane had long been impressed by the stylish but affordable paperback editions of British classics produced in Germany by Tauchnitz and Albatross, which sold successfully across Europe. The standard size and design of the Albatross series undoubtedly influenced the design of Penguins. There is evidence that H.A.W. Arnold, an office junior at The Bodley Head who loved books but couldn't afford to buy them, had also suggested the idea of sixpenny paperbacks.

Whatever the origins, Allen Lane was spirited into action after attending a conference of publishers and booksellers in 1934, where there was great concern about poor book sales and reduced profits due to rising costs. Lane decided to launch a series of stylish sixpenny paperbacks to increase book sales and attract those not currently buying books. He wanted these books to be sold not only by bookshops and station book stalls, but through non-bookshop outlets as well, such as Woolworths.

Allen Lane's plan was set at a much lower price and on a much bigger scale than similar schemes by the likes of Heinemann and Dent before him. His idea was bold and audacious, and many thought it would fail, but they had reckoned without Lane's enthusiasm, grit and determination, attributes that would underpin the success and growth of Penguin Books in the years to come. Lane shared with Dent and many others the desire to make great books available to readers from all walks of life. 'A man who may be poor in money is not necessarily poor in intellectual qualities,' he said. 'The thing to aim at was the sixpenny book, something that could be bought as easily and as casually as a packet of cigarettes.'

He was determined to publish good-quality literature that would be available to all: 'I wanted to make the kind of book which, when the vicar comes to tea, you don't push under the cushion. You are rather more inclined to put it on the table to show what sort of person you are.'

Edward Young, part of The Bodley Head team, remembers a brainstorming meeting to decide on a name for the new imprint. 'Phoenix' was one suggestion and the team, being very much inspired by the example of Albatross, were considering similar names when Allen Lane's secretary, Joan Coles, suddenly said, 'What about penguins?' Lane liked the idea and Young was duly despatched to London Zoo to sketch a penguin for the colophon that would be used on all the covers.

Lane launched Penguin Books with ten titles priced at 6*d* a copy in July 1935. The titles were reprints of existing hardback titles and one of Lane's challenges was to persuade hardback publishers to sell him the rights to produce cheap editions of their books in paperback.

Books were generally sold first in a 7s 6d hardback edition, with a cheaper 3s 6d edition following a couple of years later. Most publishers were understandably wary of selling their books for just 6d, finding it hard to believe that they could make money out of this idea and concerned that this could devalue books in the eyes of the consumer – all very valid arguments.

Jonathan Cape was the first publisher Lane persuaded to sign up, despite Cape thinking that the venture wouldn't work. The low pricing of the Penguin edition meant that the company needed to achieve huge sales to make a profit. Other publishers did follow Cape in due course, but many only after Penguin had established its success.

The first ten Penguins (all issued together) were *Ariel* (Andre Maurois), *A Farewell to Arms* (Ernest Hemingway), *Poet's Pub* (Eric Linklater), *Madame Claire* (Susan Ertz), *The Unpleasantness at the Bellona Club* (Dorothy L Sayers), *The Mysterious Affair at Styles* (Agatha Christie), *Twenty-Five* (Beverley Nichols), *William* (E.H. Young), *Carnival* (Compton Mackenzie) and *Gone to Earth* (Mary Webb). The list demonstrated the mix of highbrow literature and middle-brow popular fiction that would become part of Penguin's USP, not dumbing down for its readers but rather respecting their intelligence.

Lane ordered a print run of 20,000 copies per title, but the company struggled to get booksellers behind the venture many of them worried about selling books at such a low price that could damage the profitability of their businesses. Advance orders were initially very poor. Neither W.H. Smith nor the wholesaler Simpkin Marshall showed any interest, although Lane was told that Selfridge's were going to devote a window to Penguins and the renowned London bookseller Bumpus were also on board.

It was only with the co-operation of Woolworths that Penguin avoided failure before they had even begun. Legend has it that the Woolworths buyer, Clifford Prescott, who already sold cheap children's books and downmarket novels, was not initially impressed with Penguins, until his wife looked at the list of titles, recognised several that she knew well and persuaded her husband to give them a go. Woolworths subsequently submitted an order for 63,500 copies and the Penguin phenomenon was underway.

A few days after publication, Allen Lane popped into Selfridges to check on sales and was told that the retailer had almost sold out of all titles, having initially ordered 100 copies of each. Buoyed by this success, Selfridges promptly reordered 1,000 of each book, based upon the public demand. Lane's gamble about attracting a wider audience with good books at affordable prices was clearly paying off.

More titles promptly followed and, in due course, most publishers and booksellers came to see the value in Penguin books, despite a swathe of initial resistance. In a review of a clutch of later titles in *New English Weekly* in 1936, George Orwell argued that it was 'a great mistake to imagine that cheap books are good for the book trade'. A bookseller needed to sell a lot of books at sixpence to compare to sales of more expensive books. Lane's argument was that the paperback revolution created a much wider reading public and a bigger book-owning public – and the gamble did pay off, despite scepticism from Orwell and many others.

Lane achieved massive sales and attracted customers who hadn't previously bought books on a regular basis. Very quickly, Penguin expanded its range, with Pelicans as a separate non-fiction imprint and Penguin Specials publishing current affairs titles, which were particularly relevant in the run-up to and during the Second World War. The company was a huge success in its first few decades and, buoyed by this, it kept adding new imprints. Penguin published Shakespeare plays in individual editions, introduced the King Penguin series and published *Penguin New Writing*, a leading literary journal edited by John Lehmann. Lane also introduced Puffin Books for children.

The first Penguin Classic appeared in 1946: E.V. Rieu's translation of *The Odyssey*. By 1960, it was one of twelve Penguin titles that had sold over one million copies, demonstrating the success of Allen Lane's philosophy of bringing great literature to a wider audience. Other million-sellers included Kitto's *The Greeks* and Orwell's *Animal Farm*.

In launching Penguin Books, Allen Lane had shown how the book market could widen and grow. Penguin's success led to the mass market for books that we know today, with books being routinely purchased by a larger proportion of the population. Paperbacks became the most popular form of book published. The low price and portability of the paperback format is responsible for the massive growth in book sales in the second half of the twentieth century. And, inevitably, the success of Penguin inspired other publishers to follow their lead and launch rival paperback publishers, too.

Pan Books and Other Paperback Publishers

Pan Books was launched in 1944 and, from its inception, was deliberately aimed at being less highbrow than Penguin. Its origins were in a consortium of Collins, Heinemann, Macmillan and Hodder, joining together as competition to Penguin. Its original MD, Aubrey Forshaw, stated, 'We are in middle-of-the-road entertainment.'

Pan was less concerned with developing a huge backlist and more interested in selling huge quantities of popular titles that appealed to a mass market, often to those who weren't traditional book buyers. The company not only sold to bookshops but made a point of targeting the CTN sector (confectioners, tobacconists, newsagents), which was so important in the second half of the twentieth century but has almost vanished today. It was very much the norm to see spinners of popular paperbacks in these outlets during the 1960s, 1970s and 1980s.

Pan gained a reputation for more lurid, brighter covers than Penguin, styled more like the American pulp-fiction market, and it achieved early success with action-packed war stories such as *The Dam Busters*, a title that Penguin had turned down and that went on to sell over one million copies in paperback. Pan published thrillers, crime novels and popular fiction by the likes of Edgar Wallace, Nevil Shute and Georgette Heyer. By 1972, Pan had sold over 30 million copies of Ian Fleming's James Bond novels.

Forshaw's successor as MD in 1970 was Ralph Vernon-Hunt, who had started his career as an assistant bookseller at Hudson's in Birmingham before becoming sales director at Pan. He was famous for telling booksellers that their shops were quite forbidding to would-be customers – an argument that Terry Maher of Dillons would also later champion – and he helped, through the paperback revolution and Pan's publishing programme, to make some bookshops a little less intimidating. He also continued the focus on selling large numbers of books through non-bookshop outlets.

As a result of this success, more paperback imprints joined the market, including Panther, which was a bit more literary than Pan, publishing Doris Lessing, Jean Genet, Norman Mailer and Nabokov. Corgi, another new paperback imprint, was similar to Pan in generating huge bestsellers, including titles by Frederick Forsyth, Joseph Heller, Catherine Cookson and J.T. Edson. Collins introduced the Fontana list, which included several different imprints such as the Crime Club, the Modern Masters and the children's Armada list. And Hodder introduced New English Library, an offshoot of the New American Library.

At the early stages of mass-market paperback publishing in the UK, Penguin, Pan, Corgi and the rest were buying rights from the original hardback publishers to produce a cheaper paperback edition. From the 1960s and 1970s onwards, however, hardback publishers started to set up their own paperback imprints and retained the rights to their titles, publishing their authors originally in hardback and then, generally a year later, releasing a paperback edition themselves. This was called vertical publishing, and it became very much the norm towards the end of the century, although it took several decades to become established; it is standard practice today.

Puffin Books

Puffin Books was launched in 1940 as the children's imprint of Penguin, just four years after Allen Lane had revolutionised the British publishing world with the launch of Penguin paperbacks. Puffin was the brainchild of publisher Noel Carrington, who had wanted to produce inexpensive educational titles for children and approached Allen Lane with the idea. The first books published were the non-fiction titles *War on Land* and *War at Sea*, but the series went on to encompass a wide range of topics, including natural history, reference, history and hobbies. In 1941, a paperback fiction series was launched, starting with *Worzel Gummidge* by Barbara Euphan Todd.

Puffin's first editor, Eleanor Graham, had reviewed children's books for *The Sunday Times* and had worked in the children's department of Bumpus, the famous bookshop in Oxford Street, before joining Puffin

Books. She initially experienced the same problems as Penguin's adult imprint – namely, the reluctance of hardback publishers to grant Puffin the rights to release cheap paperback editions of their bestselling titles. But the paperback revolution was proving that, in this new cheaper format, publishers could reach a much wider audience and thereby make more money.

In time, and with persistence, Eleanor Graham managed to change publishers' thinking and during the 1950s Puffin started to achieve success, publishing the likes of *The Lion, the Witch and the Wardrobe* by C.S. Lewis, *Charlotte's Web* by E.B. White, and *The Family From One End Street* by Eve Garnett, plus novels from Noel Streatfeild, Ian Serraillier, Norman Hunter (the Professor Branestawm books) and many more. Some 150 titles had been released by the time Eleanor Graham retired in 1961.

Puffin's most amazing period of growth, though, were the five years between 1963 and 1968, under the stewardship of Kaye Webb, when sales trebled; by 1970 it was the fastest-growing of all the Penguin imprints. Kaye Webb was a successful journalist, editor and broadcaster, who had worked for *Lilliput* magazine and edited *The Young Elizabethan* – a sort of 1950s precursor to *Look and Learn* or the modern-day *Aquila* – magazines for bright children. She had interviewed Allen Lane and met him several times before becoming his choice to succeed Eleanor Graham as Puffin editor.

Her journalistic life and the society she mixed in (friend to writers, artists and actors, and wife of the ubiquitous Ronald Searle) gave her the nous and the necessary connections to transform Puffin into the publishing juggernaut it became in the subsequent two decades. She was able to bring a multitude of existing authors into the stable as well as searching out new talent and unleashing a tide of wonderful new writing to an enthusiastic and growing audience. The 1960s was a boom time for children's writing and illustration, and Webb's eye for the next big thing coincided perfectly. She brought on board a plethora of fantastic authors including Leon Garfield, Alan Garner, Joan Aiken, Nina Bawden, Margaret Mahy, Peter Dickinson, Helen Cresswell and Penelope Lively.

One of the titles she discovered was *Stig of the Dump* by Clive King, a favourite of mine as a child in the 1960s. The manuscript had been rejected by several publishing houses before Puffin published the book in 1963; it has remained in print ever since. She also introduced the Puffin Club and its magazine, *Puffin Post*. The magazine featured competitions, jokes and puzzles but, most importantly, interviews with the authors themselves. The Puffin Club provided a haven for children who loved books. Webb organised events, competitions and holidays, bringing the readers closer to the authors.

Puffin Books was enjoying its classic period during my childhood, and we had many Puffin books in the house. One of the advantages of having older brothers was being able to share their books, including the Puffin Professor Branestawm and Dr Dolittle books, as well as books by Rosemary Sutcliffe, Leon Garfield and Alan Garner.

As with any successful publisher, however, competition soon arrived, as it had for Penguin Books. Following Puffin's lead, the Armada Lions paperbacks and Picture Lions became increasingly successful, publishing the likes of *The Tiger Who Came to Tea*, as well as later reclaiming the rights to the Narnia books. And Piccolo Books, How and Why, and many other children's publishers were starting to make their mark.

Roald Dahl was one of the authors introduced by Kaye Webb, although initially she had reservations about the cruelty in his books. He insisted that children loved it (he was right) and she was finally convinced by his astonishing hardback sales. He was published in Puffin with a higher royalty payment than other authors, but the investment was repaid many times over as his books became massive bestsellers. Originally a writer of stories and film scripts for adults, he had achieved success with his collection *Tales of the Unexpected*, which subsequently became a successful TV series. He began writing for children in 1961 with *James and the Giant Peach* and possibly his most famous book, *Charlie and the Chocolate Factory*, followed in 1964.

At the time we opened our bookshop in the early 1980s, Roald Dahl was the bestselling children's author in Britain, with several big sellers already available in Puffin paperbacks. The brilliant Quentin Blake illustrations captured Dahl's wicked humour perfectly. Dahl's sales continued to increase dramatically during the 1980s and 1990s. Any new Dahl release during that time was a massive seller for us. *Matilda*, released in 1988, was one of our most memorable successes. We had a big cardboard display bin full of the Puffin paperback – known in the trade as a 'dumpbin' – halfway down the shop and had to constantly keep refilling it, as the books were selling so fast.

Puffin Books still thrives, like its grown-up parent, Penguin Books. But there are a wealth of other great children's publishers vying for readers' attention today, as this sector continues to thrive and expand.

Ladybird Books

Another important and innovative children's publisher of the post-war period – and another important part of my childhood – was Ladybird Books. Whereas Puffin Books had published mainly fiction, Ladybird was responsible for growing sales of children's non-fiction in another publishing revolution.

Ladybird Books had started back in 1914, the children's imprint of established publishers Wills & Hepworth. But its transformation and huge success began in the 1950s and was very much the brainchild of one of its salespeople, Douglas Keen. He thought that the standard cheap, small hardback storybook format could be used for educational books, priced at 2*s* 6*d*.

Keen had a great belief in encouraging children's learning across a wide range of topics. To demonstrate his idea, he designed a mock-up of what became the first non-fiction title, *British Birds and their Nests,* on his kitchen table at home, with the help of his wife and watercolour illustrations by his mother-in-law. Keen's boss at Wills & Hepworth, Jim Clegg, loved the idea, and in 1954 the first Ladybird non-fiction title was released.

The finished book was written by esteemed naturalist Brian Vesey-Fitzgerald, who subsequently authored several other Ladybird books, as well as editing sixty volumes of the County Books series for publisher Robert Hale. It was illustrated by the great nature artist

Allen W. Seaby in some of the last work he produced before his death. The book was a beautiful production of its time and is a much sought-after edition today.

A whole swathe of brilliant and innovative publishing followed, all driven by Keen and Clegg. Keen masterminded the introduction of the various series as the list grew, including the long-running Nature titles and the History series, which answered a need from teachers and readers for better factual books. There then followed the Learning with Mother series, People at Work, the Science titles, How it Works series and the Key Words reading scheme.

Keen brought in many talented artists and writers, including Frank Hampson, creator of *Dan Dare*, and John Berry, a renowned war artist who illustrated the People at Work series. Many readers will have fond memories of illustrations by the likes of John Leigh-Pemberton, S.R. Badmin, Charles Tunnicliffe (who produced the Nature titles, such as *What To Look For in Autumn*) and Harry Wingfield (from the Key Words scheme), as well as individual titles that were prized and much-loved.

Other Ladybird artists who had renowned careers beyond these children's books included Rowland Hilder, 'the Turner of his generation' and a renowned landscape artist, John Kenney, illustrator of many of the history titles but arguably more famous as illustrator of *Thomas the Tank Engine*, and Ronald Lampitt, who also illustrated for *John Bull* magazine, *Readers Digest* and *Look and Learn* magazine.

Keen managed all of this from a small extension at the back of his house, which became the hub of the Ladybird operation throughout those golden years, with authors and illustrators coming and going. Even at its peak, the Ladybird operation was centred on Keen's house, with much of the success based upon Keen's amazing rapport with his writers and artists.

Keen continued to work for Ladybird until 1973, when the company was sold to Pearson, leaving behind him an amazing achievement and a rich heritage of children's educational titles that were so much a part of millions of children's lives. So many of the iconic Ladybird books produced at that time seemed to have been standards on children's bookshelves in the 1960s and 1970s. They contributed towards a general perception that books were a vital part of children's lives – an essential resource for facts and learning as well as for stories.

Almost as soon as we opened our shop, we started receiving visits from publishers' reps. One of the first to visit was the rep from Ladybird Books. Following his advice (or persuasion), we promptly installed a big red stand to display Ladybird books in our children's section and, to be fair to the rep, brilliant sales of their books followed, contributing not just to the continued growth of our shop but to the growth in importance of our children's section.

At that time, in the early 1980s, Ladybird was still a big name in children's books and very much a trusted brand, founded on three decades of success. But Ladybird's position was under threat, with the likes of Usborne Books (launched in 1973) and Dorling Kindersley, or DK, (launched in 1974) already snapping at its heels by the time we opened our shop. In fact, in that first year, we also installed an Usborne spinner (another rep visit) and, within a few years, our sales of these books overtook Ladybird.

Usborne Books was started by Peter Usborne, who sadly died in 2023, just before the company's fiftieth anniversary. Their books were brighter and had a more contemporary look than their more-established rival, with a much more appealing approach for children than the rather dry style of Ladybird.

However, nothing stays the same in publishing or retail. Change, competition and innovation bring continued improvement. Ladybird Books' heyday was sadly behind it and the company was absorbed into Penguin Books in 1988, part of a general trend as bigger publishers gobbled up many smaller companies. Another much-loved and iconic independent publisher that was acquired by Penguin around this time (in 1983) was Frederick Warne, publisher of the Beatrix Potter books and the Observer series of nature guides, another memorable staple of my childhood and a cherished part of British life in the post-war years.

Very quickly, the prominence that we afforded to children's books in our shop began to bear fruit. From the outset, our shop attracted parents with children – from the very young in prams or pushchairs to older ones merrily browsing among the shelves themselves. Being the only ground-floor bookshop in town played a massive part in this, as parents didn't have to struggle upstairs with pushchairs or try to find a lift. Our shop was small but easily accessible and soon became part of the local community and part of parents' lives – a place to bring children after school or on Saturday mornings. Puffin and Ladybird played their part in this.

6

Bookselling in the
Twentieth Century

Foyles bookshop in Charing Cross Road, London. (Alamy)

The paperback revolution and the subsequent expansion in publishing created a growing mass audience for books. This resulted in significant growth in the number of bookshops across the UK during the twentieth century. The expansion of the education market in Britain, particularly in higher education in the aftermath of the Second World War, presented great opportunities for bookshops to develop very profitable businesses. And some larger bookshops began expanding into international markets too, doing very good business in Africa, Asia and beyond.

London was always at the centre of these developments, spearheaded by Foyles, Dillons and Hatchards – iconic bookshops that are still an important part of our modern British book trade. Dillons, situated in Bloomsbury, was founded in 1936 by Una Dillon, a pioneering bookseller who developed the business from nothing to become one of the capital's leading bookshops. After the war, the shop moved into the beautiful Gower Street building designed by architect Charles Fitzroy Doll, where it still stands today (although it is now branded as Waterstones). The shop benefitted from its proximity to the University of London and included extensive academic and general selections on several floors. Its importance grew immensely in the post-war period and it was one of many bookshops to capitalise on the growing market for educational books.

Other notable London bookshops of the century included Claude Gill, one of the best-known booksellers in London in the 1960s, with its flagship 8,000-square-feet store at the Marble Arch end of Oxford Street, near to Selfridges. At one point, Claude Gill had six sites in and around the capital. However, the shop was in decline by the 1980s and its stores became remainder outlets, finally closing in the 1990s – a sad end for one of the famous names in post-war bookselling.

Another bookshop of great renown, particularly in the early part of the twentieth century, was Bumpus. Originally started in Bond Street in 1790, it moved to Oxford Street in 1903. It was in the 1920s and 1930s, under the reign of John G. Wilson (said by many to be *the* London bookseller of his day), that the shop achieved its peak, selling to the carriage trade as well as to tourists. Bumpus later moved to Baker Street under the aegis of Tony Godwin, who had made his name at Better Books, an avant-garde bookshop in Charing Cross Road, opposite Foyles. Better Books had been founded by Godwin in 1946 in Charing Cross Road and became a significant player in the counter-culture movement of London in the 1960s. But Bumpus' glory days were behind it – times had changed and the business closed in the early 1960s. Tony Godwin subsequently went to work as an editor for Penguin Books, recruited by Allen Lane.

Another similar London bookshop worthy of note was Compendium, opened in 1968 on Camden High Street. Compendium took over from Better Books as London's radical bookshop, itself surviving until 2000. The shop was a mecca for those seeking a range of books beyond the mainstream, including radical fiction, poetry, books on music and politics as well as more esoteric subjects.

Bookshops thrived throughout the UK. Beyond the capital, most towns boasted an independent bookshop of their own as well as a branch of W.H. Smith, although some smaller towns or villages could support only a newsagent or stationers that also sold books (the CTNs). Each town has its own memories and unique history, each bookshop its own story.

Among those independent bookshops, some of the more significant were Blackwell's, situated in Broad Street, Oxford, founded by Benjamin Henry Blackwell as a general and academic bookshop in 1879; James Thin, founded in Edinburgh in 1848; Sherratt & Hughes in Manchester, founded in 1896; Hudson Books in Birmingham, founded in 1821; John Smith in Glasgow, founded in 1751; Bowes & Bowes in Cambridge, dating from 1843; and Heffers, also in Cambridge, dating from 1876. Other regional booksellers included Sisson & Parker in Nottingham, Lear's in Cardiff, Bisset's of Aberdeen, Goulden & Curry in Tunbridge Wells and George's in Bristol. There were hundreds more.

At least the first half of the twentieth century was defined by these strong, independent bookshops and small chains, together making up the interwoven fabric of the British book trade. Many of them still exist today and remain a vital part of the bookselling landscape, much loved by book buyers. Until the challenges towards the end of the century, this passionate and dedicated cohort of booksellers drove the book trade onwards, aiding its expansion and growth.

W.H. Smith

In many ways, W.H. Smith is the great unsung hero of the book trade in the twentieth century and its retail backbone throughout this time. We have seen how W.H. Smith first grew its book stall network on the railways before opening a succession of bookshops in towns throughout the country; but in the twentieth century its importance grew further still. Many British book buyers today will think of Waterstones as the dominant bookshop chain but, for most of the last century, Waterstones did not exist, and W.H. Smith was very much the dominant retailer.

By the early 1980s, when I started out in the book trade, W.H. Smith was the only bookshop chain of any decent size, accounting for about 35 per cent of the English market at that time (John Menzies held a similar position in Scotland, as did Eason's in Ireland). W.H. Smith is the oldest chain bookseller in the UK and is still a familiar feature of many high streets across the land today, as well as in train stations, airports and motorway service stations (the 'Travel' stores). It performs a vital function, mainly through the Travel stores, selling bestsellers, guidebooks and children's books in vast quantities, as well as being the UK's largest newspaper and magazine retailer. However, there is a strong argument that the high street shops have diversified too much and are often packed full of almost anything but books – greeting cards, stationery, toys, drinks, sandwiches and even post offices.

Throughout the twentieth century, W.H. Smith continued to adapt and grow, including a move to a new purpose-built warehouse and office site in Swindon in 1967, where it is still based today. In 1966, W.H. Smith set up Book Club Associates (BCA) in partnership with American publisher Doubleday. The book club business grew dramatically in the 1970s and 1980s, mainly through advertising in Sunday newspapers, only finally disappearing in 2012 as retail fashions changed again to online selling. Before the days of the internet, many booksellers viewed such book clubs as a threat to their sales of full-priced books. The bookshop business expanded further in the post-war period, including the airport shops, beginning with Gatwick Airport in 1958.

Further opportunities arose because of government policy towards higher education changing dramatically in the post-war period. The

Robbins Report of 1963 envisaged a doubling of the higher-education student population which, in turn, opened up a wider market for educational books, textbooks, literature and reference books. W.H. Smith decided to enter the field of more specialised 'quality' bookselling with a clear aim to open what the company termed 'pedigree bookshops' to capitalise on this market. Other bookshops also took advantage of this trend, including Blackwell's, Heffers and Foyles.

Since the 1920s, W.H. Smith had owned a small chain of three bookshops under the Truslove & Hanson name in London, as well as other regional bookshops not branded as 'W.H. Smith'. After acquiring two strong local bookshop names in Bowes & Bowes and Sherratt & Hughes, W.H. Smith turned both independent bookshops into small 'pedigree bookshop' chains, retaining their well-known names and opening more shops under these brands, thus expanding their reach beyond the W.H. Smith chainstore look and running well-stocked, upmarket bookshops that looked and felt like independent shops.

Bowes & Bowes was originally founded in Cambridge in 1843 by Daniel and Alexander Macmillan, trading as Macmillan & Co until 1907, when it became Bowes and Bowes, managed by their nephew Robert Bowes. John Sherratt and Joseph David Hughes had opened their bookshop in Manchester in 1898 and subsequently opened a shop in Long Acre in London. There were thirteen Bowes & Bowes branches by 1971, demonstrating once again W.H. Smith's ability to adapt and change to survive and grow. In many cases, W.H. Smith bought up and absorbed local independent bookshops into these chains and, in most cases, they took on the existing staff too.

Foyles

Once listed in *The Guinness Book of Records* as the largest bookshop in the world, Foyles was founded in 1903 by brothers William and Gilbert Foyle. Originally started as a small second-hand book business in their kitchen, they opened their first bookshop in Peckham soon after and, within ten years, had four branches across London, subsequently opening the famous mammoth shop in Charing Cross Road in the 1920s. Foyles remains one of Britain's most iconic bookshops to this day, famed throughout the world, particularly the flagship Charing Cross Road bookshop.

William became the head of the main bookselling business while Gilbert concentrated on their educational company. The Foyles business originally grew from huge sales of second-hand books but soon embraced new full-price books, too. William was a great booklover and believed in creating a welcoming environment to encourage more people to buy books, echoing James Lackington's motives back in the eighteenth century. William was also a benevolent employer, nurturing and encouraging his staff and building a multifaceted business with their expertise.

The shop became a destination, not just for its amazing depth of book stock across many floors, but also for its craft department (selling wool and other accessories), as well as philately and travel departments. It embraced the export business and turned over a great deal of money by supplying educational books to all parts of the globe. The company also built up a massive international mail order operation and, in its early days, had over 4,000 lending libraries around the country.

The shop's reputation grew further from the 1930s with the introduction of the Foyles Literary Lunches. These became greatly renowned and featured many famous names and celebrated authors over the years, including Haile Selassie, Evelyn Waugh, Charlie Chaplin, Dylan Thomas, Ian Fleming, Laurie Lee and John Lennon. However, when Christina Foyle, daughter of William, took over more of the running of the business, things changed. Christina was a stubborn eccentric, who refused to introduce modern technology and didn't treat her staff with the same affection as her father had. After William's death, the shop developed a quirkier and more negative reputation.

It was a running joke in the 1970s and 1980s that a customer had to queue at three separate points within Foyles to be able to purchase a book – a ridiculous system set up because Christina didn't trust most of her staff to handle money. When Christina died in 1999, the members of her family who took over discovered widespread fraud within the company (some in collusion with publishers' sales reps), to no great surprise in the book trade, where this had been an open secret for many years. It was a company in decline and running at a loss, although it was still a destination for tourists and had retained its international reputation. It was a multi-floored warren with many hidden riches and a great stock of books, but it was very much in need of a total makeover. Following the subsequent changes after Christina's death, the shop was transformed and restored to full strength as a key destination bookshop once more.

Heffers

The huge Heffers shop in Trinity Street in Cambridge, with its many nooks and crannies on different levels, is a seemingly endless wonder of literary delights. It is the sort of shop that gives the impression that there is always more to explore. Like Foyles, it was a long-established family business and proclaimed itself as 'the bookshop that is known all over the world'. But while Foyles was suffering from poor management by the 1980s, Heffers, in contrast, had a deserved reputation as a well-stocked bookshop for both academic and general interest. Indeed, its huge stock holding had been an inspiration to a young Tim Waterstone when he was a student.

Heffers seemed to almost happen by chance. William Heffer had held various jobs in Cambridge, including groom and publican, before taking on the tenancy of a small shop selling stationery, books and educational supplies in Fitzroy Street in Cambridge in 1876. Despite his lack of experience, William excelled in the role of retailer and the business grew successfully. In 1896, a separate bookshop was opened in Petty Cury, which eventually expanded across into the neighbouring premises and onto five floors to create a destination bookseller with an unrivalled reputation for service and expertise. Only in 1970, as this street was being redeveloped, did Heffers relocate to its current location in Trinity Street, where it has remained ever since.

Along the way, Heffers opened various other branches, including a music shop, art shop, paperback shop and a specialist children's bookshop in 1969. There was also a map shop and a stationery shop. At one time, Heffers had ten different outlets in Cambridge – a great example of a large, well-stocked independent bookshop outside the capital, staffed by enthusiastic and knowledgeable staff, several of whom were still family members and many of whom had worked for the company for years.

Heffers obviously benefitted from the university business, but it was also popular with non-academic townsfolk, as well as with the thousands of tourists who visited each year, hence its glowing international reputation. Like many well-established independent booksellers, the shopfloor book business was just part of its success, and the business was underpinned by several other operations. Heffers had at various times been a printer and a publisher, a big university and schools supplier and, like Foyles, ran a very large mail order business across the globe. It also supplied libraries throughout the world, at one stage employing salespeople to tout for business from libraries across Europe, the Middle East, Africa and Canada.

Blackwell's

Benjamin Harris Blackwell opened a bookshop in St Clements High Street in Oxford in 1846, but the shop closed after his death. However, his son Benjamin Henry Blackwell, originally apprenticed to another Oxford bookseller, subsequently opened his own bookshop in Broad Street in 1879. His son, Basil Henry, was born in 1889.

Basil joined the family firm in 1911, but he initially focussed on developing the publishing side of the business, before becoming one of the most important booksellers of the twentieth century. Basil Blackwell (known to all as 'The Gaffer') was devoted to the bookshop. As an early riser, he arrived at Broad Street by 7.15 each morning and was known to walk around the large shop at least once every day, talking to as many staff as possible and always encouraging them to put forward ideas. Like William Foyle, he was an inspiring and innovative bookseller.

In the 1930s he became involved in the Associated Booksellers of Great Britain, serving as president in 1934 and 1935. He also played a key role in the introduction of book tokens in 1932. Blackwell was passionate about his job and company and, as the Broad Street business grew, Blackwell opened separate shops for art books, children's books and music.

The Gaffer's elder son, Richard, joined the company in the late 1940s but didn't officially take over the reins until Basil's retirement in 1969 (the latter still being very involved even at an old age). The younger son,

Julian (known as Toby), joined the company in 1952. He oversaw the expansion of the Broad Street premises to create the huge 10,000-square-ft Norrington Room, which allegedly has 2.5 miles of shelving and for some time was the largest room of books in Europe.

In the 1960s, Blackwell's partnered with Oxford University Press to form a company called University Bookshops, subsequently opening several shops in red-brick university towns, capitalising on the growth in student numbers just as W.H. Smith, Foyles and Heffers did. This became the backbone of the Blackwell business for the next fifty years or more.

Basil Blackwell died in April 1984 and there were multiple tributes to him, full of adulation for this giant among booksellers, who had grown his father's small shop into a huge global business. *The Times* called him 'a legend in his lifetime', while *The Oxford Times* boldly stated that he was 'the greatest bookman of his time'. His office is still preserved in the Broad Street building, just as it was in his day, complete with his original chair and desk, coat and hat, and his pipe.

At the end of the twentieth century, Blackwell's had over seventy shops, having bought up the James Thin chain as well as Heffers in Cambridge. But the dramatic changes that were to follow in the book trade, particularly online bookselling and the emergence of digital books, severely affected the Blackwell's chain, particularly its academic and educational business. In 2022, the remaining stores were bought by Waterstones, although currently the Blackwell's and Heffers names have been retained.

Simpkin, Marshall & Co.

One of the key elements in a good supply chain for bookshops is the existence of an efficient and capable wholesaler. Simpkin, Marshall & Co. had started life as a bookseller in 1819, founded by William Simpkin and Richard Marshall but, by the early twentieth century, it had grown to be the first major trade wholesaler in the UK book trade. Most book-shops did not have direct accounts with all publishers at this time, so the ability to order almost any book from one central account was vital. Simpkin's was based in Paternoster Row, the historical centre of the book business and, from there, supplied many single-copy customer orders and small stock orders.

Many publishers were still based in and around Paternoster Row at this time, although booksellers had spread further afield across the city and country. These were still the days when each publisher, particularly those that were London-based, had its own trade counter, which bookshop 'collectors' would visit regularly to collect orders for stock or specific customer enquiries. Obtaining these small orders from one general wholesaler was obviously much easier than having to visit each individual publisher and became an essential part of how the book trade worked during the twentieth century.

However, tragedy struck during the Second World War. The persistent German bombing raids from September 1940 onwards had a devastating effect on several publishing houses, destroying many of their premises as well as those of Simpkin Marshall. On the night of 29 December 1940, Paternoster Row and many nearby streets were demolished by German bombs, destroying much of the British publishing business. Simpkin's premises and their entire stock were obliterated.

This was a huge shock to the entire British book trade. *The Bookseller* reported, 'The hub of the English book trade lies in a smoking ruin', and it went on to report that 'Simpkin's, Whitaker's, Longmans, Nelson's, Hutchinson's and, further afield, Collins and Eyre and Spottiswoode, are gutted shells'. It should also be noted that many booksellers and publishers around the country suffered too. Collier's bookshop in Coventry was destroyed and so were Philip, Son & Nephew and Henry Young's in Liverpool. It is estimated that over 20 million books were destroyed in these raids.

Simpkin Marshall continued despite this enormous setback, moving into temporary premises in St John's Wood, but it was never the same again and its demise left a huge hole in the trade. In 1951, the company was sold to Robert Maxwell, who famously ran the company into the ground. It was declared insolvent in 1954. Maxwell seems to have bought the company to help raise funds and make interest-free loans to his own private companies. According to publisher Lionel Leventhal (who founded Arms & Armour Press and Greenhill Books), this behaviour 'sounded a warning to the book trade about Captain Robert Maxwell's way of doing business', a sadly prescient statement for those involved in the Mirror Group debacle in later years.

Bertram Books

The loss of Simpkin Marshall was felt throughout the book trade and the repercussions resonated for many years to come. There was no immediate successor to replace them, although W.H. Smith ran a small wholesale operation, as did Gardners of Bexhill. For some time, though, there was a gaping hole that remained unfilled.

Bertram Books originally started from a small chicken farm in Norwich, run by Elsie Bertram. Her son, Kip, was a sales rep with Pan and, at some point, she became his assistant before deciding to launch a small wholesale operation of her own, distributing Pan paperbacks and others from a small van to shops in the East Anglia area.

Elsie's big break came in 1968 when the publisher Paul Hamlyn was desperate to get his bestselling books to bookshops but was being thwarted by a strike at the IPC warehouse (owners of Hamlyn at that time). Hamlyn used Bertrams to supply his books to bookshops in the run-up to Christmas, providing a huge service to the trade. From that lucky break, the reputation of Bertrams grew and bookshops who had been seeking a successor to Simpkins Marshall flocked to the company in droves.

The business' success was based upon a real demand combined with excellent personal service, provided by Elsie and Kip. The company was always renowned for its personal, friendly but hard-working approach and the staff always felt very invested in the business. Mike Butler, who joined the business in 1977 and rose to become head of buying, says that, initially, 'there was no staff structure, everybody, including the Bertrams, was expected to do everything'. There was a company ethos that nobody went home until the last order that day had been despatched.

As the business grew, many small bookshops ordered most of their stock from Bertrams, rather than dealing with lots of different publishers. The company grew significantly in the 1980s and 1990s. We were one of the bookshops that used Bertrams for the bulk of our stock orders. For most of our bookshop's life, we received a daily delivery from Bertrams, which included a large volume of customer orders. As long as we placed an order by 5 p.m., we received the books the next morning. This was before the days of Amazon Prime – not only was this service speedy and efficient, but it was more personal and encouraged human contact. Like most independents of that era, we received a lot of customer orders each day, which in turn encouraged repeat regular visits from our customers.

Sadly, after Elsie's death in 2003, the company was sold. In the following years, Bertrams changed ownership several times and things were never the same. It finally went into receivership in 2020, a sad end to a vital cog in the bookselling world. By that point, Gardners of Eastbourne had become the dominant UK wholesaler. Gardners of Bexhill had been acquired in 1986 by Alan Little and it remains under the ownership of the Little family to this day, another family firm that has grown tremendously from that time. Gardners now supplies books globally and to online retailers as often as to bricks-and-mortar shops. The company now boasts the personal approach and attention to detail that marked Bertrams out in its heyday. It is likewise a great supporter of independent bookshops and runs an annual trade show alongside the BA Conference, as well as supporting the BA Catalogue each Christmas, too.

Paul Hamlyn – Selling Beyond Bookshops

As Britain moved into the 1960s and beyond, book publishing had become a huge industry. The success of Penguin, Pan and the rest led to the expansion of the industry and the growth of the paperback, making books more affordable and more widely used. Still, publishers and booksellers continued the quest to expand the books market.

One of the key players from the 1960s onwards was Paul Hamlyn, born in Berlin in 1926 as Paul Hamburger, the fourth child of a middle-class Jewish family. The family moved to Britain in 1933 but, after his father's death, Paul left school at 15, working first at *Country Life* magazine as office boy before starting in the book trade at Samuel French, publishers of plays, and then Zwemmer's art bookshop in Charing Cross Road.

Paul was ambitious and, using a small inheritance from his grandfather, set himself up in business, graduating from first running a book stall in Camden Town Market to selling remainders and then setting up his own publishing company and, ultimately, amassing a fortune. Coupled with an ambition to grow rich was a desire to disrupt his adopted industry. Soon after establishing himself in the book trade, Hamlyn was very critical of high prices for books and the trade's inefficient distribution. He was convinced that books could be sold in greater volume and to a much wider readership.

His experience selling publishers' remainders (overstocks of books that had ceased to sell at full price) led him to start reprinting his own 'remainders' cheaply in eastern Europe. He bought up the cheap rights on books from foreign publishers, such as a deal he struck with the Czech publisher Artia for a low-priced book on Rembrandt. By printing a large quantity, he was able to publish the book in English at a very keen cover price and it quickly became the bestselling book on the painter in Britain.

Based on this success, he launched his own publishing company, Books for Pleasure, later renaming it Hamlyn. He published inexpensive editions of what became known as coffee-table books, on subjects such as art, cookery, gardening, DIY and interior design.

The importance of Paul Hamlyn is the huge change he brought to the industry. He saw himself as an outsider in the world of publishing and he worked hard to bring books to customers beyond the traditional bookshop market. To keep costs down, he printed in huge quantities and then sold his books less through the usual bookshop channels and more significantly through department stores and supermarkets, aiming at the non-traditional book buyer. This revolution in how books were sold also included custom-made stands and spinners to display the books to potential customers. The books were stocked in quantity and positioned face-out or piled high for maximum effect, in stark contrast to the traditional spine-on shelves of most bookshops at the time.

Hamlyn didn't operate like other publishers, sifting through manuscripts to decide which books to publish. Instead, he set up a small team who decided the subject to publish, then designed and commissioned books accordingly. In this way, for example, Hamlyn dominated the cookery book market, producing titles such as the *Hamlyn All Colour Cookery Book*, which sold millions of copies.

Paul Hamlyn was another key figure, like James Lackington and Allen Lane before him, who was keen to expand the book market but not afraid to be a disruptor to achieve his goals. In a speech to the Society of Young Publishers in 1960, he reiterated a recurring theme, arguing that most people were terrified of going into bookshops. While bookshops would always be important for the regular 'bookish' book buyers, there was also a place for the supermarkets, department stores and more general outlets like W.H. Smith, playing an important role in delivering books to the wider population. Hamlyn was successful at selling large quantities of books through such outlets to non-traditional book buyers.

He was so successful that he eventually sold his eponymous company for a fortune but almost immediately went on to set up another publisher, Octopus, repeating the same formula of producing great books on similar subjects at affordable prices. Hamlyn's methods, once seen as outrageous to many traditionalists in the industry, very quickly became the norm and his success led to multiple imitators. The inexpensive coffee-table book became a staple of the industry from that point.

PART TWO

The Way
We Live Now

7

Tim Waterstone
and the Bookselling and
Publishing Transformation
of the 1980s

Waterstones bookshop in Reading, Berkshire. (Alamy)

Running a Bookshop

Our story now reaches the 1980s and the time when I started my career in the book trade. When my father and I opened our bookshop in Chelmsford, we were joining a long tradition of independent bookshops that together made up a sizeable portion of the British book trade at this time. I was in my early twenties with no actual idea of what I wanted to do as a career, working in a very dull insurance job, when my dad, Peter, was made redundant from his job importing and exporting fruit and vegetables. (He had originally started his career in publishing, working as an office boy for Allen & Unwin.) He was now due for a decent redundancy package and so we revived, somewhat speculatively at first, the family discussion about opening a bookshop, funded by this golden handshake.

As the months went by and my dad's redundancy date moved closer, our discussions became more serious. We began subscribing to *The Bookseller* magazine. In the early 1980s, there were over 2,000 independent bookshops around the UK, very much the backbone of the book trade, and the only real bookshop chain of any size was W.H. Smith. The pages of *The Bookseller*, therefore, were mostly concerned with independent bookshops.

One week, we read an article about a man who had recently opened his own new bookshop in a busy town in the London commuter belt. We got in touch and visited him at his shop, learning how he had accomplished what we were still only dreaming of. He was incredibly helpful and told us where to obtain equipment, which shop fitters he used, which book wholesalers to contact and what the BA could do to help. It was an exciting meeting, and our dream seemed within our grasp. We now understood the nuts and bolts of how we could make this happen. The dream was becoming much more serious – something tangible – and starting to become a genuine possibility.

In the next few months, I continued working away in insurance, but I was living a double life, secretly plotting alongside my dad for a completely different career. We contacted estate agents looking for suitable local properties and had several potential locations sent our way, but none were quite right. It quickly became clear that a town centre or high street position was going to prove too expensive, as is often the case for independent businesses. We widened our search and eventually came across a new building planned in an area just off the High Street, in a well-established secondary shopping area that had several strong, independent businesses, including cafés, restaurants and an art shop with gallery. The proposed site had room for a 1,000-square-ft shop floor plus a small back office, parking and two floors of offices above.

We visited the prospective site, which at that stage was just a pile of mud between two existing buildings and started investigating footfall and viability. Our research data was based on little more than me standing opposite the shop counting passersby at several times of the day and comparing that to the centre of the town. The signs, though, were good. This was a busy location, near a bus stop, and a passing place for thousands of people walking to and from the town centre every day, as well as students going to the further education college nearby. It was close to a well-established residential area of the town and seemed the perfect location for a dedicated bookshop. Only many years later did I make the serendipitous discovery that there had been a bookshop very close to the same position almost 100 years earlier.

We signed up for the site and, from that point, things snowballed. Our dream was now being built in the physical world. We were aiming to open in time for Christmas 1983, but inevitably the building work was delayed and we had to settle for the start of February the following year.

I was more than a little overjoyed to escape the world of insurance in December and promptly dedicated myself to planning for our opening date. I was just turning 22 when we opened our bookshop, and it was to be staffed initially by just my father and me with a Saturday assistant. Our single qualification for the job was our love of books and we could not pretend to have any extensive knowledge beyond our own tastes.

Among many problems to be solved was how to stock a new bookshop from scratch. In her novel *The Bookshop*, set in a small Suffolk town in the late 1950s, a thinly disguised depiction of Southwold, Penelope Fitzgerald's bookshop owner Florence Green has certain ideas about the sort of stock she wants to have and how to display it:

The heavy luxurious country-house books, the books about Suffolk churches, the memoirs of statesmen in several volumes, took the place that was theirs by right of birth in the window. Others, indispensable, but not aristocratic, would occupy the middle shelves. That was the place for the Books of the Car – from Austen to Wolseley – technical works on pebble-polishing, sailing, pony clubs, wild flowers and birds, local maps and guide books.

When we first planned our shop, we had some ideas about the kinds of books we would stock, but not as much as we probably should have. Luckily, Hammick's, one of the book wholesalers that we were in touch with, supplied a computer printout of suggested stock based on the size of our shop. I spent several weeks poring over this list, adding quantities, deleting some titles, bringing in others.

We were already subscribers to *The Bookseller* magazine, which I had been reading avidly for the past few months – and that certainly helped. And I had been engaged in a considerable number of recent spying missions to other bookshops locally, in nearby towns and London to see what those shops stocked. I had quickly got up to speed on current titles in the market across multiple categories. So, while we went into the venture naively, we were learning more all the time and gradually building a vision of what our shop would look like.

As for the competition, W.H. Smith were much better-stocked shops than their modern-day counterparts and the local book department held a decent range of general-appeal titles and bestsellers, across a wide range of subjects. The independent Clarkes were quite serious booksellers, albeit this was very much second fiddle to their large stationery and office supplies departments on the ground floor. But we felt our town had room for a dedicated bookshop, as both the other retailers sold stationery and multiple other lines.

Our instincts were proved right. We opened our doors in February 1984 and for the next sixteen years enjoyed running a profitable and much-loved business.

As time passed, I felt comfortable as a bookseller and believed that I was not only good at what I was doing but was performing an important public service. I firmly believe that a bookseller is the gatekeeper to all the treasures of world literature, supplying these precious goods to local readers, whether adults or children, whatever their tastes.

I soon recognised that I really cared about this bookshop: it had become an integral part of who I was. I now had skin in the game and was passionately invested in this entity we had created and in the role of bookseller. As the years went by, the bookshop increasingly became a vital part of my being and, to quite a large extent, defined who I was.

We worked hard to grow the business both on the shopfloor and through outside activities such as events and supply to schools, businesses, the local college and local university. I spent the greater part of each week at the shop, including many long evenings, and it became like a second home. I had no idea other than that it would exist forever.

It is this sort of passion and devotion that underpins most successful independent businesses. But it means that the fall will be that much harder if things should one day take a turn for the worse.

The Changes Begin

There have been many upheavals and changes during the long history of bookselling and publishing. Retail is a constantly evolving and changing environment but, for the book trade, the last forty years have arguably seen more changes than ever before. From the 1980s onwards – coincidentally, when I joined the business – there would be a significant overhaul in the way the book trade operated and a shift in power.

The first big change was the enormous growth of chain booksellers in the 1980s and 1990s. This was followed by the abolition of the Net Book Agreement (NBA) in 1995, which meant the end of fixed pricing for books and the introduction of heavy discounting. As the new century dawned, the dramatic growth in online selling, particularly through Amazon, transformed the market even further.

As if that wasn't enough, the introduction of digital publishing and the e-book, coupled with the massive growth in audiobooks and the rapid development of self-publishing online, brought another revolution to the whole trade. Added to this, the way books were produced and printed was undergoing major changes, as the trade moved towards twenty-first-century digital printing. And publishers themselves were experiencing huge structural change as several joined forces or were bought up by larger international conglomerates to better cope with the more international aspects of the business and global supply chain challenges.

Each of these developments on their own would have resulted in dramatic alteration to the book trade but, taken together, these changes occurring in rapid succession have resulted in the landscape today being almost unrecognisable from what it was four decades ago. Looking back now from forty years later, the 1980s seems a different world, a more innocent time perhaps. These were the twilight days of a certain kind of independent bookselling, which our own bookshop epitomised.

As we have noted, the trade in the early 1980s was still dominated by independent bookshops and W.H. Smith. It was still the only major chain, also owning the upmarket Bowes & Bowes and Sherratt & Hughes mini-chains. Blackwell's had several university bookshops throughout the country and its shops across Oxford, while Heffers had multiple sites in Cambridge.

A commonly held view of UK independent bookshops at that point was that they were rather old-fashioned, possibly dry and dusty, although also in many cases much loved. Book distribution was still quite antiquated, and reorders of stock could often take weeks. Some shops were still collecting customer orders by hand from publishers' trade counters in London. Stock control systems were generally manual and inefficient.

Bookshops themselves were not always welcoming and there was anecdotal evidence of grumpy owners and their rudeness to customers. Many shops hid in back-street locations and were often subject to strange opening hours. There was a sound argument that some change was necessary, systems could be improved and bookshops should appeal to and attract a much wider market.

Penelope Fitzgerald's novel *The Bookshop*, although first published in 1978, paints a rather quaint image of a Suffolk bookshop in the late 1950s. To some extent at least, not a great deal had changed by the early 1980s, and the trade needed a kick up the backside. While there were many brilliant and commendable independent bookshops, in retrospect we can see that new ideas, new visions and an element of disruption were needed. The book trade was to get all of these in spades.

The Rise of Literary Fiction

There were changes to how books were being sold and promoted. In 1983, the Book Marketing Council launched a promotion called the Best of Young British Novelists. The campaign was promoted in heavyweight newspapers and magazines, bookshop windows and table displays, in a special issue of *Granta* magazine, edited by Bill Buford, and nationwide through the W.H. Smith high-street bookshops.

For those involved in bookselling today, it will sound quite remarkable that W.H. Smith took part in such a promotion, giving over table space to literary fiction. It now has much less space for books in its shops and generally focuses on more mainstream and mass-market fare, but things were very different forty years ago. Indeed, for several decades from 1959 until 2005, long before Waterstones and Dillons arrived on the scene, it even ran its own literary book prize, the annual W.H. Smith Literary Award, predating the Booker Prize. Its aim was to 'encourage and bring international esteem to authors of the British Commonwealth' and winners included Laurie Lee, Jean Rhys, Nadine Gordimer, John Fowles, Anthony Powell, Ian McEwan, Doris Lessing, Vikram Seth and Simon Schama.

The Best of Young British Novelists campaign included Julian Barnes, Graham Swift, William Boyd, Kazuo Ishiguro, Ian McEwan and Salman Rushdie, as well as Jeanette Winterson, Pat Barker, Adam Mars-Jones, Rose Tremain and Lisa St Aubin de Terán – all relative unknowns at this point. I can recall picking up a promotional leaflet from W.H. Smith and subsequently purchasing several books in the promotion. This introduced me and thousands of other book buyers to authors I had barely been aware of beforehand. Julian Barnes, Graham Swift and Ian McEwan remain authors I have read consistently ever since.

There is obviously lots of brilliant new fiction being written by today's young writers, but it's fascinating that these three and many others from the list are still releasing powerful new works to this day.

In 2022, for example, Ian McEwan released one of his greatest works, *Lessons*, a bestseller and great bookshop favourite. The Best of Young British Novelists campaign gave a significant boost to his fledgling career.

The campaign capitalised on the growth in serious fiction that had been taking place since the mid-1970s and the increased importance of literary fiction as a genre separate from general mass-market fiction. Recent years had witnessed many broadsheet newspapers, particularly the Sundays, giving an increased amount of space to book reviews, with papers such as the *Sunday Times* even having its own extensive separate books section.

The space devoted to book reviews would be boosted further by the launch of *The Independent* in 1986. These newspapers often contained in-depth interviews with the big names of this rising genre, including many from the Best of Young British Novelists campaign. And big-money advances for literary novels, a recent development, made the news pages, creating hype around these books. Likewise, the advent of the Booker Prize was given widespread coverage in the press, all increasing the public profile of literary fiction.

D.J. Taylor rightly reports that 'books were more fashionable in the late 1980s'. Until this point, authors had continued to struggle to make decent money from their profession, apart from a few mass-market exceptions. Most novelists wrote, on average, a book a year and generally had to support their writing with another form of income, whether that was journalism, teaching or something more prosaic. Martin Amis was literary editor of the *New Statesman* while starting out as a novelist, later writing for *The Observer* too. Anthony Burgess wrote book reviews for *The Sunday Times,* while Peter Ackroyd subsidised his revenue from book sales by working for *The Spectator* as literary editor and film critic at different times. This is no different from George Orwell, back in the 1930s, surviving by penning book reviews and magazine articles until the success of *Animal Farm* late in his career gave him financial security.

Advances, even for the best writers, were still often quite low in the 1980s, but for first-time novelists you would be lucky to receive more than £250. Indeed, this was the amount that Martin Amis received for his first novel, *The Rachel Papers*. But the tide was changing and the success of many of the writers in the Best of Young British Novelists campaign, particularly Ian McEwan, Kazuo Ishiguro and Graham Swift, alongside other more-established names, led to improved advances for their new books. This enabled growth in the importance of literary agents, who duly touted for even bigger advances for future novels from certain key novelists in well-publicised bidding wars. All of this in turn helped bring literary fiction more into the public spotlight, growing book sales and authors' salaries.

One of the key publishers at the heart of the growth in literary fiction was Jonathan Cape, led by Tom Maschler. Jonathan Cape had been founded in 1921 in Gower Street in Bloomsbury. The company initially made its name publishing Hemingway and Christopher Isherwood and continued to develop in the subsequent decades. But its immense success really came after Maschler joined the company.

Tom's father, Kurt Leo Maschler, had worked in the book trade in Germany publishing, among others, Erich Kastner, author of *Emil and the Detectives*, before emigrating to the UK in the 1930s. Tom Maschler's first job in publishing was working for Andre Deutsch, before he joined Cape in 1960. As Maschler says in his autobiography, *Publisher*, 'Most people working in publishing would concede that from the late sixties to the early eighties Cape was the greatest literary publishing house in England. We had the best authors, we produced the best promotions and our production was the best.'

Maschler was a publishing wunderkind, a workaholic, a bon viveur, a great talent-spotter and talent-nurturer. As his successor at Cape, Dan Franklin said, 'He was much the most brilliant publisher of his generation.' He worked with some of the greatest and most successful writers of this period, including Peter Mayle, Kurt Vonnegut, Philip Roth, John Fowles, Doris Lessing, Bruce Chatwin and what Maschler calls the 'triumvirate' of Martin Amis, Ian McEwan and Julian Barnes. These were among the biggest names of the 1980s publishing boom and very much the talk of the literary world.

Maschler also had a strong line in children's authors and illustrators at Cape. He inherited Erich Kastner (an interesting coincidence), Hugh Lofting, Arthur Ransome and Joan Aiken on joining the company, but also added such esteemed names as Roald Dahl, John Burningham, Quentin Blake, Nicola Bayley and Russell Hoban – all subsequent bestsellers and many of them prize-winners. It was an exciting era in publishing and Maschler was right at the centre of it.

Publishers differentiated between the more serious 'literary' fiction and mass-market fiction by publishing them in separate paperback formats. Thrillers, romance, crime fiction, horror, science fiction and other genres were still issued in small 'A' format editions (height approximately 180mm), but literary fiction and non-fiction were published in larger 'B' format paperbacks (198mm). The likes of Picador and Faber were in the new 'B' format, as were other new literary imprints introduced by paperback publishers to capitalise on the growth of literary fiction – for example, Flamingo, Minerva and King Penguin.

Our bookshop boasted a Picador spinner, which was responsible for massive sales and attracted a certain sort of discerning literary customer. Julian Barnes, Graham Swift and Ian McEwan were some of our bestselling authors from Picador and it was the leading literary paperback list at that time.

It is also worth mentioning that, alongside the growth of literary fiction, there was a similar growth in the importance of more serious non-fiction throughout the 1980s and 1990s. This would include big history titles from Anthony Beevor and Antonia Fraser, important biographies by Richard Ellmann (of Oscar Wilde), Anthony Burgess (D.H. Lawrence), Claire Tomalin (Jane Austen), Michael Holroyd (George Bernard Shaw) and Peter Ackroyd (Dickens), plus a wealth of brilliant travel writing from Eric Newby, Dervla Murphy, Paul Theroux, Jonathan Raban, Gavin Young and William Dalyrmple.

These sorts of books were promoted by the rising chains of Waterstones and Dillons and would be one of the masts upon which they staked their expansion – and the accompanying publicity and press coverage that these books attracted underpinned their growth. In our own small fashion, many of these titles were ones we and other independents did rather well with, too. Ellman's Oscar Wilde book and Ackroyd's *Dickens*, the latter being one of my personal favourites from that era, were huge sellers for us.

The Booker Prize

Tom Maschler also played an important role in creating the Booker Prize. He had always thought that Britain didn't seem to care about literary prizes. The importance of literary prizes, the prestige connected with them, the publicity they gave to the industry and the sales they created were well recognised in France, Germany, the USA and elsewhere, but not in Britain. Maschler gave a talk to the Society of Young Publishers way back in the 1950s, talking about how the winner of the Prix Goncourt would sell as many as 500,000 copies.

Building on this enthusiasm for prizes generating book sales, Maschler worked with Martin Goff at the National Book League, in association with Booker Brothers as sponsors, to create the inaugural Booker Prize in 1969. The first winner, *Something to Answer For* by P.H. Newby, only saw a slight boost in sales. It was really from 1980 onwards, with the increased spotlight on literary fiction, the televising of the Booker Prize ceremony and blanket press coverage from the broadsheets, that the prize finally achieved Maschler's original aims.

The 1980 contest came down to two literary heavyweights: William Golding's *Rites of Passage* was up against *Earthly Powers* by Anthony Burgess. This great battle between these two big-name authors made headline news, particularly when Burgess refused to attend the prize-giving ceremony unless his victory was confirmed in advance. In fact, it was Golding who eventually took the prize, but both books and their authors benefitted from the publicity, as did booksellers across the land.

The importance of the Booker Prize grew throughout the 1980s, particularly with more large, upmarket bookshops to sell through as Waterstones and Dillons expanded. Bookshops focussed on the six-title shortlist, which was announced six weeks ahead of the winner, giving them an opportunity to sell all six books before the prize-giving ceremony itself.

In 1984, our first year in bookselling, Cape's Anita Brookner won the prize with *Hotel du Lac* and Cape sold 80,000 hardback copies in total – an amazing result. Brookner's previous novels had never sold more than 7,000 copies. This was testament to Maschler's belief that book prizes could deliver increasingly brilliant book sales. Our bookshop sold large quantities of *Hotel du Lac* as well as Brookner's backlist and we enjoyed regular success every year around Booker time. Some years, the choice was rather too eclectic or obscure, but most years saw a significant sales boost. Our bestselling Booker winners included *Moon Tiger* by Penelope Lively in 1987, *Paddy Clarke Ha Ha Ha* by Roddy Doyle in 1993 and *Last Orders* by Graham Swift in 1996. Each of these had a knock-on effect on the author's backlist sales, too, and we would enjoy brilliant sales again when the book was released in paperback the following year.

Following the Booker's success, the UK now has several book prizes that help generate book sales, including the Nero Book Awards, the Baillie Gifford Prize, the Women's Prize, the International Booker Prize and the Waterstones Book of the Year.

Virago Heralds Change

There had always been women in publishing, but often just in minor office roles. During the twentieth century, the situation gradually improved as more British publishers employed female editors. At the same time, women writers continued to grow in importance. This was the century of Virginia Woolf, Rebecca West, Jean Rhys, Iris Murdoch, Elizabeth Bowen, Margaret Drabble, Muriel Spark and countless others. But this was still an industry dominated by men.

The role of women in society had become a huge subject of debate during the 1960s and change was very much in the air. In the early 1970s, a group of women working in the book trade decided to set up a publishing house to focus exclusively on books by women, both new titles and out-of-print titles that deserved a new lease of life. It was the brainchild of Carmen Callil, who had become friends with Rosie Boycott and Marsha Rowe, founders of the feminist magazine *Spare Rib*. Callil wanted to do for books what the other two had done for magazines; indeed, her original idea had been to call her venture Spare Rib Books. It was Rosie Boycott, going through a book of goddesses, who came up with the title Virago.

Carmen Callil had emigrated from Melbourne to Britain in 1960 after graduating. She had held several jobs in publishing, mainly in marketing and publicity, working her way up the ranks, first with Hutchinson, then Panther, Granada, Anthony Blond and Andre Deutsch.

Virago was launched in 1973 by Callil, with Ursula Owen and Harriet Winter. Initial funding was raised from several sources, including from fellow publisher Quartet Books. Virago's mission was 'to champion women's voices and bring them to the widest possible readership around the world'. Although money was certainly tight at first, the small group were buoyed up by a wave of support.

The publisher used a group of twenty-eight women from publishing, journalism and academia as advisors. This assistance and goodwill helped the fledgling list find its way. The company produced twelve books in its first year, kicking off with *Fenwomen* by Mary Chamberlain, setting a standard for depicting a wide variety of women's lives in fiction and non-fiction.

Virago Modern Classics were launched in 1978, with the now-famous green spines, a celebration of women writers that the book trade had either forgotten or ignored, but who returned to prominence as a result. It was a rejoinder to the male-dominated Penguin Classics adorning booksellers' shelves,and the series found immediate success with its first title, *Frost in May* by Anthonia White. Other great authors in the series included Molly Keane, Angela Carter and Rosamund Lehmann. Virago also revived *Testament of Youth* by Vera Brittain and were rewarded when it was serialised by the BBC the following year, enormously boosting sales. By the time I entered the trade, six years later, this Virago Modern Classics series was already well established and many of its titles were strong, steady sellers for us.

Virago still thrives today, although it is no longer independent. It became part of the CVBC group (Chatto, Virago, Bodley Head & Cape) in 1982, when Carmen Callil was headhunted to run Chatto, but she only agreed to take up the role on condition that Virago came with her. Lennie Goodings, who had been with Virago since 1978, took over as publisher. However, there was discontent within the company and most of the staff voted for a self-funded management buyout to return to independence in 1987.

Virago is not just Callil's story. Goodings and many others helped create, maintain and grow this publisher into the wonderful list that has delighted so many readers over the years. Like many publishers, Virago struggled in the vicious price wars of the 1990s that ended with the abolition of the NBA. To secure the company's future, it was sold to Little, Brown in 1996 and today is part of the Hachette conglomerate, one of the 'Big Four' publishers. It continues to be a major publishing force, combining classic women's writing with the best in contemporary fiction and non-fiction. Among its modern cohort are Natasha Walter, Sarah Waters, Marilynne Robinson and Maya Angelou.

Virago released *I Know Why the Caged Bird Sings* by Angelou in 1984. The book had been issued in the USA back in 1969 but had been repeatedly rejected by publishers in the UK, who didn't think that the British reading public would be interested in the story of a poor black child from the American South. Virago made the book into a massive bestseller.

Virago was a pioneer – a game-changer that helped move the dial. As a result, women's writing became more prominent and women became more dominant in publishing. Today's publishing world has many women in key roles (Macmillan and Bonnier, for example, both have female CEOs) and books by women dominate our bookshops and, increasingly, the literary prizes. Change has been slow and there is more work to do, but Virago set a trend. To date, it has published over 1,200 authors and over 3,500 titles.

Waterstones and Dillons

The growth in literary fiction was a hugely positive and exciting development for bookshops and, as the 1980s began, the previously staid and stale bookshop landscape of Britain was on the verge of undergoing another huge change. Storm clouds were gathering for independent bookshops, and W.H. Smith was about to face stiff competition and lose its position as the only major chain.

There were two men at the heart of this upheaval. They were Terry Maher, head of Pentos PLC, and Tim Waterstone. Both men had a passion for books and bookshops, and both were to dramatically transform the bookselling landscape of the UK in the 1980s. They achieved this separately, through the Dillons and Waterstones chains, and only later did their paths converge.

Tim Waterstone had a long-held dream of launching a chain of large, well-stocked literary bookshops that would sit in prominent positions on high streets across the country. This vision would lead to a revolution and change bookselling in the UK forever. Always a man who loved books, Waterstone had worked for his local bookshop, The Book Club in Crowborough in Sussex, during his school holidays in the 1950s, although he had also been a frequent visitor to the shop as a child, being allowed to sit and read despite not having money to buy books. He learned a lot from observing how the owner, Miss Santoro, ran her business, how she marketed the shop (she 'never missed a promotional trick') and dealt with customers. This experience seemed to tether him to the world of bookshops and sow the seeds for his future endeavours. 'She taught me what proactive, imaginative, knowledgeable bookselling is all about, even on her relatively modest village scale.'

But it was while studying at Cambridge and regularly visiting Heffers that Tim Waterstone had an epiphany, formulating his plan that would take another sixteen years to realise. His vision was to open a chain of bookshops, a mixture of the size and range of Heffers combined with the devotion and book knowledge demonstrated by Miss Santoro.

He spent several years in business unconnected to books, gathering experience and honing his skills. He moved closer to his goal in the 1970s, accepting a management role working for W.H. Smith running their distribution department. Only on being made redundant from that role did Tim Waterstone put his grand plan into action, pulling together finance to open his first eponymous bookshop on Old Brompton Road in London in 1982.

Waterstones stores held a much higher volume of stock than existing bookshops and were tilted towards literary fiction, art, poetry and weighty non-fiction. In addition, Waterstones employed intelligent, book-loving staff – mainly graduates, many of whom would become writers or publishers themselves. Some would even start their own bookshops.

Tim Waterstone empowered his managers to make their shops unique and gave them carte blanche to stock books they believed in – in complete contrast to the central buying that was taking hold at W.H. Smith, which would later be the norm for large retail chains. His booksellers hand-sold countless great books that they loved and believed in, bringing a refreshing new enthusiasm to the trade. He combined the passion and specialism of the best independent bookshops with strong financial backing, delivering a much larger stock range.

Waterstone wanted to encourage people to browse in his shops, to pick up and handle the books and read bits of them. He believed that, given this freedom, browsers became book buyers, often buying much more than they had ever intended when they entered the shop.

His hunch paid off. The growth in book sales and the greater publicity for literary titles meant Waterstones was entering the market at exactly the right time. His first shop was a huge success and more followed, initially in other London locations (Charing Cross Road and High Street Kensington followed swiftly after the first store), but they soon opened beyond the capital too, across the country, often going head-to-head with independents that struggled to survive against this new behemoth. This is not to criticise most of these independents, but they were up against bigger bookshops with deeper pockets and, in most cases, this ended with the independent having to close.

Interestingly, when Tim Waterstone was looking for premises for his second shop, Christina Foyle contacted him and offered him very cheap rent on the building next to Foyles in Charing Cross Road, which Foyles also owned, and this is where Waterstones opened its next store. This demonstrates something important and possibly unique about the book trade: there is a very high degree of interaction between competitors and between retailers and their suppliers. All are joined by a love of books that often seems to supersede the desire to make money. Although famed for her difficult personality, the act of offering cheap rent to Waterstones and inviting a competitor to open next door to her shop reveals another side to Christina Foyle's character.

There was definitely an arrogance about Waterstones, but there is an argument that the trade needed that. While it avoided going head to head with decent independent bookshops, if Waterstones felt that the incumbent bookseller wasn't up to the mark, it launched itself into the area with gusto. Independents (perhaps unsurprisingly) didn't take kindly to Waterstones, and the BA initially refused it membership, although this situation changed years later.

Tim Waterstone justified his methods, saying, 'It is difficult to over-state how lamentable the bookselling scene of the time was.' Many – me included – would argue with that characterisation of the independent sector, while also recognising that Waterstones has been a force for good in the UK book trade.

Within ten years, Waterstones was the largest bookseller in Europe. Tim Waterstone's vision for larger, well-stocked bookshops, that were open for longer hours, with enthusiastic staff and an emphasis on more literary titles was all eagerly received by the book-buying public. In 1992, *The Independent* wrote, 'It would be difficult to overstate Mr. Waterstones impact on the book trade ... he has made book-buying a pleasurable experience.'

Our own small bookshop had continued the existing status quo. Tim Waterstone was doing something very different. He started a much-needed bookselling revolution, upending that status quo and bringing better bookshops to British high streets. He created an outstanding legacy and paved the way for multiple other changes in bookselling and publishing, including more in-store bookshop events, author tours, book groups, literary festivals and higher engagement by authors with their audience. Today, Waterstones has over 290 stores and, although somewhat changed from its early days, these remain exemplary literary beacons across the country.

★ ★ ★

Before Waterstone began enacting his plan, in 1977 Dillons in Gower Street had been bought by the Pentos group. Pentos, with Terry Maher as chairman, was building a retail portfolio which was to include Athena and Rymans.

The Pentos group had already bought up some thirty-four bookshops over nine years, including the Hudson chain in the Birmingham area.

Prior to this, the three children of E.F. and Elsie Hudson had expanded the family business by enlarging the New Street shop and opening shops in Aston and Edgbaston Universities. Medical and art bookshops were opened in Birmingham, new branches started in Wolverhampton and Coventry, and an existing shop purchased in Loughborough. In the late 1970s, Pentos also bought Sisson & Parker in Nottingham, Hodges Figgis in Dublin and the Pilgrim's Bookshop in Canterbury. These were early shots across the bows of the independent bookselling sector, presaging a future that would soon reveal itself.

Pentos set about refurbishing and redesigning Dillons in Gower Street in the early 1980s, making it into the largest bookshop in the UK, overtaking Foyles. The redesign also included a new 'Dillons the Bookstore' logo and signage. Over the next few years, Pentos transformed the regional bookshops that they had acquired, including Hudsons and Sisson & Parker, into Dillons-branded stores and began opening in other new locations.

Other mini-bookshop chains that Dillons acquired in 1990 included Claude Gill and Hatchards – the latter was one of the key flagships of the British book trade that we first encountered in the eighteenth century. Hatchards had been bought by Sir Thomas More MP in 1938 in association with Clarence Hatry, a convicted bankrupt and fraudster, who was newly released from prison. Between them, they had revamped and rejuvenated what was then a tired and ailing business. However, by the 1950s, Hatchards was in trouble again and in 1957 Billy Collins, of the publisher William Collins, decided it was too important to the British book trade to be allowed to fail. He tried to persuade W.H. Smith to buy the company but, in the end, Collins acquired the company itself, later absorbing the Claude Gill shops too.

When Pentos bought the company from Collins, Hatchards and Claude Gill between them accounted for twenty-six shops, some of which were subsequently closed, but many were transformed into the new Dillons brand. The Hatchards Piccadilly store itself was a major purchase for Dillons, as a prestige bookseller and the leading retailer of hardback fiction in the country. Dillons retained the Hatchards branding for this store alone, as have Waterstones, the current owners of this important bookshop.

Like Waterstones, Dillons stores provided a shot in the arm for the book trade. They were generally much bigger than existing independents, in better locations and with a much heavier stockholding. Dillons tended to be a little less literary-focussed than Waterstones, with a broader appeal that was more inclusive of all tastes.

Terry Maher's contention was that the book market could be expanded if bookshops were better stocked and more welcoming to the reader, and he backed this up with witty marketing campaigns, such as 'Foyled again? Try Dillons', aimed at the renowned difficulties in purchasing a book for customers of Foyles. The success of his stores proved him right. In later years, he was to be the driving force behind the campaign to get rid of the NBA, which fixed prices and prevented discounting or special offers.

Many viewed his tactics as quite aggressive, and he was not a universally popular figure in the trade. Maher's formula was, however, massively successful and, by the 1990s, Dillons had 140 stores in locations across the country. Maher shared Tim Waterstone's view about the state of bookselling in the UK and, between their two chains, they brought about seismic change. Maher said that 'many people were intimidated by the prospect of entering a bookshop'.

They certainly ruffled quite a few feathers and were the cause of many independent bookshops going out of business, but they also raised the bar and created a much-improved retailing environment for the book buyers of the UK. British high streets were witnessing the opening of new bookshops on an increasingly regular basis. This expansion continued throughout the 1980s and into the 1990s, with more bookshop chains joining in. These included Ottakar's (founded in 1987 and named after a character in the Tintin books), opening in smaller market towns across the UK and very much stepping directly into independents' territory. Other chains that expanded at the same time were Hammicks, Books Etc, Methvens and the US giant, Borders, set up in the UK in 1998, opening several out-of-town megastores.

Terry Maher and Tim Waterstone were to represent the 'new wave' that would do so much to shake up bookselling in the 1980s and 1990s, a change that was much needed. But that is not to ignore the fact that hundreds of independent booksellers were put out of business because of their actions. Some of these were not of the highest quality, but many more were hard-working key retailers in their communities, who were simply forced to close by competition from a much bigger retailer. This sort of thing happens repeatedly in all forms of retail, but those independents were the collateral damage as the book trade transformed and modernised.

There are always two sides to every story and the aggressive expansion by the chains was heavily criticised by many within the trade. Most publishers recognised it as a positive change and supported the growth of bigger outlets for their wares, but they would also experience tougher negotiations on terms from these new, larger retailers. This period of growth was not without its challenges across the whole book trade.

Interlude

The Closing
of a Bookshop

Robbs Bookshop, closing-down notices. (Author's collection)

While Waterstones and Dillons rapidly expanded elsewhere, our small bookshop enjoyed continued success in the subsequent years. We recorded decent annual growth and firmly established the shop as part of the local community. The business had become much more of a family affair after Kathleen joined the staff in the early 1990s. We had dated soon after and married in 1995. Kathleen managed the growing business alongside my father and me, between us managing staff, buying stock, developing the children's department and our further expansion in schools and education supply. We had recently opened a satellite shop in the further-education college a mile up the road, confirming our dominance in that sector, but this growing business required more hands on deck.

Despite this success, we were not unaware of the changes taking place across the country. Reading *The Bookseller* every Friday revealed a constant stream of new chain bookshop openings, as Waterstones and Dillons expanded. By the mid-1990s, we had also become very aware of the Ottakar's chain, which had been growing steadily since its launch in 1987. Ottakar's generally opened smaller shops than Waterstones or Dillons and targeted market towns across the country – previously prime independent bookshop territory. Indeed, to many of its customers, Ottakar's felt just like a local independent bookshop, with friendly, engaged staff who were empowered to embed their shop into the local community in much the same way that we had done, connecting to schools and institutions. The difference was that the local Ottakar's shop was backed up by the finances of a national chain. The inevitable downside of these developments were the regular reports in *The Bookseller* of independent bookshops closing, one after another.

Of course, we would have been blind not to have considered that this relentless wave sweeping across the bookshop landscape might one day arrive at our door. As well as reading about this, I heard a great deal of chatter from the sales reps visiting our shop – many were fairly buoyed up by the increased sales possibilities that more shops afforded. They gossiped about which shops were opening and which had been forced to close. I was also in touch with several fellow booksellers who had been forced to close after Ottakar's had opened in their small town.

Sometime around 1996, one of our reps told me he had heard a rumour about Dillons potentially opening a shop in the town. Inevitably, Chelmsford, as a large and growing commuter town, would eventually be targeted, but it still came as a shock to hear it spelled out. Feeling very uneasy, we kept a close eye on the weekly news pages of *The Bookseller*, but in the end nothing happened, and the Dillons threat receded.

However, we now understood that it was probably just a matter of time. And so it proved to be. At the start of 1998, another rep told me he had discovered that Chelmsford was on Ottakar's target list for upcoming stores. This was quickly confirmed by *The Bookseller*, reporting that Ottakar's would indeed open a large store in Chelmsford in May. The new store would be in a much better location than ours, in the High Street. It would comprise 8,000sq ft, which was eight times our floor space. This was to be one of their new wave of larger stores, on two floors, complete with a café.

It is an understatement to say that my world was suddenly turned upside down, but, perhaps foolishly, until that moment I had thought that our shop would last forever. Now we knew we faced the possibility of the entire house of cards tumbling down around us.

My life had changed a lot in the fourteen years since we first opened our doors, but the bookshop was still a central and defining part of my being. Kathleen and I had moved out of our flat into a three-bedroom house and, in 1997, our daughter Emily was born. There was now a lot more at stake.

After digesting the news, Kathleen and I took a day trip to Bromley, where the nearest large Ottakar's store was situated, a similar size to what was destined for Chelmsford. We wanted to get a measure of our rivals-to-be. The Ottakar's store seemed enormous, spacious and welcoming, with sofas and armchairs dotted around, a beautiful children's section with its Tintin rocket display, an impressively large range of books – and a café, too. The whole store looked to us like the future of bookselling.

As Kathleen wrote in an article for *The Bookseller* in March 2000, talking about these larger stores with sofas and cafes, 'if we had not had our own shop we would have chosen to shop in them ourselves'. I have always thought of myself as first and foremost a reader and, as such, I could not fail to be impressed and excited by such a bookshop. This was a booklover's dream. Visiting that store and seeing what we were up against really brought home to us the harsh reality of the situation. We both realised that the writing was on the wall for our shop.

On our return, we sat down with my dad and planned what we should do. Despite our strong feeling of what the result would be, we decided to fight it out and see how things fared for at least a year. We turned for advice to other booksellers who had either closed or were facing similar competition. I kept mentioning how we could rely on our hundreds of loyal customers, but one bookseller who had been forced to close was adamant that they too had thought they had loyal customers until the competition arrived. I still refused to believe that our loyal customers would desert us.

We devised a new loyalty scheme, which essentially offered regular customers discounts on future purchases, and we backed this up with advertising in the local papers and a poster campaign on the backs of local buses – new territory for us. In those months prior to Ottakar's' opening, we had a brilliant response from our customer base and much rallying round and vocal support. Perhaps it might be alright, we thought.

Then, just before Ottakar's opened, *The Bookseller* announced that Waterstones would be opening a large store in Chelmsford High Street. We initially thought that the magazine had made a mistake, naming Waterstones instead of Ottakar's. But it turned out to be the truth, and Waterstones would open just a few months after Ottakar's. By Christmas, Chelmsford would boast two large chain book retailers. Our situation was clearly untenable.

Once Ottakar's was open, we popped in regularly to assess how things were going. The vast store was always busy, and the café had a buzz about it. Ottakar's hosted several celebrity book signings, including footballers and TV chefs, and a few of these events had queues around the block. Within weeks, we noticed that our takings through the shop till were dramatically reduced.

In the autumn, with Waterstones open as well, our sales were taking a severe hit. Despite our loyalty scheme and constant reassurances from many loyal customers, by Christmas our sales were down over 45 per cent and in ongoing decline. For me, the defining feature of this period was repeatedly seeing regular customers coming into our shop brandishing dark-green Ottakar's carrier bags as if it was the most natural thing in the world. One regular customer, a heavy book buyer, who would often come in to buy a pile of hardbacks from us, shamelessly sought me out to order the one book he hadn't been able to buy in Ottakar's (these I could see in his two bulging Ottakar's carrier bags). I felt deeply hurt, but I also understood that the other bookseller had been right: when push comes to shove, there really is no such thing as loyalty. And, hurtful as it was, I tried not to attach blame to customers: I understood.

By that Christmas, 1998, we knew we were finished. I felt very bitter and quite down throughout 1999. For the first time, I found I didn't care about new books coming out. The pages of *The Bookseller* held no excitement for me anymore and I felt the book trade was slipping away from me.

We went through the first part of that next year trying everything, including special offers, both in store and to schools and businesses, discount promotions and more loyalty offers. We garnered some decent press coverage to celebrate our 15th birthday, but it was all to no avail. The sales kept going down. We even reduced staff numbers, but nothing we did made any difference. We were up against two massive behemoths: both much larger and better stocked than us, both sited in the centre of town and both backed up by better resources.

Before the summer, we decided that we would have to close and so we opted for one last Christmas to maximise sales as we did so. We were liable for the lease of the property for another nine years, but luckily we found a local independent sports shop to take it over, who were keen to move out of the town centre and avoid spiralling rents.

The 1980s and 1990s had seen huge retail expansion, with bigger and bigger shopping centres built across the UK, such as Lakeside in Thurrock, the Metro Centre in Gateshead, Meadowhall in Sheffield and Manchester's Arndale Centre. Every town seemed to boast a new shopping precinct. Allied to this was the expansion of many retail chains to fill those malls. Waterstones, Dillons and Ottakar's were part of this, alongside Athena,

Thorntons, Next, Our Price, Dixons and many others. It seemed like everything was getting bigger and the space for decent independent businesses was shrinking. The small local shop was going out of fashion, and we were one of hundreds of victims of this trend. Throughout the 1980s and 1990s, retail in the UK had become bigger, brasher and more American, with the same large chains in every town. There was less and less room for the small, the independent, the local.

However, while it lasted, our bookshop was important to its customers and the local community. It was so much more than just a shop. It had become a public space and an important part of our customers' lives. Looking back with hindsight, I can easily recognise that we just weren't strong enough or good enough to withstand the competition we faced, but we can still look back proudly on what we achieved. Retail is an ever-changing environment and these things happen repeatedly.

To maximise our last Christmas, we did not publicise our forthcoming closure. It was business as usual that December with the Christmas window, Christmas lights and our last-ever Christmas catalogue. We didn't tell the customers, we didn't tell the reps and we swore our small cohort of staff to secrecy. We kept up the facade right through to the end.

However, after closing the doors on a quieter than usual Christmas Eve at 4 p.m., we put posters up in the window announcing a 'Closing Down Sale' starting on 4 January, with '40% Off All Stock'. We had also arranged articles in both local newspapers for the first week of the New Year. We locked up the shop and went home to enjoy our last Christmas as booksellers and coincidentally celebrate the Millennium, too.

When we reopened on 4 January, there was a significant queue outside the shop. As soon as we opened our door, we faced a barrage of familiar and unfamiliar customers, all bemoaning our impending closure. This was all completely unexpected, and I had to ring Kathleen to get her to come in to help cope with the crowds, as we just hadn't anticipated how busy it would be. We had customers in tears, some pleading with us not to close. They told us what the shop meant to them, how it was a part of their lives. If you've watched the film *You've Got Mail*, it was exactly like that. Even now, more than twenty years later, I well up just thinking about this.

Throughout that day, a huge queue snaked through the shop. In monetary terms, 4 January 2000 was the biggest day's takings for our shop ever, by some margin. Throughout the next two weeks, the sales continued at full strength, only petering out towards the end of the second week. We had cards and gifts from customers and a seemingly endless repetition about how sad everyone was that our shop was closing. Every night, I went home emotionally drained. Later in January, we started selling off the fixtures and fittings too, right down to the till, the chairs, the office desks and even the shop fan, with the last books and shelves going to a local second-hand bookseller.

By the end of January, the stock was gone, and even the shelves were gone. The inside of the shop looked bare. All that remained were the marks on the wall where the shelving had stood. It looked just like it had done when we first took possession of it all those years ago, eager and ready to kit it out with shelves and books and excited for our new venture.

In the first week of February, exactly sixteen years after we had first opened our doors, seemingly a lifetime ago, we finally closed the door for the last time. I cried when we turned the key in the lock and walked away, and I'm crying again now writing this. Work is not everything, of course, and I am incredibly lucky to have a loving wife and family and all the happiness that brings, but the bookshop was a huge part of my identity for sixteen years. My dad and I had created the shop from nothing, and I will be forever grateful for the opportunity and the tremendous experience it afforded.

We were one victim of the chains' expansion, like so many others. I am pleased to report that many hundreds of independents survived the onslaught of the chains and continue to thrive to this day. And recent years have witnessed a revival in independent bookselling once again. But on that wintry day at the start of February 2000, the story of our bookshop was over. We had reached the final lines of the last chapter and were now faced with those immortal words, 'The End'.

8

Selling Books in the
New Millennium

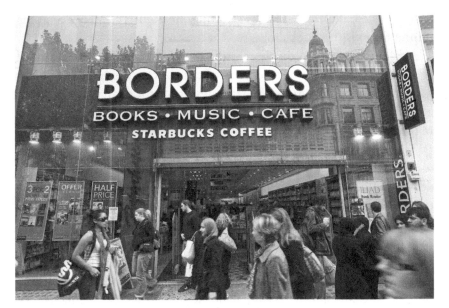

Borders bookshop in Oxford Street, London. (Alamy)

In the late 1990s, with a new century about to dawn, the British book trade was in the full throes of dramatic change. As we have seen, the growth of literary fiction and the increased media attention for books had helped give book sales a significant lift in the 1980s and 1990s. At the same time, the introduction of the new book chains, led by Waterstones and Dillons, but also including Ottakar's, Hammicks and Borders, had transformed British high streets and taken book sales to a new high.

But more change was already underway. To detail all the many changes, we will deal with each subject separately, rather than strictly chronologically. In this way we will build an overall picture of how the trade changed even further as the new century progressed.

We will look at how the Net Book Agreement was repealed in the 1990s and how this paved the way for heavy discounting of lead titles and enabled more retailers to get involved in bookselling at scale. And we will examine further developments happening to the big bookshop chains, including continued expansion but also the first signs that the growth could not be sustained in the long term. We will also look at how the structure of publishing was transformed during this period, with the rise of mighty conglomerates as more companies joined forces. We will examine these multiple changes affecting the industry and the ongoing impact for existing bookshops.

Amazon came into existence in 1995 and grew fast. The rise of Amazon would turn out to be one of the two biggest game changers for the industry, alongside the later development of digital books, or e-books. We will come back to those two huge changes and their impact in the following chapters.

Those working in the industry, me included, were caught up in this maelstrom of dramatic changes, holding on for dear life, akin to being on deck during a terrible storm at sea. It is important not to sound too negative throughout all of this, as many of the changes that have occurred in the past four decades have transformed publishing and bookselling for the better and have forced the trade to up its game and produce better books for readers. But no bookseller or publisher was unaffected by these changes as they swept through the industry one by one. It was frenetic, exciting and worrying all at the same time and, arguably, the changes are still going on to this day.

The Death of the Net Book Agreement

The Net Book Agreement (NBA) had underpinned the British book trade since 1900, providing a level playing field for all booksellers. It helped support the publishing of niche, lesser-selling titles and encouraged booksellers to hold a wide range of stock. Under the terms of the NBA, all retailers had to sell books at the same recommended retail price. The only exclusions were non-net educational titles supplied at lower discounts, sales through book clubs whose members had to pay a subscription fee to receive discounted prices, and an annual post-Christmas book sale that gave publishers the opportunity to sell off slow-moving stock. There had been one legal challenge to the NBA in 1962, but the Restrictive Practices Court rejected this and argued that the NBA should remain in place because it protected the publication of more specialist titles that didn't necessarily generate profits but were nonetheless important to the nation.

But in the late 1980s, murmurings started again. There was a lot of talk about wanting to expand the book market and grow book sales further. A very vocal minority of booksellers and publishers claimed that books would be cheaper for book buyers if the NBA didn't exist and this would promote a further democratisation of reading, rather than books being an exclusive club for heavy book buyers. With bigger publishing conglomerates and ever-growing bookshop chains needing to show profits, all ideas to grow sales had to be considered. On the opposing side, however, there were still many, both booksellers and publishers, who felt that books should be treated differently from other products – that discounting was unnecessary and a somewhat crude instrument.

It was the Dillons chain, run by Terry Maher, that was the most determined to see books operating in the market just like other products. Maher was not popular with other booksellers and had been quite dismissive of the BA, reluctantly joining it only to enable Dillons to sell book tokens, a nationwide scheme managed by the BA. In 1988, though, he was invited to speak at the annual BA Conference in Bournemouth. His speech, entitled 'The Impact of Change', on the theme of expanding the market for books, caused an uproar. He railed against the NBA and argued that its abolition would help grow book sales. Maher argued that in all other areas of business the retailer dictates the price, not the supplier.

Maher thought that, prior to Dillons and Waterstones entering the market in the early 1980s, bookselling was in a parlous state. 'Book retailing was fragmented,' he said, with no national chain and 'tiny shops, most of them in poor locations'. The expansion of Dillons and Waterstones was part of the answer, but Maher felt that a further shake-up in the way books were supplied was necessary. He felt that the public had no awareness of the NBA or fixed pricing and, from market research conducted by Dillons, the public 'actually thought books were cheaper in Smith's', even though W.H. Smith sold at the same price as everyone else. For the opposing camp, Clive Bradley of the PA felt that the poor economic situation added pressure to abolish the NBA: 'In times of recession, people were keen to sell more books come what may.'

As well as causing controversy at the conference itself, Maher's speech attracted a lot of press coverage, with both the BA and the PA speaking out against him. Clive Bradley promised to take Dillons to court if they broke the NBA.

However, as Maher had hoped, this speech and the resulting controversy did prompt a public debate about the NBA and what it was for. Maher's argument advocating for cheaper books, attacking the alleged snobbery of the book trade and its failure to make books available to all, struck a chord with the book-buying public. In conjunction with other like-minded souls within the book trade, the media and politics, Maher and Dillons plotted a campaign to force the issue.

In 1990, Dillons declared it would sell the Booker Prize shortlist at discounted prices. Maher was interviewed widely, on TV and in the press. The publishers of the shortlisted titles seemed to initially support Dillons, but soon rallied together with the PA to bring legal action to stop the campaign. Blackwell's and many independent bookshops also fought hard against the move. However, Dillons ran more discount promotions in the following years and the battle within the trade continued amid ongoing publicity.

In 1991, the Reed Group declared that it would no longer be bound by the terms of the NBA and Dillons price-promoted several of their titles, including new books from bestselling authors such as David Lodge and Roddy Doyle. This eventually prompted the Office of Fair Trading to review the NBA in 1994 and refer it to the Restrictive Practices Court.

Hodder Headline, Random House and HarperCollins all subsequently announced that they would no longer operate under the terms of the NBA, and then W.H. Smith did the same. At that point, the NBA was as good as dead already. The Restrictive Practices Court announced their conclusion in 1997 after much deliberation and hearing of evidence from all sides, declaring that the NBA was no longer in the public interest. The abolition of the NBA would deliver cheaper books to consumers and that was seen as a good thing.

While the NBA's removal allowed bookshops to price promote, it also opened the door to wider competition, particularly at that time from the large supermarkets. These had only dabbled in book sales before, mainly selling bargain books. But now they ramped up their offer, selling some new books at half-price or less. The supermarkets started by selling best-selling paperback fiction at £2 or £3, an easy amount for shoppers to add to their trolleys without much thought. This was so successful that they expanded their range into new hardbacks (fiction, popular biography and cookery) and children's books. Tesco, Sainsbury's and Asda appointed specific book buyers and publishers' sales managers added these important new customers to their roster of key accounts.

This certainly hit the chain bookstores, but was yet another problem for independent bookshops, who were already reeling from the growth of the chains. Mass-market fiction titles, cookery titles and celebrity biographies were suddenly being sold at ridiculously low prices.

This situation reached a head with the publication of the final Harry Potter book in hardback, which Asda sold well below half-price. Bookshops were forced to reduce their prices to compete, and the result was that virtually every retailer sold this million-selling title at a loss.

The importance of the supermarkets grew during the late 1990s and early 2000s, particularly for publishers of popular, mass-market titles. By the mid-2000s, supermarkets accounted for 25 per cent of some publishers' sales. Arguably, book sales grew, and these offers reached many who were not habitual book buyers. But publishers had to give supermarkets very high discounts, reducing the profit for themselves and their authors, and they also received very big returns (unsold copies sent back) – these could be many thousands of copies. As soon as a book stopped selling, a supermarket removed it from its range and returned all stock. This produced excess stock in the publisher's warehouse and reduced profitability.

Nobody at the time could have foreseen the rise in importance of the internet or Amazon, but the lack of a NBA made Amazon's rise all the easier. There are now a lot fewer bookshops than there were in the 1990s and early 2000s, and the NBA's abolition contributed to this. Book sales have continued to grow, but publishers, booksellers and authors now make far less money from the sale of each book than was the case before the collapse of the NBA, due to Amazon, supermarkets and others demanding more margin.

Other European countries, particularly France and Germany, still have laws that restrict the price books can be sold at and support bookshops against the threat of Amazon and online retailers. In France, no retailer can discount the RRP by more than 5 per cent and a recent update to this law means that online retailers must also charge a minimum fee of approximately £2.50 for postage, thus enabling bricks-and-mortar bookshops to compete fairly against online competition.

France still has over 3,500 independent bookshops, whereas the UK has just over 1,000, despite having a very similar population size. Over 140 new bookshops opened in France in 2022 alone. Germany has fixed pricing and still has over 6,000 bookshops. In addition, several countries in the EU give 'culture vouchers' to young people to encourage them to spend money on books and the arts generally. Although many countries are now reviewing the amounts given due to budget constraints, the Association of Italian Publishers reported in 2021 that young people spent 80 per cent of the 500 Euros from the '18App' on printed books. Likewise, German youngsters are given 100 Euros through the 'KulturPass', demonstrating how other countries support their bricks-and-mortar bookshops.

Giving books special treatment is what many publishers and booksellers argued for in the 1990s, but they lost out to the call to open books to the market. It is highly unlikely that the NBA will ever be revived, but introducing restrictions on the levels of discounting permitted and taxing online retailers equitably with bricks-and-mortar shops deserves examination if we want to preserve our bookshops.

Like many independent bookshops, we were against the abolition of the NBA. Now, with Pandora's box open, it is difficult to see how the trade can row back from the current state of affairs. But the law currently does nothing to protect and support bookshops or, indeed, authors, and I feel the country is the poorer for that.

Bookselling in a New Century

Although the first decade of the new century did witness continued growth from many bookshop chains and the ongoing closures of independents, it paradoxically also signalled the beginning of the end for the chains' expansion. With Amazon growing at a startling rate and then digital books (or e-books) starting to impact the industry, even bigger seismic change was underway and, amazingly, there would be a collapse of most of these bookshop chains before the 2000s decade was concluded.

However, as the new century dawned, the UK book trade was in rude health and seemingly unaware of its impending fate. The huge growth in the number of booksellers and the square footage of their shops gave an impression of a booming industry. Following the collapse of the NBA, publishers and booksellers hoped to increase book sales significantly and, brimming with optimism, felt enabled to continue their ambitious growth plans.

Publishers seemed to be mightier than ever, following a series of mergers in the past two decades, which had created bigger and stronger international conglomerates that were better equipped to take the industry into this new century. Alongside this, improved printing technology enabled publishers to print better, cheaper and faster.

The massive success of Waterstones and Dillons had demonstrated that there was a huge public audience who were eager to buy more books. This led to other bookshop chains joining the party, identifying opportunities for their own success. One of the most successful was the Ottakar's chain, launched by James Heneage in 1987.

Heneage had served in the military and enjoyed a successful career in advertising before deciding to start Ottakar's. He sensed an opportunity in smaller market towns – places that had been largely ignored by Waterstones and Dillons. His hunch paid off and Ottakar's very quickly developed a chain of what felt very much like independent bookshops. They were smaller bookshops than Waterstones and Dillons, friendlier and less literary in approach, but arguably much better at integrating into the local community. The shops felt like independents but enjoyed the financial backing that a big chain could bring. Heneage empowered his booksellers and championed their individuality, running a personable operation that the staff loved being part of and, in return, their enthusiasm drove the company's success.

The company expanded rapidly throughout the 1990s at the expense of many independent booksellers whose territory Ottakar's were now occupying. As the new century dawned, Ottakar's also opened larger stores in areas such as Bromley, Milton Keynes and Norwich. Along the way, the chain bought out some independents and acquired eight stores from James Thin in Scotland, as well as twenty-four branches from Hammicks, who had also previously expanded strongly in this boom time. Like Ottakar's, Hammicks had targeted smaller market towns and had enjoyed considerable success before being sold. What this all amounted to was that by 2006 Ottakar's had 140 stores across the UK, which was phenomenal progress and testimony to Heneage's vision. Our bookshop was just one of the many victims of this expansion.

The success of Ottakar's' approach demonstrates that there is no single way to sell books. There were plenty of book buyers who loved the intellectual approach of Waterstones stores, but equally there were others who were intimidated by this. The smaller, friendlier Ottakar's approach was certainly more appealing to a less-highbrow book-buying audience, just as there will always be those who love books but prefer to buy them from W.H. Smith station book stalls, supermarkets, CTNs or, these days, from online retailers.

Borders, one of the USA's mega-bookstore chains, also entered the UK market in 1998 – a late entrant to the feast but a hugely significant one. Borders' new UK stores were massive, more the size of a B&Q than a regular bookshop, often including Starbucks and Paperchase concessions within them, taking the Waterstones and Dillons ideas of what a bookshop could look like to a whole other level. The Borders model was the 'lifestyle' store, selling books alongside magazines, CDs, videos and stationery. The aim was to encourage customers to spend more time in the stores, which would ultimately lead to higher sales.

At its peak, Borders had forty-one megastores in the UK, and most were very successful. To give itself a decent foothold in the UK market, Borders had first acquired the small Books Etc chain, including its Charing Cross Road flagship store, across the road from Foyles. Books Etc had been set up in the early 1980s by Philip Joseph, who had originally founded the Exclusive Books chain in South Africa in the 1950s, a company that still exists to this day with over forty stores. Working with his son, Richard, Philip Joseph had grown the Books Etc chain to forty stores, mainly in and around London, before selling the company to Borders. Another unique chain, Books Etc was very London-centric with a more modern and fashionable feel than other rival bookshop chains.

Borders opened its first British megastore on Oxford Street in August 1998 – a massive store across four floors, covering 40,000sq ft. This was a completely new sort of bookshop for UK customers. As Philip Downer, chief executive of Borders UK, remembers, 'We were carrying 120,000 different book titles (including remainders), 40,000 CDs and around 6,000 videos (numbers that may have become inflated in the retelling), plus 3,000 newspaper and magazine titles from around the world.'

Borders imported the idea of the huge US-style megastore, not just to city locations such as London, Oxford and Cambridge, but also to traditionally less 'booky' locations in out-of-town shopping centres, such as Lakeside in Thurrock. In this fashion, they helped widen the book market even further and expand the public's perception of what a bookshop could be.

Borders, originally started in Michigan in 1971, had over 500 megastores across the USA by this time. Its own major expansion there had come after being bought in 1992 by Kmart, which also owned the Waldenbooks chain of smaller, mainly mall-based bookshops. Waldenbooks, named after Henry David Thoreau's book *Walden*, dates back to 1933 and, before its eventual demise, owned over

1,200 bookshops across the USA. The other major US bookshop chain, Barnes & Noble, had an even bigger footprint in the USA than Borders at the time but opted not to expand internationally in the 1990s.

There was an argument that the UK now had too many bookshops and, while most publishers loved having this increased space to display their wares, some privately wondered if the trade could sustain quite this number of shops. Various reasons would contribute to the collapse of this impressive house of cards, including the growing influence of Amazon, but the excess of bookselling space itself was also a big factor. Not all of these bookshops could make enough money to sustain this number of stores and the vast amount of retail space they occupied, and some necessary realignment was necessary. Indeed, it was already underway and had actually been happening for a few years.

The first signs had come early in the 1990s when the Pentos chain, which owned Dillons, Ryman and Athena, started experiencing financial difficulties due to the increased costs incurred by rapid growth. As a result, Pentos was sold to Thorn EMI, which also owned the HMV chain of music and video stores.

Change was afoot at Waterstones, too. In 1990, W.H. Smith had taken a minority stake in Waterstones with a view to buying the chain a few years later, which it eventually did in 1993. The ongoing expansion of Waterstones required extra capital. Like Dillons, Waterstones was discovering that such growth came with associated costs.

The sheer number of stores demanded a certain level of bureaucracy – however much power was devolved to store level – and kitting out new stores was expensive. Improved technology was required, stores needed better point-of-sale equipment to record sales and enable them to order stock. Distribution was also a factor. A small chain could get by ordering stock from wholesalers or direct from publishers, but eventually economies of scale demanded some form of central distribution warehouse. W.H. Smith had long embraced this model and Waterstones would eventually decide to do the same.

The new ownership by W.H. Smith not only offered more secure financial backing but helped Waterstones to grow even more. Forty Sherratt & Hughes stores that had previously been owned by W.H. Smith were rebranded as Waterstones stores.

Tim Waterstone left the company at this point, believing it was in good hands, but he was forced to return a few years later, unimpressed with the managerial direction of travel as the chain stumbled with the costs of computerisation and ongoing supply chain issues. He led a takeover bid in league with HMV, which consequently acquired the Waterstones chain in 1998. As a result, he became chairman of the new HMV Media Group.

As noted above, HMV already owned the Dillons bookshop chain. Following the takeover of Waterstones, the Dillons brand ceased to exist, and the shops were either absorbed into the Waterstones brand, closed down or, in a few cases, sold to Ottakar's.

These were difficult years for Waterstones as the chain flailed around, trying to adapt to the new realities confronting it. At this time, under HMV stewardship, it lost its way somewhat, moving to central buying, with the individual shops losing their autonomy and their unique offer.

There were various disagreements among staff as HMV failed to recognise the unique nature of bookselling and was treating books like any other product in its portfolio. There was increased emphasis on a discounted frontlist and a move to reduce the range of titles stocked – an attempt to mimic successes in the HMV shops. But this was a complete reversal of Tim Waterstone's ethos when setting up the chain and, after three years in charge, he resigned.

HMV appointed a succession of MDs in the next decade as both Waterstones and HMV struggled against the rise of Amazon and, for HMV, the rise of digital downloads. I was present at various Waterstones presentations to publishers during this period, which were trying to assuage concerns about the chain's direction. Indeed, it would take some years for Waterstones to find its way out of this mire and reestablish its dominance. These were, though, the first signs that the winds of change were now affecting the UK bookshop chains, too.

Life on the Road

While these huge events were happening, our small bookshop was now closed, and I had decided to move to the publishing side of the business by becoming a sales rep. After our son Edward was born in 2000, Kathleen would also eventually return to work, first managing a new local children's bookshop before herself becoming a sales rep. She now works for Bounce Sales and Marketing, the UK's leading children's book supplier, working on behalf of a range of great children's publishers.

Sales reps are often overlooked and don't always receive the recognition they deserve for their integral role within the book trade. When we first opened our shop, we were buying all our books from one wholesaler, but it quickly became apparent that this would not suffice. We felt we needed more in-depth knowledge about the key books we were buying. And we needed to see sales reps from local book publishers, map publishers and a host of specialist publishers.

In those first few months, we were inundated with visits by a variety of reps from multiple publishers, all keen to sell us their wares. Naïve and inexperienced, we were persuaded to buy all sorts of things that weren't suitable for our small shop; but we also met many wonderful reps, some of whom became good friends and called on our bookshop throughout our two decades in business.

A publisher generally has a team of reps to cover all regions of the UK, varying in number depending on the company's size. Reps are unique within a publishing company, occupying a strange position as they are not office-based but instead operate on their own timetable, out on the road and one step removed from the day-to-day business of the company. Publishers employ a sales manager or key accounts manager to look after the head-office calls to national accounts, while the field sales reps will visit all the individual bookshops on their territory. Between them, they aim to maximise the sales potential of the new books on their list as well as reminding retailers about key backlist titles that are worth stocking.

The good rep takes time to understand a bookshop's business and works with you to grow sales and, crucially, is honest about the things that he or she thinks won't work for you. I would single out for special mention our reps from Ladybird, Usborne, Pan, Faber and Penguin, but there were numerous others who played a part in helping us learn the business and grow our sales. Many of the reps calling on our shop had vast experience of the book trade stretching back many years. They would tell stories about the 'glory days' of life on the road and gossip about publishers like Victor Gollancz, Robert Maxwell and Andre Deutsch. These reps connected us to the whole world of the book trade, enriching our business and giving us a wider perspective on what we were doing.

Lewis Buzbee's homage to bookselling, *The Yellow-Lighted Bookshop*, has a very good section about the importance of the book sales rep. The sales rep travels across the country, visiting many very different bookshops, talking to booksellers about the books he or she is selling. In turn, the rep learns from the booksellers. Buzbee talks about this 'excitement [...] in being the messenger, saying to one bookseller a hundred miles distant that another was having luck with this memoir about the circus'. This excitement, this buzz, gets passed on by the rep to the buyers. It 'does matter that one rep can be a strand of the web, that even though publishing is a complicated, messy business, good books still find their way to the hands of readers'.

After the closure of our bookshop, I was very fortunate to get a job as sales rep for the wholesaler Bertram Books, covering the south-east. We had used Bertrams as our main wholesaler for many years and had built up a close connection with them. Now, I would be an ambassador for their service. I quickly started learning about journey plans and things like the locations of car parks and toilets across my new territory – the essentials underpinning a rep's success.

After a year, I moved to a new role with Harvill Press and, three years later, to a key accounts manager role with the art publisher Taschen. My 'territory' varied during that decade but encompassed East Anglia, Kent, Sussex, London, Oxford, Cambridge and even further afield. As I moved up the pecking order with the Taschen role, I became a regular visitor to the head offices of Waterstones, W.H. Smith and Blackwell's, among many others.

I experienced a rapid education about the rest of the book trade beyond our small bookshop. I normally visited about three or four shops a day and had my eyes opened about how different and wide-ranging these were. I met booksellers of all stripes, most of whom were incredibly devoted and hard-working. I was fascinated to see different booksellers in action, many who were far more knowledgeable than me, doing the job in very different ways to us.

Most rep visits were conducted on the shopfloor and were subject to interruption from customers, and it was great watching how the other booksellers responded. I started to get a better understanding of how many talented and passionate people there were working across the entire book trade.

Not only was I learning about the wider business, but I was also seeing at first hand the changes that the book trade was undergoing. During the early 2000s, I visited several struggling independents who were engaged in a battle against a recently opened chain bookshop in their town, replaying events very close to my own experience. I also had the opportunity to visit Waterstones, Ottakar's, Books Etc and Hammicks stores and understand how much they offered, and often how good their staff were too. I recognised that the chains weren't the enemy; they were just another style of bookselling, in most cases bringing a better offer to the end customer.

I visited the long-established Heffers in Cambridge and much-revered London booksellers, such as Hatchards, Foyles and John Sandoe – all brilliant and useful experience, providing a window into a wider world of bookselling. It was a great education and made me proud to be a part of this business. In long-established large bookshops like Foyles and Heffers, I had to seek out and visit multiple buyers in their own departments – the fiction buyer, history buyer, politics buyer, children's buyer and so on, each of them incredibly knowledgeable about their subject area.

In Heffers and many of these larger London bookshops, I frequently bumped into other publishers' reps and realised that the reps shared a camaraderie, often meeting to exchange gossip in coffee shops and pubs near Hatchards and Foyles. I was soon part of this loose-knit club. However, the impending changes meant that within the next decade there would be far fewer reps to meet up in this way. Today, Heffers, Foyles, Hatchards, Dillons and Blackwell's are all owned by Waterstones

and are all subject to buying from head office, limiting the role of the
sales rep in those shops.

★ ★ ★

The Harvill Press was started in 1946, its strength built mainly on international fiction in translation. As a Harvill rep in the early 2000s, I was
selling the likes of Henning Mankell (whose Wallander novels were just
taking off), Richard Ford, Haruki Murakami (another whose reputation
was just starting to grow), as well as W.G. Sebald, who sadly died during
my time with Harvill.

I had to do a lot of background reading across these authors to get
up to speed, but I also learned a great deal from the buyers I talked to.
They gave me information and recommendations that I could take to
other shops, just as Lewis Buzbee recounts in his book. For example, I
met several Waterstones buyers who championed Murakami and Sebald
in particular, hand-selling these books to their customers, demonstrating
the crucial role that booksellers perform. This is so often how books
become bestsellers, by word of mouth alone, without advertising or
hype, succeeding on readers' shared enthusiasms.

Sadly, just a few years later, during the HMV years, Waterstones
moved to central buying and these intelligent and experienced booksellers across the branches had the buying role taken away from
them. This was a major shift away from Tim Waterstone's original vision for his bookshops and many booksellers left the chain.
Much of this talent was lost to the trade, although some buyers
went on to jobs in publishing and some even set up their own
independent bookshops.

Harvill Press also had an agreement to sell the John Murray list,
which meant a connection with one of the oldest and most revered
publishers in the country. I attended several sales conferences at the
John Murray offices in Albemarle Street, just off Piccadilly, the historic building that had hosted the likes of Byron, Jane Austen and
John Betjeman in its illustrious past. I worked for the seventh John
Murray, who told us many great stories about these famous authors,

and I feel lucky to have played even a small role in the history of this great publishing company.

Sadly, both Harvill Press and John Murray were to lose their valued independent status during this period. The whole Harvill team, led by publisher Christopher Maclehose, was incredibly talented, but the numbers were not adding up and the company was sold to Random House in 2002. It now exists as part of Harvill Secker, within the huge Penguin Random House conglomerate.

A few months later, John Murray, which dated back to 1768 and was the oldest surviving independent publisher in the UK, was also sold due to ongoing economic difficulties. Murrays was bought by Hodder & Stoughton, which itself became part of the multinational conglomerate Hachette just a few years later. Yet again, I was seeing the multiple changes in the industry at first hand, the increased instances of large publishers swallowing up the independent minnows. It was such a shame to witness these unique publishers losing their independent status. Not only do many staff members lose their jobs because of these changes, but I would argue that the individual lists lose some of their unique identity too.

My education in the wider industry also meant that I became a regular visitor to the Waterstones head office, particularly after the move to central buying. I attended several annual presentations to publishers and was witness to the changes going on behind the scenes at the chain. These were the troubled HMV years and Waterstones struggled to forge a new identity during this time.

I also made similar visits to the W.H. Smith HQ in Swindon. The company moved to this huge, sprawling 15-acre site in 1967, which includes its own distribution warehouse as well as the large office complex. I got to see the machinations inside this long-surviving company, so very different to Waterstones and one that has seen multiple changes over the centuries of its existence. W.H. Smith is the great survivor of the book trade and has been its most significant player for much of its existence. Only in recent decades, with the advent of Waterstones and other chains, and then Amazon, has it lost its dominance. But it remains a major player and these iconic offices, well-known to those within the trade, are part of that.

I also began regular trips to Slough, to the headquarters of Amazon, a company that was almost unknown at the turn of the new century, but, that within a few short years, was already becoming hugely important. For many years, my life included these regular long drives to Swindon, Chiswick, Slough, Norwich (for the wholesaler Bertrams) and Eastbourne (for the other main wholesaler, Gardners) alongside multiple other locations.

9

Changes to the
Wider Book Industry

Penguin Random House UK offices in Vauxhall Bridge Road, London. (Alamy)

The Discounters

We have seen that supermarkets and other non-book retailers benefitted from the abolition of the NBA, but another sector to benefit from this change were the bargain book retailers or discounters. There have been bargain bookshops of one sort or another for centuries – an outlet for the industry to get rid of unsold books at cheap prices. Publishing is not an exact science and there have always been books that don't sell at all or books that did well initially but then stopped selling, in both cases leaving a large unsold quantity in the publishers' warehouses. The trade has had to find ways to dispose of these excess copies and that usually means selling them cheap to try to clear them. If all else fails, books will get pulped.

Cheap books were one of the main attractions at James Lackington's massive Temple of the Muses bookshop in the eighteenth century. Our own bookshop, like many others, included a table of cheap remainder titles.

But times were changing. The abolition of the Net Book Agreement (NBA) enabled supermarkets and other non-book retailers to sell the latest bestselling books at heavily discounted prices. This wasn't selling cheap to clear excess stock, this was selling cheap to try to attract more customers. A few leading booksellers, most notably Dillons and W.H. Smith, also offered high discounts on key titles with the same aim. And the absence of the NBA made it much easier for Amazon to establish itself – its business model based on heavy price reductions. This sort of discounting had been the norm in America for decades but was an entirely new development for the British book trade.

Several other companies on the periphery of the existing book trade also benefitted from the NBA's demise and subsequently enjoyed massive growth in the first decade of the new century. One of these was Sussex Stationers, started in 1971 by brothers Michael and Jonathan Chowen when they bought an existing shop called Sussex Stationers in Haywards Heath. They gradually added more shops and, during the 1980s, added books into the mix. Without the NBA, cheap front-list books became their key offer and grew to be the major part of the business.

By the turn of the decade, Sussex Stationers had fifty stores and its own distribution warehouse in Hollingbury, near Brighton. The growth continued into the new century but, in 2011, the company went into administration, undoubtedly due to the competition posed by Amazon, which was fast killing off many bricks-and-mortar retailers.

Another retailer that has benefitted from the deregulation following the NBA's abolition is The Works. Founded by Mike and Jane Crossley in 1981, it was always a shop selling remainders but in the past few decades it has been able to sell current bestsellers at cheap prices alongside other books created specifically for the chain. The Works bought up the Bookworld and Bargain Books chains in 2007 and then was purchased by Endless in 2008. Today, the chain still thrives, with over 500 stores across the UK.

Perhaps the most significant of the discounters, though, was The Book People, originally set up in 1988. The company was the brainchild of Ted Smart, an ex-policeman and salesman, and Seni Glaister. Together, they had the idea of selling books to people who weren't habitual book buyers and who never entered a bookshop. As this narrative has shown, this has been the holy grail for booksellers and publishers almost from the days of Caxton and De Worde. Many others, including Lackington, Allen Lane, William Heinemann, J.M. Dent, Pan Paperbacks, Paul Hamlyn and Terry Maher, have tried to reach this larger market. All of them succeeded in some way, but Ted Smart believed that there was still more untapped potential – and he would be proved right.

The Book People's business involved taking a range of popular titles into offices or workplaces and offering these to the workers at bargain prices. The Book People salesperson would leave the samples in the office, usually displayed on a prominent table, so that the workers could look through them and then place orders. The salesperson would return a week later to retrieve the book samples and collect orders.

Many of the books they sold were general titles such as cookery or mass-market fiction from many of the biggest names in the business, offered at a huge discount. After initially starting out selling publishers' remainders and overstocks, the abolition of the NBA gave The Book People the opportunity to do deals with publishers, enabling them to offer current bestselling books to their customers at massive discounts.

As the company grew, they were able to place increasingly large orders with publishers and buy these books firm sale (i.e., non-returnable). For a book that would have previously only sold 10,000–20,000 copies in the market at full price, The Book People might buy 50,000 copies firm sale from the publisher at something like 80 per cent discount (most booksellers received around 50 per cent discount). The publisher would see this as easy additional revenue and a difficult deal to refuse. The Book People's customer could then buy the latest Jamie Oliver or Maeve Binchy title at a much cheaper and more affordable price, tempting many to buy who would previously not do so.

As this selling wasn't ever advertised and much of it was direct to the consumer, it rarely affected mainstream sales through bookshops. But it increased the sales for the publisher and author, albeit at very reduced margins, and did reduce the value of books in the public's perception. Inevitably, many booksellers and publishers grumbled at the margins publishers gave, but The Book People had proved that it was possible to sell large quantities of books to those elusive customers who previously weren't buying books at all, expanding the book market. The company grew rapidly on this model, offering ever more books and taking on a bigger and bigger sales team. Soon, The Book People were selling well across all categories – cookery, gardening, non-fiction, literary fiction too, and huge quantities of children's books.

These three different booksellers demonstrate wider changes to the trade after the NBA's abolition. These changes continue but, of our three examples, only The Works still survives (The Book People also finally collapsing in 2022). The abolition of the NBA provided many different sorts of companies with an opportunity to make huge profits by selling large volumes of new books at cheap prices, but that window of opportunity lasted for twenty years at the most. The coming new world would be dominated by Amazon, offering cheap books across all categories and titles – and delivering direct to the consumer.

Alongside the supermarkets, the three discounting retailers used the NBA's abolition to massively increase their book sales. One of the most significant factors was that key titles, particularly mass-market fiction, cookery and celebrity biography, were now regularly sold at heavily discounted prices, often at half-price or less. This increased sales of such titles and produced sales to customers who were not regular book buyers. But this discounting took a large proportion of the key title sales from the bookshop market and transferred it to discounters and non-book retailers.

Before the abolition of the NBA, when pricing was the same wherever a book was sold, most of these sales would have been through bookshops. Our own independent bookshop was a good example. While we catered for more literary and highbrow fiction, some of our biggest sales would be mass-market fiction from the likes of Jeffrey Archer, Dick Francis, Maeve Binchy, Danielle Steel and Stephen King, as well as big TV tie-ins such as Michael Palin's *Around the World in 80 Days* or *Pole to Pole*, or the latest cookery titles from Delia Smith. We would sell hundreds of copies of new titles by these authors. These were bread-and-butter sales that helped underpin the business and enabled us to offer a wide range of slower sellers, including the more literary or niche titles. In the post-NBA bookselling landscape, independent bookshops' sales of such key lines became greatly reduced and their job is that much harder.

The other side of the argument is that the relaxing of rules post-NBA has widened the book market and achieved sales to customers who were not buying books previously, either because books were perceived as too expensive or because they never visited bookshops. There are at least two sides to every story.

The Rise of the Conglomerates

In addition to the changes in how books were sold, major changes were happening to many publishing companies. Publishing in the nineteenth and early twentieth centuries had been defined by its strong, independent companies, many of which were family-owned businesses or driven by one strong-willed and determined owner with a vision. Names such as John Murray, Thomas Longman, Jonathan Cape, J.M. Dent, William Heinemann, Allen Lane and many others detailed in earlier chapters created a unique cohort of brilliant British publishers.

But post-war Britain was much more subject to global forces and the requirements of the international market. As book sales grew, so did the costs of publishing, printing and distribution, and it made increasing sense for publishers to join forces to reduce costs. This had been happening gradually during the 1950s and 1960s but became more of an issue from the 1970s onwards, as economic realities started to bite, and it was increasingly obvious that many companies could not survive alone.

Most British publishers hadn't changed their way of doing business for decades. With new printing techniques available, European publishers were becoming more efficient and seemed more willing to embrace new working practices. Britain, in the midst of an economic crisis and often subject to the demands of the print unions, was getting left behind. Joining forces or selling out to a bigger and better European competitor seemed the only answer for many.

An early example of this was Cape, Chatto and Bodley Head joining together to share distribution. Max Reinhardt of Bodley Head set up a company for the three publishers to work together, with Graham C. Greene, MD of Jonathan Cape (nephew of the novelist Graham Greene), and Ian Parsons of Chatto. The company became four with the later addition of Virago Press, publisher of women's writing, founded by Carmen Callil.

The company they created, Chatto, Virago, Bodley Head and Cape, known as CVBC, retained the editorial independence of each imprint but shared distribution through a new facility based in Grantham in Lincolnshire, situated right alongside the A1. CVBC provided centralised invoicing, credit control, stock control and customer services operations, helping to reduce costs. The new arrangements inevitably caused internal ructions for each publisher, due to streamlining and staff reductions, but clearly this was a way forward – a way that more publishers adopted in the ensuing years. Bigger, streamlined operations delivered efficiencies and reduced costs.

In another example, Pearson, a huge newspaper publishing company, owning, among others, the *Financial Times*, had moved into book publishing when it bought the educational publisher Longman in 1968. This was followed by the significant purchase of paperback publisher Penguin

Books in 1970, children's publisher Ladybird in 1972 and then Pitman, another key educational publisher, in 1985. The company consolidated its position as one of the key players in the academic and education market with other acquisitions, including Prentice-Hall and Addison-Wesley, and likewise enlarged its holding in the general trade when it purchased Michael Joseph in 1985, Hamish Hamilton in 1986 and the illustrated publisher Dorling Kindersley (DK) in 2000.

Pearson Longman remains one of the giants in the education market and this became their area of focus after they sold off the Penguin division (which included DK, Ladybird, Michael Joseph and Hamish Hamilton) to the German Bertelsmann media group in 2013. There, the Penguin Group joined with the huge US publisher Random House, already owned by Bertelsmann, to form the international powerhouse Penguin Random House.

Random House is older than Penguin, having been founded in the USA in 1927 by Donald Knopfler and Bennett Cerf, who later became famous as one of the panel on the hit TV show *What's My Line*. Cerf and Knopfler joined together to publish the Modern Library series, which they had bought rights to, and then to publish books 'at random', hence the name. During the twentieth century, Random House grew to dominate the US book market.

Random House already had a long-established presence in the UK before the merger with Penguin, through having bought the CVBC group in 1996. Penguin Random House now counts Chatto, Bodley Head and Cape among its many imprints, alongside a whole host of other once-independent publishers it has purchased along the way. Virago returned to independence before selling to Little, Brown, now part of the massive Hachette group. Penguin Random House is now the largest book-trade publisher on earth and employs over 12,000 people worldwide. It is one of the 'Big Four' publishing conglomerates operating in the UK, alongside HarperCollins, Hachette and Macmillan.

HarperCollins is another company formed from a merger between publishers from either side of the Atlantic. William Collins was founded in Glasgow back in 1819 and built its reputation by publishing Bibles, other religious books and educational titles. During the twentieth century, the company widened its net to publish all manner of subjects, not least general fiction and children's books, while retaining a strong presence in religious, education and reference publishing.

Collins was bought by Rupert Murdoch's News Corporation in 1989, which had also purchased the US publishing giant Harper & Row two years previously. Harper & Brothers date back to 1817 and had themselves previously merged with Row, Peterson & Company. HarperCollins has continued to absorb many other publishers along the way, including Thomas Nelson, Harlequin, Avon, Egmont and, most recently, Pavilion in the UK and Cider Mill Press in the USA.

Macmillan dates back to 1843 and historically was the publisher of *Alice in Wonderland* and *The Jungle Book*. Over the years, it too has absorbed other publishers, including Pan Books, Tor Books and St Martin's Press, and now has a huge mainstream trade list as well as the massive Macmillan Education offering. Macmillan is owned by German company Holtzbrinck Publishing Group, which had previously purchased the Springer academic list, now also part of the Macmillan stable.

There are many other conglomerations and joint ventures, but it is important to recognise that some publishers still opted to remain small and independent. As we have seen, John Murray remained independent until 2002, although it is now part of Hachette and still thriving there. Faber remains a strong independent publisher and, indeed, has linked with others of similar ilk to create the Independent Alliance sales force to bring their books to market.

One of the consequences and concerns with conglomeration is the loss of identity for individual imprints within the new, larger company. There is no doubt that many editors who defined a certain list lost their jobs when the publisher was absorbed into a bigger rival. The big companies have, however, generally been adept at retaining the strengths of the individual brands after purchase, although some would argue that certain imprints have never been the same since conglomeration. As with many things in this narrative, we will always find opposing views for each development.

Another consequence of this process was the reduction in the size of rep teams across the country as combined publishers rationalised their sales needs. This coincided with a general move towards central buying from the larger chains. Waterstones took the decision to move to central buying in the early twenty-first century under HMV's ownership, at a stroke destroying a huge part of many reps' jobs and resulting in inevitable redundancies.

In the modern book trade, there are far fewer reps than would be seen just a few decades back. Buying is in the hands of a small group of buyers at head office in many companies, which in Waterstones' case, dramatically changed the look and feel of their stores and completely changed the dynamic from Tim Waterstone's original vision of autonomy at store level. Arguably, this is just the reality of the changed market that now exists, but is also another contributing factor to the transformation of the book trade.

Printing Techniques in the Late Twentieth Century

The mechanics of the book trade were being transformed too. Technological change was being experienced across the printing industry. Since the original invention of the movable type printing press in Gutenberg and Caxton's time, there had been ongoing improvements in printing methods. These included the introduction of steam printing and then the invention of the hot metal typesetting machine such as linotype in the late nineteenth century. The latter sped up the process and was the standard method for printing books and newspapers through to the 1970s.

The 1970s and 1980s saw rapid developments in photo typesetting, electronic setting of text with automatic relineation, as opposed to its more manual predecessor. In the late 1960s, the first dot matrix printers were introduced, and this was followed by developments in laser printing in the early 1970s. Each of these developments underpinned the expansion of the book market and enabled mass book sales during the second half of the twentieth century.

As computer and digital technology improved, so did printing processes and today digital printing is the industry norm. The first digital printing models were introduced in the early 1990s, but digital technology has improved by leaps and bounds in the subsequent decades. We are now at the stage where publishers no longer need to print large quantities of books on a speculative basis. Instead, an increasing number of books are either printed in very short runs or only printed when a customer orders that title (print on demand). This is particularly true of specialist or academic titles but could become the industry norm going forward.

Richard Charkin, who has had a distinguished career working for Oxford University Press, Reed, Macmillan and Bloomsbury, announced at the end of 2023 that henceforward his recently formed company Mensch Publishing, in association with Ingram Content Group, would publish all its titles using print-on-demand (POD) technology. In essence, the Mensch titles will only be printed when a retailer or customer places an order. Advances in digital technology mean that books ordered in this way take no longer to deliver than just taking pre-printed stock from shelves. This new method will reduce publisher costs and cut down on waste, doing away with the historical issue of excess stock in the warehouse. This is a bold and innovative move, likely to be followed by many others, and it will be very interesting to watch this concept develop further.

10

Jeff Bezos and the Rise of Amazon

The Amazon logo. (Alamy)

Amazon's Origin Story

We have seen that the book trade was undergoing massive change at the start of the twenty-first century. Publishing was now dominated by huge multinational conglomerates and bookselling by the big chains. But an even bigger transformation was also underway, which would be a game changer for both publishers and booksellers. That tremendous change to the book-trade status quo was the arrival of the internet and online bookselling, more specifically Amazon.

The rise of the big book chains throughout the 1980s and 1990s was based upon their desire to transform bookselling by offering customers a huge range of books, whether new or backlist, popular or niche. This happened in the UK through the massive expansion of Waterstones and Dillons and in the USA through Barnes & Noble and Borders. In doing this, these new chains stole business from the long-established independent sector.

As the new century dawned, Amazon now offered readers access to an infinite range of books at much cheaper prices – books that could be ordered with one click of a mouse and delivered direct to the customer's house. Amazon's comprehensive and completist title listing introduced the concept of the 'long tail', reaching countless potential buyers who had never previously been able to find obscure or specialist titles. Amazon uncovered niche markets that publishers had always hoped were out there but had never been able to service successfully before. Amazon's unlimited range went far beyond what the largest Waterstones, Barnes & Noble, or Borders could offer in their stores. Amazon was now the range bookseller.

Amazon would do to the chain stores exactly what they had done to the independents and, in many cases, would kill their businesses. In all other cases, booksellers' sales would be dramatically reduced because of this new online competitor. For just two short decades – some less than that – the chains had ruled supreme. These chain bookshops had barely got used to enjoying their day in the sun before the cataclysm arrived. None of them were at all aware of the internet's potential for their business, let alone prepared to exploit it in any way.

Jeff Bezos was fond of saying, 'Amazon isn't happening to the book business, the future is happening to the book business'. But for publishers and booksellers in the early 2000s, it certainly felt like a very personal assault on their home turf.

The Amazon story is an amazing one: a brilliant idea, conceived and executed in spectacularly assured and successful fashion. At a very early stage in the 1990s, Jeff Bezos had recognised the huge potential of the internet, long before most of us were even aware of its existence. Like many Silicon Valley entrepreneurs, he possessed a brilliant business vision, with the associated talent to keep updating and improving upon that vision to make his company more and more successful.

Bezos' teachers remember him being competitive from an early age. He graduated from Princeton in 1986 and worked for various Wall Street traders, utilising his computer skills, but he became increasingly frustrated with the reluctance of most financial companies to understand the potential that computers could deliver. He joined D.E. Shaw & Co. in the early 1990s, a more go-ahead Wall Street company headed by entrepreneur David Shaw. Like Bezos, Shaw was an ideas man who would go on to amass a fortune by developing several companies from new thinking. Shaw understood the potential of the internet and both he and Bezos developed various ideas to exploit this potential.

One such idea was the 'everything store', an internet-based company that could sell virtually anything by acting as an intermediary between supplier and customer. Bezos had been researching the growth of the internet and been blown away by how much it had grown in such a short time and what its projected future growth pattern could be – this was still the early 1990s, when few possessed even the most basic dial-up internet connection.

To develop the idea properly, Bezos felt he had to leave D.E. Shaw and set up on his own, swapping a decent Wall Street salary with stock options for an uncertain future. Bezos considered how he could set up his 'everything store' and duly made a list of twenty products that he could sell initially as a building block for the expansion of the company.

There are many apocryphal stories of the early days of Amazon, with Bezos and two or three others working from his garage, gradually building up this small internet bookseller. From that working list of twenty products, Bezos chose books as his first product. It is important to recognise that he chose books not because of a burning love of them or the passion that drives most booksellers (although Bezos is an avid reader), but because it was the simplest category to work with to achieve his goals. Unlike William Caxton, James Lackington, Allen Lane or Tim Waterstone, Jeff Bezos was not driven by a love of books per se or a desire to bring books to a wider audience, although he did obviously achieve the latter in spades. He viewed this purely as a business opportunity – a starting point for his concept of an internet retailer.

A book is identical wherever it is sold, as opposed to something like electrical goods, for example, where you can buy several competing versions of the same product. In addition, there were over one million books in print, a vast number that no physical bookstore could hope to stock, and each easily identifiable by its unique thirteen-digit ISBN. An online retailer like Amazon could list them all and the ISBN made it very easy to order electronically. Bezos said he was building 'a true superstore with exhaustive selection – and customers value selection'.

Bezos didn't invent online bookselling. Several attempts at selling books on the internet already existed in the USA, including Book Stacks Unlimited and WordsWorth. But none of these were thinking on the scale of Bezos. His vision can perhaps be compared to Allen Lane's concept when developing Penguin Books – a radical upheaval of the market, which would initially be viewed with scorn and disbelief by most in the trade.

Bezos moved to Seattle and set up a prototype internet business from his garage. He employed several computer programmers and built a functioning website, one that enabled customers to search for books and order them easily. The company then rented offices in Seattle and used the basement as a packing room, with the Amazon website going live on 16 July 1995. Bezos set up accounts with Ingram and Baker & Taylor, the two main book wholesalers in the USA, then attended a course for new booksellers run by the American Booksellers Association.

At the beginning, the company had no stock and no warehouse. When a customer ordered a book, Amazon placed an order with either of the wholesalers. The book then arrived at the office, was repacked and sent to the customer. Average turnaround time was less than a week, although more obscure books that the wholesaler would have to order in from the publisher took a bit longer. Bezos' plan was that, once he had established a way of supplying books to customers, he would have a customer base he could then sell other products to, and he could grow the business based upon that starting point.

Bezos was a disruptor, bringing new ways to business, as so many tech companies were doing – taking an idea and getting big fast. He was keen to establish Amazon rapidly as the leading internet retailer before others got a foothold. He always wanted to be the first, the biggest, the best.

Developing the Concept

From these small beginnings, the company grew rapidly, with customers responding very positively to the new convenience of home delivery. In early 1996, Bezos secured $8 million of funding from venture capitalists, which helped propel the company forward. He negotiated better terms from suppliers, improved the service for the customer and grew the business. The company began building their own warehouses and holding stock, and increased its staff levels, bringing in expertise from other retailers.

By 2000, Amazon's annual sales in the USA had ballooned to $2.76 billion. Already, at this very early stage, internet book sales accounted for 10 per cent of the book business in the USA, most of which was through Amazon. Within the next decade, and with the introduction of e-books – a market that would be completely dominated by Amazon – their share of the book business grew considerably.

By 2010, Amazon's dominance had dramatically altered the landscape. At that point, not only was Amazon the world's biggest retailer of books, both print and digital, but it was also dominating sales of music, video games, film and TV as well as multiple other retail categories.

During that first decade of the new century, Bezos introduced several extra features that helped reinforce Amazon's dominance, which are now taken for granted across the e-commerce sector. The first of these was allowing customers to leave reviews of the books they ordered, which built ratings for each title and provided more information for the customer. Several publishers complained that Amazon was including negative reviews and couldn't understand how this helped sales, but

Bezos always believed that the customer was king and was determined to design the Amazon experience around the customer.

Amazon also introduced a different approach to bestseller lists. 'Why do we stop at a hundred?' asked Bezos, looking at the usual top 100 bestsellers list. 'This is the internet … we can have a list that goes on and on!' The multiple bestseller lists Amazon introduced for many categories played to the customers' interests, but they also became an attractive tool for authors and publishers, helping them to keep a much closer track of sales. With the internet, anything was possible, and this included many new ways to sell books.

In addition, Amazon consistently built greater personalisation into the ordering process. From the outset, Bezos had been keen to personalise each customer's experience when they visited the site. Companies had never previously 'had the opportunity to understand their customers in a truly individualised way. E-Commerce is going to make that possible.' Amazon developed a feature called 'similarities', directing customers to books bought by other customers with similar purchasing histories. This feature would grow with improving algorithms, trying to mimic the job of a real-life bookseller recommending further reading to a customer.

Initially, Amazon used editorial staff to decide which books to promote and to produce the content supporting these titles. In the first decade of the new century, I visited Amazon's head office in Slough, like many other publishers, and talked to the editors and buyers about key titles. But this was a short-lived process. The editors were soon replaced by algorithms, which selected how books were promoted based on views and sales. This was seemingly more efficient and would be Amazon's way forward henceforth. Any future communication between Amazon and publishers was less about specific key titles and more about terms.

Amazon also spent a great deal of money getting search engines and other websites to refer customers to the Amazon site. Building on this, the development of the 'associates' programme, which invited other retailers to sell through the Amazon site, was another game changer. Amazon Marketplace allowed other retailers to sell the same product alongside Amazon, including having second-hand books listed alongside the pristine version. Once again, publishers hated it, but Bezos believed it gave more choice and added to the customer's experience. Thousands of businesses now exist as secondary sellers on Amazon, making money for themselves but coincidentally driving even more traffic to Amazon, substantiating its position as the go-to place to buy books and multiple other products. Amazon, of course, benefits from a commission on every sale.

In 2004, Amazon Prime was introduced as a special deal for regular customers, similar to the buying clubs pioneered by Costco or loyalty schemes, such as Tesco Clubcard. For an annual fee, customers got free next-day delivery on all orders in addition to other offers, such as access to video content, an area that Amazon would grow hugely in the following years. Prime tied the customer more closely to Amazon. Next-day delivery became the norm, and customers became addicted to the convenience.

In similar fashion, but on a much smaller scale, our bookshop used to offer next-day delivery for customer orders back in the 1990s. We would have approximately fifty or sixty customer orders per day at our peak. About 60 per cent of these could be obtained from our wholesaler from whom we had a daily delivery. The difference was that the book was delivered to us, meaning the customer had to come to the shop to collect their order. This lacked the convenience of home delivery that Amazon Prime offers, particularly for those not living near the bookshop. But it did mean that the customer engaged in human connection and conversation – and experienced the joy of visiting a bookshop and the serendipity of being tempted by even more books. This was obviously an advantage to the bookshop too. Most independent bookshops still offer this valuable next-day service.

It is not difficult to see that the existing bricks-and-mortar book trade was rocked to its foundations by all of this. The very rapid rise of Amazon and the seismic changes it brought to the book trade left the traditional businesses reeling and blindsided by this interloper. By 2010, many in the book trade felt like they were the victims of an alien invasion and were now under the rule of beings from another planet. The existing status quo had been ripped to shreds. There was now a new world order.

In the next decade, Amazon's dominance would only increase. Today, it is estimated that as much as 50 per cent of UK print book sales are through Amazon and almost 90 per cent of the UK e-book sales.

The Immediate Impact

Amazon launched in the UK in 1998, having bought up an existing British online bookseller called Bookpages. In the latter years of our bookshop's existence, we were starting to use the internet and were aware of this nascent online retailer. To us and many booksellers, it was another threat but, in its early days, less troublesome than the rampant expansion of the chains or the newly unleashed supermarkets gobbling up huge volume sales of the biggest bestsellers. But in the coming years, it would grow to be the biggest threat to both chains and independent bookshops.

As with the expansion of book sales to supermarkets, there were huge implications for publishers too. In its bid to establish market dominance, Amazon constantly lowered prices to be the cheapest, often losing money on a sale. The theory was that lower pricing delivered more customers, which delivered more sales. Eventually, the sales would make money, Amazon would have driven most competitors to the wall and grown its market share, and Amazon could then go back to publishers asking for better terms. This was to be repeated for all other categories Amazon sold.

Most of the battles between Amazon and publishers were fought in the USA first and then the outcome became the norm in all other territories, including the UK. In the first ten years of Amazon's existence, its massive growth meant that the company became incredibly important to publishers. It became *the* range bookseller, and it could supply any book, far exceeding the range of even the biggest Waterstones store.

The main consequence for publishers was that, due to their increased reliance on the massive revenue generated by the internet retailer, Amazon was in a very strong position to demand better terms (i.e. higher discount) from publishers. Amazon's power became even more stark when some large publishers tried not to give Amazon the higher terms it demanded. At several points, Amazon simply removed that publisher's titles from its pages, meaning the publisher would get zero sales and zero revenue.

The more important Amazon became to publishers' sales, the more power Amazon wielded and the better terms they demanded. This obviously resulted in decreased margin for publishers and their authors.

This was nothing new in retail. In the USA, large chains such as Walmart had acted like this for years, and British publishers were seeing similar demands from the supermarkets. But this was now the new norm – books sold to large retailers at much higher discounts and then sold to customers at cheaper prices. In many cases, publishers increased their RRPs to accommodate this, but generally the end customer was getting cheaper books overall. However, the traditional book trade, both booksellers and publishers, was now making a lot less revenue from book sales.

The Fallout for Bookshops

During that first decade of the twenty-first century there was a power shift in bookselling. Whereas during the late 1980s and throughout the 1990s, the bookshop chains dominated book sales, their supremacy was now being threatened by supermarkets and Amazon. As Amazon's reach grew and as customers became more internet savvy and more comfortable ordering products online, the entire bricks-and-mortar book market was in freefall.

Waterstones launched its website in the late 1990s but, lacking the expertise or a system to fulfil orders, they then invited Amazon to run the website for them. In retrospect, this was a terrible decision, akin to the Three Little Pigs inviting the Big Bad Wolf into their house for dinner. But, in their defence, Waterstones and HMV, like most retailers at that time, had no ready means of setting up or running a website.

Only in 2008, after installing a central distribution centre in Burton upon Trent, did Waterstones pull out of the agreement with Amazon. At that point, the company relaunched its website, using its own dot-com to fulfil orders. However, Amazon had long established its total dominance of online book retail and all other competitors were left picking up the scraps. Amazon were the experts in this area by a huge margin, and it showed.

With the management of Waterstones now under the auspices of the HMV Group and with Tim Waterstone now gone, the chain tried several manoeuvres to boost sales in difficult trading conditions. The most successful of these was the '3 for 2' promotion on paperbacks (both fiction and non-fiction), which was a feature of Waterstones' front-of-store table and window displays for the next decade. This was a big success, and publishers vied to get their books included in these promotions.

But the bricks-and-mortar book market was suffering and, as hinted previously, the trade could not sustain the huge number of bookshops across the UK. The next major change was the sale of Ottakar's to the HMV Group in 2006. Despite Ottakar's' huge success, a tribute to the vision of James Heneage, it could no longer compete in the very difficult trading conditions as the book trade struggled against the relentless assault from Amazon. All Ottakar's' stores were rebranded as Waterstones and many eventually closed, where there were duplications.

The next casualty was Borders, which had been struggling against the threat from Amazon on both sides of the Atlantic. The chain went into administration in 2009. All of the Borders megastores in the UK closed – empty relics of the heady days of 1990s expansion. Waterstones bought up eight of the Books Etc stores in and around London and rebranded them, but the rest were closed.

There had been a few other smaller bookshop chains riding on the coattails of Waterstones' and Dillons' expansion, including Methvens, which had opened a number of stores in the south-east, in places such as St Albans, Canterbury and Worthing. They too went into administration in 2009. And Maher the Bookseller, launched in the late 1990s by Tony Maher, son of Terry Maher from Dillons, opened three shops but these too were closed by 2014.

The British book landscape was starting to look bleak, although it should be stressed that Waterstones remained the key survivor and, although it experienced difficulties, it battled through these and emerged strongly after a tumultuous decade. But the HMV Group was struggling too, and in 2011 it sold Waterstones to Russian billionaire Alexander Mamut, a bookshop lover.

In an astute move that many claim saved the chain, Mamut appointed James Daunt as MD. Daunt had made a name already as head of a small chain of independent bookshops, Daunt Books, with its beautiful flagship store in Marylebone. Under his expertise, a complete overhaul of Waterstones operations was undertaken. The company was revamped, badly performing stores were closed, staffing was rationalised, and the decline was halted. But the threat of Amazon's growth had not receded, and even more challenges were just around the corner, particularly the growth in the sales of e-books.

11

The Digital, Audio and Self-Publishing Explosion

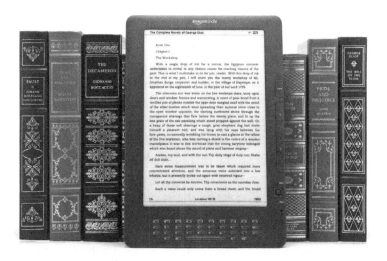

An e-reader. (Alamy)

The Introduction of the E-Book

In Stanislaw Lem's 1961 novel, *Return from the Stars*, an astronaut returns to Earth after over 100 years' absence to find it unrecognisable from the world he left. One of the many new developments he discovers is that readers access books via a device called an 'opton'. This is an electronic device that shows only one page to the reader at a time but moves onto the next page with a simple touch. Lem, like countless other science-fiction writers, was predicting a future where the print book would be replaced by an electronic book or 'e-reader'. In my early teens, I devoured many books of this ilk – books that predicted an amazing future with robots, machines and various electronic devices taking over the jobs currently performed by humans.

As we headed towards the end of the twentieth century, many of science fiction's predictions were already coming true. The dawn of the electronic book no longer seemed like science fiction, more like science fact. Since the development of the home computer, many books (particularly those out of copyright) had been available to read in a digital format. But this meant reading books on a large screen and, while plenty of academics would read texts online in this fashion, for the general reader the print book remained far and away the preferred format. It was only really with the introduction of smaller computers such as laptops, tablets and then mobile phones that developers got closer to producing a handheld reading device.

It's important to state that Amazon did not invent digital books or e-readers. As computer technology developed, there had been several attempts at creating handheld reading devices, including the Dynabook in the 1970s and Sony's Data Discman in the early 1990s.

In 1997, a company called NuvoMedia in California, led by Martin Eberhard and Marc Tarpenning, introduced the Rocketbook. Eberhard and Tarpenning were both keen readers and they too envisaged a future where people could access books via digital means. The company pitched the Rocketbook to Jeff Bezos and Amazon.

The device was well ahead of its time but needed to be connected to a computer to download books. Bezos wanted a device that enabled readers to download books wherever they might be, such as at the airport just before boarding for a long flight. Also, Amazon wanted the Rocketbook as an exclusive, which NuvoMedia weren't prepared to agree to. Instead, they offered the product to Barnes & Noble, who duly agreed a deal and subsequently sold 20,000 Rocketbook units that year.

Although this was early days in the development of handheld devices, the Rocketbook was an impressive start. But most publishers hadn't digitised their backlist, so the titles available were limited to the current mass-market bestsellers. As it had been with online retailing, the book trade just wasn't ready for this next development and the widespread availability of books in digital format would not happen for several years. After a strong start, Rocketbooks stumbled and, in need of extra capital, NuvoMedia was sold to Gemstar, who eventually ceased production.

During this period, as publishers started to be more aware of the possibility of e-readers, they recognised that existing contracts didn't grant them the rights to publish their books in digital form. So, from the early 1990s, this was included in standard publisher contracts. However, on all books published prior to that date, publishers had to go back and renegotiate those rights with the author or their estate. This process was ramped up in the early 2000s as more e-reading devices were launched on the market.

Rocketbooks probably came too early, but it was an important step in the right direction. Other e-reading devices were released in the following years, including the Sony Reader. Many other companies continued to work on better designs, including Amazon. Bezos was keen not to release the Amazon e-reader until the product did everything he wanted it to. So, it wasn't until 2007 that Amazon unveiled its first Kindle. Its release was spurred on by the success of Apple's iPod and a mounting concern that Apple could do the same to books that it was doing to music and establish an early dominance in the market.

The development process at Amazon went through many ups and downs. Developing this sort of hardware was difficult and Amazon initially lacked the expertise within the company. Others, meanwhile, were developing e-readers with varying levels of competence. Bezos employed Steve Kessel, who had worked for Netscape, to create the perfect e-reader. 'I want you to proceed as if your goal is to put everyone selling physical books out of a job.'

Bezos wanted something that mimicked the way people read print books, making a reader forget about the device and get lost in the book. This device had to be light, simple to navigate, easy to turn pages and comfortable to read. At the same time, Amazon was encouraging publishers to make more of their books available in digital format, using its growing power in the market established through sales of print books. Bezos wanted all the current bestsellers but also a strong range of backlist too. As always, he wanted the customer experience to be the best it could be.

Needless to say, Amazon was also aggressive in terms discussions for digital books, at times being accused of bullying tactics. Bezos wanted to make e-books cheap at a flat US price of $9.99, which initially horrified publishers. This bears comparison to Allen Lane wanting to sell paperback books for just sixpence in the 1930s. Eventually, Amazon would mainly get its way. It did produce a game-changing e-reader, with wireless connection that could download e-books anywhere – and it would transform the market.

The first Kindle was boldly unveiled in November 2007 and touted as the successor to the printed book. Costing $399, it could carry about 200 books. Having seen various e-readers, like the Rocketbook, come and go, the book trade initially thought that this was going to be another non-starter, not really believing that the future of the book could be in digital form. Barnes & Noble would also eventually develop their own e-reader, the Nook, which was sold by Blackwell's and later Waterstones in the UK, but this would never trouble the dominance of Kindle.

The first Kindle had supply issues because the company underestimated demand; but, it was still a massive success and this would escalate in 2009 with the introduction of the Kindle 2, a much-improved and more user-friendly design.

Amazon succeeded in getting ahead of the rest of the market and established early dominance. The Kindle still dominates e-reader sales to this day, with over 80 per cent of the UK market. Its nearest rival, Kobo, has 13 per cent of the market. (The Nook does still exist too.) Amazon also dominates the supply of e-books, with over 90 per cent of UK sales going through the platform. This all bypasses the traditional book retailers, who are cut out of the loop.

The Trade Reaction to Kindle

During the 2000s, with the existence of a decent e-reading device and the increased availability of more books in digital format, the sales of electronic books multiplied at a rapid rate. By 2012, e-books were accounting for over 30 per cent of book sales revenue. This was phenomenal growth from zero just a few years earlier.

I was at London Book Fair in 2012 when all the talk was about the death of print books, the basis upon which the entire book trade was founded. Understandably, publishers and booksellers foresaw e-books sales continuing to grow in the years ahead and print book sales going into freefall. The talk was that what had happened to the music industry, the physical format (the CD) being replaced by digital downloads, was now happening to the book business. There was massive panic throughout the trade and a huge undercurrent of concern. It really did feel as if the entire book trade was under threat, and I shared this feeling of panic and gloom. We were all wondering whether the codex format, the print book that had supported the book trade for 2,000 years, had finally had its day. It seemed like an enormous turning point.

But then something very strange happened.

After 2012, e-book sales plateaued and ceased to grow. In fact, after 2014, they began a very gradual decline. Many better and much-improved e-readers were introduced into the market in the next few years, but it made no difference.

Today, some twenty years after e-readers and e-books were first introduced, digital sales account for approximately 20 per cent of trade publishing sales, of which up to 5 per cent are now audiobook downloads. For some publishers, focussing on fiction, particularly genres such as romance or science fiction, the percentage of e-book sales is certainly higher; but, overall, that percentage has settled at around 20 per cent.

There are many possible reasons why digital sales did not take over the industry as so many of us had feared. Not least of these is that publishers and booksellers, faced with potential oblivion, launched a strong defence of the print book. Publishers have worked hard in the past two decades to improve upon book design and production, so that the print book is not only easier to use than its digital equivalent but is a more beautiful and desirable object.

At the same time, the reading public seemed to decide that many books simply worked much better in print format. These included children's books, cookery books, art books and illustrated non-fiction. For all of these, the print book continues to deliver a far superior reading experience.

It would seem also that most readers still believe that the print book is easier to use, and it is generally preferred to an e-reader. I stated my belief right at the outset of this book that the print book is a brilliant invention, and so it remains.

E-readers do offer great convenience for travelling on a train or by plane, so that the reader doesn't have to pack a whole pile of books. In this way, e-books have certainly earned their place. But reading digitally, like listening to an audiobook, remains just another way to access books. Crucially, though, it is not the preferred way. The print book has weathered the storm and remains supreme, which has been quite inspiring for those of us in the industry who had been concerned at its potential demise.

It would also seem that readers and book buyers still value and appreciate their bookshops and are keener than ever to attend author events and signings and buy exclusive or unique editions. None of this is possible with a digital book. Booksellers have worked hard to make their shops a more interesting destination to facilitate this. The job of a bookseller today is so much more difficult than it was back in the 1980s, with most bookshops having to run coffee shops, book clubs, in-store events, storytimes, author readings and all manner of things to entice customers to spend time in their shop.

But the great fear that digital books would wipe out the print book did not happen.

We can't say what will happen in forty years' time but for now the print book has withstood the assault, and both print books and bricks-and-mortar bookshops have seen a healthy resurgence in recent years. The book trade, as on so many previous occasions, has faced the threat of the new, absorbed it, then adapted, changed and grown as a result. Arguably, the availability of e-books and audiobooks simply offer readers wider choice and enable more people to enjoy books, bringing more readers into the fold. This can only be a good thing.

E-book sales for now will remain an important part of publishers' offer to their readers. For the most part, e-book sales mirror the sales for print books – many of the same books are bestsellers and in many of the same categories. As stated, certain categories (such as cookery) don't really figure in the e-book charts and, if anything, e-book sales are skewed towards fiction and, within that genre, to fantasy, romance and crime novels.

The Growth in Audiobook Sales

Audio versions of books have been available since the invention of the phonograph. The first format was on a vinyl LP, with an actor or the author reading the text of a book or, in most cases, an abridged version thereof. These were known as 'talking books', with the term 'audiobook' only really being adopted later as different technologies developed. Many of the early talking books were created for libraries, often for use by the blind and disabled.

From the 1970s, cassette tapes enabled a new format for the talking book. The cassette tape and the cassette player were smaller, more portable and more user-friendly, creating a surge in usage among a wider range of readers or listeners. A listener no longer had to be sat in a room with a record player to hear a book; they could now listen on the move with portable cassette players and headphones.

Several companies that specialised in publishing talking books or audiobooks grew their range during this time, including Chivers Press, Naxos, Penguin and even the BBC, marketing many of its radio adaptations. In our bookshop, we always kept a few shelves of audiobooks, initially on cassette and then, later, on CD. The most popular categories for us were children's books, which were great for parents to entertain children on car journeys, and classics such as Jane Austen or George Eliot. Throughout this time, audiobook sales steadily grew and the range of titles available increased.

The next major development was the newly formed company Audible, providing audiobooks in a digital format. As with e-books, as devices improved so did the usage of this medium. This was initially through the 'Audible Mobile Player', but eventually listeners could access digital audiobooks through their mobile phones, upon payment of a small annual subscription.

With the increased ubiquity of mobile phones and the ability to download audio files to them from a range of thousands of books, the audiobook market has dramatically mushroomed over the past two decades. It continues to grow to this day, accounting for almost 5 per cent of book sales, with Audible the main player in the market. Audible was purchased by Amazon in 2008, which means that Amazon is now the largest supplier of all three available book formats – print, e-book and audio. In the latter two formats, it has over 80 per cent of market share.

As the usage of audiobooks has grown, the industry has improved the quality of the product available, often now employing name actors to narrate some of the biggest books. Most of the larger publishers have dedicated audiobook departments, aiming to get the best narrators for their books. All of this has only added to the format's appeal.

Like e-books, audiobooks have enlarged the book-reading public. Readers or listeners can now access books at times when they would not normally be able to consume a book – while walking or running or at the gym. The publishing world now has three formats that give readers far greater choices on how to consume books than they have ever had before.

As with e-books, often the audiobook sales charts mirror the key titles in the print book charts. Audio sales do, however, seem to skew strongly towards biography and autobiography, particularly when read by a name author. Books like Michelle Obama's *Becoming*, Bob Mortimer's *And Away*, Matthew McConaughey's *Green Lights* and Matthew Perry's *Friends, Lovers and the Big Terrible Thing* have all enjoyed considerable success in the audio sphere in recent years.

The Self-Publishing Boom

At the very start of this book, I discussed the role of publishers and booksellers as gatekeepers. Since the dawn of the book industry, publishers have been constantly inundated with submissions from writers wanting to see their book in print and, inevitably, only so many from this huge number are selected to be published. In fact, it is estimated that as little as 1 per cent of submissions end up as print books. As a result, each year thousands upon thousands of books don't get published because publishers didn't deem the books good enough or didn't believe that those books would find an audience to make publication worthwhile. Even once in print, a book is subject to the market. Only so many books will be selected to be stocked by booksellers, leaving plenty of others struggling to get noticed among the thousands of other new publications.

In this way, there has always been some form of selection process before we, the reader, get to choose what we want to read. We have only ever chosen books from a very slimmed-down selection made by others, these 'gatekeepers'. Over the centuries, thousands of aspiring writers have been thwarted and frustrated by this model, even though they were convinced that their book deserved recognition and warranted its place in the market.

Many such writers have long resorted to self-publishing. This could take the form of a writer paying to get a book printed themselves or, more usually, paying a publisher to produce and print the book on their behalf. This is often known as 'vanity publishing', where a publisher agrees to print a certain quantity of the book, but with the author bearing all the costs. Some of these vanity publishers would offer marketing and sales services for an additional fee, but many just offered an author the ability to see their book in print. Sadly, in most cases, very few of such books went on to be sold and, even then, mainly to family and friends of the author.

With the growth of the internet, advances in digital printing and the development of digital books, new opportunities arose for self-publishing. Digital printing meant that very small numbers of a book could be produced by a vanity publisher, reducing the outlay for the author. But books in digital form offered a much bigger possibility – the production of an author's book as an e-book at minimal cost. Various online platforms developed to exploit this new format and the self-publishing market grew rapidly in the 1990s and early 2000s.

Once again, the game-changer was Amazon entering the self-publishing market in 2005 when it bought up two existing companies, BookSurge and CustomFlix Labs. These were merged to form Amazon's CreateSpace platform, which enabled authors to upload their books to be sold as e-books or print books (only printed on demand when actually ordered). Not only did this make the process for the author incredibly easy, but Amazon also offered the author 70 per cent of the received revenue for e-books (keeping just 30 per cent itself as a distribution fee) – much better terms than offered by traditional book publishers.

I should add a caveat that most e-books sold through CreateSpace are sold much more cheaply than books from traditional publishers, so any revenue is greatly reduced despite the higher author percentage. However, with Amazon's already massive and constantly growing online presence, CreateSpace really did offer self-published authors a much better opportunity.

Amazon did demand that authors offered them exclusivity, which became even more important when it developed the Kindle Unlimited e-book subscription service in 2014. But, in return, Amazon promoted authors' books and offered books for sale at very attractive prices. Most would-be authors loved the democratic nature of this, bypassing the traditional publishers and letting the reader choose. The downside was that there were literally thousands upon thousands of books for readers to choose from, all by relatively unknown authors, and finding the gems in this veritable haystack wasn't easy. Most self-published e-books still don't sell very many copies at all, sharing the same fate as previous vanity publishing, but undoubtedly some authors have bucked this trend and enjoyed huge success through this model.

The genres that have benefitted most are romance, science fiction, fantasy, fan fiction, crime fiction, young adult and the upcoming genre of 'romantasy'. These subject areas dominate self-publishing e-book sales – in fact, they represent a huge market of their own, in most cases entirely separate from the traditional book trade.

Some authors have made the transition to the traditional trade, as a result of publishers and agents scouring Amazon's e-book bestseller lists for potential new signings. But other successful authors have preferred to remain in the self-publishing realm, proudly wearing the badge of 'indie author'. Amazon's self-publishing programme has now established itself as another route for writers to launch their careers.

This new route is becoming increasingly important and could threaten the traditional book trade's dominance in years to come. It is estimated that about one million self-published books are now released annually, although there are no accurate figures. To prove the growing importance of the self-publishing route, many will point to crossover successes such as E.L. James, who started her career in 2011 writing *Twilight* fan fiction online before writing what would become the huge print and e-book success, *Fifty Shades of Grey*. E.L. James is supposed to have amassed earnings of over $90 million through this route, including film rights.

Others will mention author Andy Weir, who started writing science-fiction stories on his blog while working as a computer programmer. He amassed a strong following for his work and was persuaded by these fans to produce his novel as an Amazon e-book. The success of this was noticed by a New York agent, who then helped Weir sell the rights to Penguin Random House. This became the best-selling novel *The Martian*, which was also turned into a huge Hollywood film starring Matt Damon and Jessica Chastain. Both examples demonstrate that there is a route to mainstream success through self-publishing on online platforms.

Perhaps of more concern for the traditional publishers is the example of British crime author L.J. Ross, who has built up a massive following, particularly for her DCI Ryan mysteries, which have been huge sellers in print, e-book and audio formats. The author of more than twenty bestselling crime novels, L.J. Ross was a lawyer who started writing crime fiction during her maternity leave. She had some interest from the traditional publisher and agent route, but decided that Amazon Kindle offered much better royalties.

Traditional publishers generally pay between 5 and 10 per cent royalty on sales, whereas Amazon offers the author 70 per cent. As a result, L.J. Ross now publishes all her books as e-books through Kindle and in print under her own Dark Skies imprint, which she set up with her husband. This is an astonishing achievement, bypassing the normal agent and publisher model – and with brilliant success, achieving sales in excess of one million copies. Her books are sold online and in bookshops, suggesting a whole new way of bringing books to readers.

These authors demonstrate that the routes to market have expanded and that there are multiple ways to publish a book in this new world.

The Consequences for
Booksellers and Publishers

The huge changes to the way books were produced and sold, with the growth of e-books, audiobooks and self-publishing, all benefitted Amazon. From the mid-1990s, its dominance in print book sales grew rapidly, particularly once broadband became more widespread in the early 2000s and internet usage increased dramatically. Now, not only was Amazon the largest retailer of print books, but it had almost complete dominance of the sale of e-books, audiobooks and self-published books. If we estimate that these three categories accounted for just 25 per cent of all book sales, for that proportion to be in the hands of one retailer was hugely alarming for the traditional book trade. Added to this, for many publishers Amazon accounted for almost 50 per cent of their print book sales. The book trade had a problem.

Publishers now found themselves incredibly reliant on just one customer. It delivered fantastic revenue and had increased sales of the 'long tail' by being able to sell any book, including the most obscure titles on publishers' backlists. But Amazon's dominance in the market and publishers' reliance upon it gave Amazon a huge advantage whenever it wanted to negotiate terms. It held some very strong cards in any deal and publishers were in a very vulnerable position.

For booksellers, the dominance of Amazon had completely transformed the playing field. We have seen that independent booksellers were hit by the expansion of the bookshop chains in the 1980s and 1990s. The chains then struggled against the new threat posed by internet bookselling and most were forced to close. One by one, Dillons, Hammicks, Ottakar's and then Borders closed or were absorbed into Waterstones. By the 2010s, Waterstones and the old reliable stalwart W.H. Smith were the only remaining bookshop chains in the UK, and the independent sector now numbered fewer than 1,000 shops – a shadow of its former self.

For booksellers, the advent of e-books and audiobooks were yet another threat. The wider industry could pat itself on the back and say that these new formats helped expand book readership. But while this was true, sales of e-books and audiobooks completely bypassed the bookshops. They were only accessible as digital downloads, which did not require a visit to a bookshop; so, that 20 per cent of the market wasn't even accessible to bookshops. And of the other 80 per cent, a huge volume of print book sales was now being channelled through Amazon and a growing cadre of other online retailers. As the new century progressed, booksellers needed new ideas if they were to survive.

12

How the Book Trade
Fought Back

Daunt Books in Marylebone, London. (Alamy)

Books in the New Century

Throughout the multiple changes and upheavals of the past four decades, authors have continued to write brilliant, inventive and inspiring books, publishers have continued to publish them, and readers have avidly bought and devoured them. In many ways, this abundance of great books has been responsible for the recent revival of the book trade: it's the reason that readers still want to buy physical books, talk about them in book groups, visit bookshops and listen to authors talking about their book. Total UK book sales have continued to grow, and sales of print books in particular are increasing once more.

Books have continued to evolve, with new trends and styles breaking through, new authors emerging and, significantly, both a better balance between the sexes and an improved diversity in the voices telling the stories. This is an exciting time in book publishing that has brought in a wave of new readers, attracted by the diverse range of books on offer.

If we look at literary fiction and use the Granta Best of Young British Novelists as a stepping-off point, the first list back in 1983 was very 'blokey', including Martin Amis and Ian McEwan. That first Granta list of twenty upcoming novelists featured fourteen men, whereas the 2023 list (the fifth one, as Granta repeats the exercise every decade) includes only four men, demonstrating a real power shift in the literary sphere.

In recent lists, not only have women gained dominance, but the ethnic mix has improved, as has the regionality, with an increasing number of non-London voices being heard. Among 2023's intake are already established young writers such as Olivia Sudjic, Sophie Mackintosh and Eleanor Catton, the youngest-ever winner of the Booker Prize at the age of 28 with *The Luminaries* back in 2013. Eleanor Catton originally hails from New Zealand and, among the other names on this exciting and varied list, we find Graeme Armstrong from Airdrie (part of the local gang culture in his teens), Yara Rodrigues Fowler of Brazilian heritage, Lauren Aimee Curtis from Australia, K. Patrick from the Isle of Lewis (who identifies as trans-masculine) and Isabella Hammad of British-Palestinian heritage, to give a flavour of the wider pool the list now draws upon.

The Granta list has proved a reliable yardstick for the British literary scene over the past four decades. In addition to flagging up Amis, McEwan, Rushdie, Barnes and others who went on to dominate the literary scene in the 1980s and beyond, over subsequent years it has championed a whole host of young writers who then went on to achieve massive success. It's an impressive list of authors that includes Hanif Kureishi, Alan Hollinghurst, Rachel Cusk, Helen Oyeyemi, Zadie Smith, David Mitchell, Sarah Hall and Kamila Shamsie.

The Granta lists have always been controversial, with critics arguing about who has been included and who hasn't (the absentees have included the likes of Jonathan Coe and Hilary Mantel). But controversy is not necessarily a bad thing, as the lists always succeed at getting people talking about books, just as the Booker and many other prizes do, and this drives readers into bookshops. The lists invite readers to stretch themselves, to discover new authors and explore new directions. Books continue to do all of this, arguably better than they have ever done.

When I worked at Harvill Press over twenty years ago, there was still resistance among the British reading public to fiction in translation. I don't feel that is still the case, or certainly not to the same extent. The book trade has diversified and improved a great deal during this new century to become a more welcoming and all-encompassing business. And the books now available to readers deliver a much more varied offer than that of the 1980s.

The success of the Booker Prize has produced several other prizes which continue to attract attention, open readers' eyes to new authors and help to grow book sales. Among the more established prizes today is the Women's Prize for Fiction, which has now been active for twenty-eight years. It was a very new prize in the latter years of my bookselling career, starting with Helen Dunmore winning back in 1996 with *A Spell in Winter*. Subsequent winners have included Maggie O'Farrell, Naomi Alderman, Barbara Kingsolver, Kamila Shamsie, Ali Smith, Eimear McBride, Chimamanda Ngozi Adichie, Zadie Smith and Andrea Levy – an incredibly impressive list from a prize that has also been a decent weathervane of talent. It works hard to publicise the work of women writers, who are still too often overlooked by critics and reviewers.

The year 2024 also saw the inauguration of the Women's Prize for Non-Fiction. The Women's Prize is a great example of a book prize working to inspire readers and champion great writing. Its mission statement proclaims, 'We believe that reading increases empathy, expands imaginations and empowers connection – simply put, books by women can change the world.' Other notable prizes include the Nero Book Awards, the Baillie Gifford Prize for Non-Fiction and the Waterstones Book of the Year.

The past few decades have continued a golden age of literary fiction, although now very much changed from the male-dominated 1980s. One of the huge successes of recent years has been Hilary Mantel, who sadly died in 2022, but not before making her significant mark on the world of literature through her Cromwell trilogy. The first two volumes of this trilogy, *Wolf Hall* and *Bring Up the Bodies*, both won the Booker Prize, in 2009 and 2012 respectively, and these books have been brilliant bookshop bestsellers. Likewise, other authors such as Maggie O'Farrell, most recently with *Hamnet* and *The Marriage Portrait*, Bernadine Evaristo, who won the Booker with her eighth novel *Girl, Woman, Other* in 2019, Claire Keegan, with her powerful novellas and short stories such as *Small Things Like These*, and Sally Rooney have all confirmed the new dominance of female writers. All of Rooney's novels to date have been massive bestsellers and have engaged and inspired a new younger readership. Authors like these continue to drive sales and bring more customers into bookshops.

This has also been a brilliant period for more popular fiction or genre fiction. We mentioned *Fifty Shades of Grey* in the last chapter, but other big titles of this century that have enthused readers and driven book sales include *The Kite Runner* by Khaled Hosseini, *The Hunger Games* by Susanne Collins, *The Girl with the Dragon Tattoo* by Stieg Larsson and, more recently, the cosy crime novels of Richard Osman and his Thursday Murder Club series. Other recent trends that have got bookshop tills ringing have been the novels of Colleen Hoover and the huge interest in 'romantasy' fiction, from authors such as Sarah J. Maas and Rebecca Yarros, boosted by marketing on TikTok. Sarah J. Maas' most recent book, *The House of Flame and Shadow*, shot straight to No. 1 in the UK bestsellers chart in 2024, selling 45,000 copies in hardback in its first week, driven by a huge pre-publication campaign through social media as well as many bookshops celebrating by opening at midnight on publication day (in Harry Potter-style) for excited fans.

Children's literature has likewise continued to thrive following the boost created by J.K. Rowling and her boy wizard. The third Harry Potter title was released just prior to our bookshop's closure but, in the years following, the phenomenon exploded in spectacular fashion. It has been estimated that to date over 600 million Harry Potter books have been sold. Those incredible sales figures have been great for bookshops, the author and Rowling's publisher Bloomsbury, of course; but the Harry Potter series has also encouraged millions of children to read more books. Eager young readers, delighted by the stories, have gone on to find other great books and become regular readers as a result. Bookshops and libraries have helped in this and benefitted from this new generation of readers drawn to literature by J.K. Rowling's series.

Recent decades have seen a wave of brilliant children's literature, also reflecting the cultural and diverse mix of modern society in much the same way that adult books have been doing. Brilliant books by Katharine Rundell, Philip Pullman, Andy Stanton, Robert Macfarlane and Jackie Morris, Malorie Blackman, Frank Cottrel Boyce, Julia Donaldson, Liz Pichon and Jeff Kinney have captivated young readers. Children's publishing is thriving as never before, with a raft of brilliant publishers from the corporates to the inventive independents.

Waterstones Rejuvenated

Over the past few chapters, we have charted the fortunes of Waterstones since its glory days under founder Tim Waterstone. The rise of Amazon in the 2000s spelled trouble for Waterstones, and the HMV ownership struggled in the wake of this competition. With the introduction of e-books, bookshops faced the same massive threat of future sales being predominantly digital as the music industry had done. So, when book-loving Russian billionaire Alexander Mamut came knocking in 2011, HMV were more than happy to sell the Waterstones chain to him for £53m. In a bold move, Mamut then shocked the book trade by appointing successful independent bookseller James Daunt as the new MD of the Waterstones chain.

James Daunt had been working in banking for J.P. Morgan in New York in the 1980s before he decided to open his own bookshop. Combining his twin loves of books and travel, he took out a loan to rent a wonderful old Edwardian antiquarian bookshop on Marylebone High Street and transformed it into Daunt Books, which opened in 1990 and remains one of the most beautiful bookshops in Britain.

Situated in a very well-to-do area of London, the shop themes books by country rather than the traditional categories of fiction, biography, history, poetry and so on. The shop has always championed travel guides and great travel writing, alongside the best literature and writing from around the world. This eclectic mix proved to be a huge success, and more outlets followed in other upmarket areas of London such as Holland Park and Hampstead. Today, the chain has ten outlets, having bought up independents in Marlow, Saffron Walden and Kentish Town, and opened in Oxford too. With his move to Waterstones, James Daunt would retain ownership of the chain but would no longer be involved in its day-to-day management.

Many were sceptical about Daunt's skills transferring from a very select independent audience to the wider and more demanding needs of a 300-store national chain. But Daunt hit the ground running, immediately bringing change to Waterstones. He didn't return buying functions to stores, as some had hoped, but he did remove uniformity from the chain, enabling each store to play to its local strengths.

He quickly disposed of the system whereby publishers effectively paid for space in the stores, which had meant that every Waterstones store throughout the land was promoting the same list of titles. As Daunt said in an interview with the *Evening Standard* in 2014, 'My problem was that they paid you to put every book in the same place in every shop. And books that might work in Kensington might not work in Blackpool.'

Daunt also removed the popular 3 for 2 promotion that adorned the front of every store. While he was not averse to some price promotion, he didn't want the chain to rely on it. Despite the competition from Amazon, he felt that books were great value at their cover price and bookshops should stand or fall by the superior experience afforded by being in a bookshop.

While there were quite a few mutterings from publishers about the removal of their promotional options, which immediately translated into smaller initial orders for new books, most recognised that Daunt was a dedicated books man and that what he was doing did make sense. Daunt's actions also reduced returns, which had been very high on those promoted titles and, in doing so, he made the chain's stock work more efficiently and reduced costs across the board.

Daunt also performed a major shake-up of the staffing structure throughout Waterstones, abolishing several management roles. And there were missteps that proved Daunt wasn't infallible, such as the decision to sell Kindle e-readers and download e-books in Waterstones stores, essentially offering Waterstones' main rival, Amazon, direct access to its customers. This was quietly jettisoned after a year or two, although Daunt argues that Waterstones made significant revenue from this move.

More significantly, after a couple of years under Daunt's stewardship, the Waterstones chain stopped losing money and broke even, the beginning of a distinct turnaround in its fortunes. In recent years, it has been turning a tidy profit. By the time the private equity company Elliott bought out Mamut and took over ownership of Waterstones in 2018, providing even stronger financial backing, the company was already on a strong footing. Daunt had not only steadied the ship, but had transformed the company into a bookselling chain fit for the challenges of the twenty-first century.

Daunt could not return Waterstones to what it had been in the 1980s. Tim Waterstone's creation was perfect for the 1980s and 1990s but would not work in the modern bookselling environment. He had created wonderful book utopias, well-stocked bookshops that offered a brilliant range to its customers. Today, Amazon is the range bookseller, offering every possible book in print, more than any physical bookshop could ever hold.

The Waterstones stores of today must compete by offering something different. They offer a curated range, unique to every local store, playing to that location's strengths. The stores sell stationery and gifts alongside books and many stores have a coffee shop. Most will offer a range of events, book clubs and author signings. The chain also produces unique editions of key titles and supports this with a very strong web offer through its much-improved website, a Waterstones account card, regular email and social media contact with its customers and a range of awards sponsored by the chain.

Recent winners of the Waterstones Book of the Year have included *Impossible Creatures* by Katherine Rundell, *The Story of Art Without Men* by Katy Hessel, *Hamnet* by Maggie O'Farrell, *Normal People* by Sally Rooney and *The Essex Serpent* by Sarah Perry, all great bookshop books. Waterstones is a key lynchpin of the British book trade once more, with over 290 stores. It is hard to imagine the book business being without this leading retailer, and publishers are eternally grateful for its continued existence. Bricks-and-mortar retailing continues to face challenges but, for now at least, its leading chain is in good health.

In 2018, Waterstones bought up Foyles and then, in 2022, the Blackwell's chain. In both these cases, Waterstones has retained the names and strong identities of these illustrious booksellers. But it speaks volumes about the fragility of physical retailing that these two big names were struggling to survive and were forced to sell. Despite this now offering better long-term security for these great British bookselling names, it is a shame that they are now owned by Waterstones. The trade needs diversity and variety and, good as Daunt is, too many shops run by one person or company is never a great idea. We will see, though, that new independents and new mini-chains are rising from the tumult of the past few decades, too. Waterstones doesn't have a total monopoly on the British brick-and-mortar book trade.

Waterstones has absorbed Dillons, Hammicks, Ottakar's, Hatchards, Foyles and Blackwell's in the past few decades. It has also opened a few non-branded Waterstones stores that look like local independents in Southwold and Rye. And it has opened smaller stores in many towns to suit local needs. Interestingly, Elliott also bought the US bookshop chain Barnes & Noble (B&N) in 2019 and Daunt was transferred to the USA to oversee the transformation there. Kate Skipper, a long-established part of the UK management team, was promoted to run Waterstones in his absence. In recent years, Daunt has been working through a root and branch overhaul of B&N to make it fit for purpose, much as he did for Waterstones.

James Daunt is now arguably the most powerful figure in bookselling after Jeff Bezos. Despite qualms about too much power in one man's hands – a legitimate concern – Daunt is at heart a book man, a reader and booklover, who is a force for good in the industry and should be praised for his success. He has steered Waterstones and B&N down a path that demonstrates how bookshops can survive and thrive in the twenty-first century, despite the threat from Bezos' mega-corporation.

Daunt argues that bookshops offer a more personal and human approach than buying online. Reading books may be a private, solo endeavour, but most readers and booklovers enjoy talking about books with others and getting recommendations. This explains the popularity of author events and book clubs in recent decades. We still crave the human contact that online shopping doesn't provide. Daunt's argument is that buying a book from a bookshop and a real bookseller is a more pleasurable experience and, as a result, you consequently enjoy the book more. 'You'll read it quicker. You chose it with your own eyes, your hands, your ears. Now it's all about anticipation. If you buy a book from Amazon, there's a *little* anticipation as you rip the tag off the envelope. But it's generally slightly flat and disappointing.'

The Revival of Independent Publishing

Looking at the book trade today from the outside, one could be fooled into thinking that the writing was on the wall for independent publishing. In recent years, the 'Big Four' publishers (Penguin Random House, HarperCollins, Hachette and Macmillan) seem to have swallowed up smaller publishers on such a regular basis that it's hard to believe that any independents remain. In the past two years alone, Hachette has bought up Summersdale, Wellbeck, Paperblanks and Workman Publishing, while Penguin Random House has recently added Quadrille, Hardie Grant and Hay House to its stable – all long-established independent publishers. There is much to be said for being part of a large publishing conglomerate, not least having more financial support and investment for key titles and authors, but the independent sector is often where most risks are taken and new ground is broken.

But, even while the 'Big Four' have continued to expand, the trade has simultaneously witnessed a flourishing of the independent publishing sector. And some of the strongest independents have grown bigger in this new century and confirmed their dominance in British publishing, among them Faber, Profile and Oneworld.

Faber, founded in 1929, remains one of the largest British independent publishers and proclaims on its website that it is 'proud to publish the foremost voices in fiction, non-fiction, poetry, drama, film and children's books' and 'thirteen Nobel Laureates and six Booker Prize-winners have been published by Faber'. Its roster includes such massive names as Kazuo Ishiguro, Simon Armitage, Andrew O'Hagan, Sally Rooney, Katharine Rundell, Kae Tempest and Natalie Diaz, among many others, while still publishing Ted Hughes, T.S. Eliot, Sylvia Plath, Alan Bennett, Samuel Beckett, William Golding and a whole host of illustrious authors.

In addition, Faber actively helps other independent publishers through the Independent Alliance that it set up. This operation offers sales and marketing services to similar independent publishers, including Profile, Oneworld, Atlantic Books, Pushkin Press and Duckworth.

Profile Books, founded by Andrew Franklin and Stephen Brough in 1996, had early success with *Eats, Shoots & Leaves* by Lynne Truss, which sold over three million copies. Today, it has a reputation for accessible and innovative non-fiction. But, along the way, it has bought up and grown the reputations of literary fiction imprint Serpents Tail (publisher of Sarah Perry's *The Essex Serpent*) and non-fiction publisher Souvenir Press (its most recent success being the gift bestseller *Murdle*), as well as launching a new hugely successful crime imprint, Viper.

Oneworld, set up in 1986 by husband-and-wife team Juliet Mabey and Novin Doostdar, has also grown significantly and now publishes over 100 eclectic fiction and non-fiction titles per year. It has produced three Booker Prize winners (Paul Lynch, Marlon James and Paul Beatty) and won many other awards too, including the Women's Prize with *An American Marriage* by Tayari Jones in 2019. Oneworld has a reputation for taking risks on titles that have been rejected by the bigger publishing houses – a theme common to many independent publishers. The best of these are breaking new ground and discovering new voices more often than the big conglomerates. The downside and harsh reality is that this success then attracts the big publishers, who often swoop in to steal successful authors from the independents.

There seems to be a real optimism and excitement coming from the independent publishing sector today. The trade needs this as part of its ongoing growth and renewal. The economic climate continues to be tough, but this passion and enthusiasm needs to be encouraged to facilitate a lively and ambitious trade. Independent publishers have been responsible for twelve winners of the Booker Prize so far this century. This is a vindication of the hard work such publishers do in bringing new voices into the public domain and the risks they take in doing so. Faber, the oldest independent publisher, has had three winners this century alone.

Recent decades have witnessed the launch and success of multiple new independent publishers – a seemingly unstoppable wave of new lists and new ideas, with more diverse, specialist and regional publishing. There are now many more independent publishing successes based away from the London-centric publishing world of old, such as Galley Beggar Press.

Founded in 2012 by Sam Jordison and Eloise Millar and based in Norwich, Galley Press aims to support and promote 'great literary talent writing outside the norm, who push the boundaries of form and language'. In a short space of time, it has established itself as a risk-taking publisher producing brilliant books, including multiple prizewinners such as *Ducks, Newburyport* by Lucy Ellmann and *A Girl Is a Half-Formed Thing* by Eimear McBride.

Kevin Duffy runs Bluemoose Books from his home in Hebden Bridge in Yorkshire and only publishes around ten books a year, but he has already won multiple prizes, including one with Benjamin Myers (since signed to Bloomsbury). 'I think that's one of the reasons why independent presses are being shortlisted and winning literary prizes, because we are taking risks the bigger publishers aren't.' Bluemoose is very strong on discovering new literary talent and is particularly keen on working-class voices. In a recent *Guardian* interview, Duffy discussed the difference between independent publishers and the large conglomerates like Penguin Random House, 'They're not going to take risks on working-class and diverse writers because they need to get their money back – when you've got a 40m-high steel and glass edifice on the Embankment, there are costs to be taken care of.'

There are so many exciting and innovative independent publishers working in Britain at the moment that this book can't hope to list them all. But I should mention Sort of Books, which published *The Seven Moons of Maali Almeida* by Shehan Karunatilaka, winner of the 2022 Booker Prize; Swift Books, now publishing Bret Easton Ellis (once of Picador); black-owned Jacaranda Books, headed by Valerie Brandes; and Fitzcarraldo Editions, only founded in 2014, but already publisher of four Nobel winners, Svetlana Alexievich, Olga Tokarczuk, Annie Ernaux and Jon Fosse. My best recommendation would be to go and seek out these presses and discover for yourself wonderful new authors and exciting new reading pathways.

The independent publishing sector faces many challenges, but there is an energy and vitality flowing from these many varied presses that is breathing new life into the book trade. And we should value this and support it wherever we can.

The Independent Bookshop Revival

Arguably, independent bookshops have been the most affected by the huge changes of the last forty years. When my father and I opened our bookshop in 1984 there were over 2,500 independent bookshops in Britain, dominating the bookshop landscape. As well as general bookshops, these numbers included CTNs (confectioners, tobacconists and newsagents), many of which had decent book departments, over 100 radical bookshops and about 150 religious bookshops. But the subsequent dramatic expansion of chain bookshops in the 1980s and 1990s was catastrophic for the independents. By 1995, the number of independent bookshops was down to 1,894.

Over the next twenty years the combination of further expansion by the chains, supermarkets selling bestsellers as low as half-price, the dramatic growth of Amazon and the introduction of digital publishing all combined to reduce the number of British independent bookshops to a shocking 867 outlets by 2016. Approximately 1,500 closed between

1984 and 2016. This is a startling figure and underlines just how much the book trade has changed between 1984 and the present day. The independent sector has been decimated and those still surviving have struggled against multiple challenges. Most of the CTNs have either ceased to exist or no longer sell books, while the radical and religious bookshops have also suffered throughout this time, with large numbers of these closing too.

However, by 2019 the BA was starting to report positive news about new bookshop openings. By 2021 there were over 1,000 independents in the UK, eventually rising to its current level of around 1,070 shops. While this was not anywhere near its former numbers, it did reflect an improving picture. Approximately fifty new shops are now opening each year. But it remains very difficult to make money from this business. In 2023, the same number of independent bookshops closed as new shops opened, reinforcing this point.

Bookshops are still fighting against a variety of challenges, and they are not helped by soaring rents and business rates. Many feel aggrieved that Amazon gets away with a minimal tax burden for the size of its business. UK bookshops, including Waterstones, need better support from government similar to that enjoyed by our neighbours across the Channel in France, Italy and Germany. Meryl Halls, the BA's managing director, recently stated, 'Margins are extremely tight, and for bookshops to thrive on high streets they need governments to take action to protect small businesses from the cost-of-living crisis, as well as unequal tax burdens such as business rates.'

This stabilisation and slight growth in the bookshop landscape in the past few years is due to several factors. Booksellers have worked hard to offer more to customers, including regular event programmes, book groups, discussions and many other types of meetings within their shops. This is called 'experiential bookselling' and many of the big publishers have worked with booksellers to develop this concept, giving customers more reasons to visit a physical bookshop, not just to buy a book but for the allied experience too. An increasing number of independent bookshops now boast a café within their shop. And, as we have seen, bookshops have had some fantastic books to sell to help them in all of this.

Bookshops have also learned to use the internet as a weapon in their own armoury. A thriving bookshop in today's world must have a good website and be posting several times a day on social media, particularly Facebook and Instagram, building relationships with customers in new ways.

Importantly, bookshops have been helped in this by several other companies, not least the wholesaler Gardners, which offers website fulfilment for independent bookshops through its Hive programme. This is particularly useful for smaller bookshops that just don't have the resources to set up and run their own website effectively. Gardners also enables bookshops to sell e-books and audiobooks, so that those who want to consume books digitally don't have to buy through Amazon; they now have alternatives.

Likewise, Bookshop.org was specifically set up in 2020 by US publisher Andy Hunter to challenge Amazon as an online book retailer and, at the same time, support the bricks-and-mortar book trade. Bookshop. org's unique point of difference is that its customer chooses a local bookshop to receive a share of the money on each sale, thus offering the convenience of online shopping while still supporting local bookshops. Bookshops can earn up to 30 per cent on each sale without stocking or shipping the book. As the online platform Inside Hook says, 'Thanks to Bookshop.org, there is no reason to buy books on Amazon anymore.' The traditional book trade is indeed fighting back.

Additionally, the BA has proved to be magnificent at supporting its independent bookshop members and helping them fight the challenges facing their businesses. There are now more regular gatherings of booksellers; much more joined-up thinking and working together across the trade. The BA runs training courses for booksellers in addition to regular conferences. It has also established an annual Independent Bookshop Week and supplies 'Books Are My Bag' tote bags for independent bookshops to sell. The BA also produces Christmas and summer book catalogues for bookshops to use and a bi-monthly magazine about new books called *Booktime*, which bookshops give away to customers. Today's independent bookshops are not fighting in a vacuum and this has led to the growth in independent bookshop numbers.

At heart, too, there has also been a level of reaction from the book-buying public against the ubiquity of Amazon, particularly following repeated publicity about how poorly Amazon treats its warehouse staff. Amazon is a brilliant business, but most of us don't want big corporations taking over everything. In her book of essays, *Trick Mirror*, the author Jia Tolentino declared that 'to use Amazon, which I did regularly for years with full knowledge of its labour practices, is to accept and embrace a world in which everything is worth as little as possible, even, and maybe particularly, people'.

Booksellers have also been aided in recent years by Amazon's attention switching away from books. The company has recognised that it isn't financially viable to stock every book in print in all their warehouses. The concept of the long tail has now been devolved to secondary sellers, so Amazon can still list everything but doesn't necessarily supply everything direct. Its book activities are mainly focussed on the top bestselling titles, skimming the easy wins off the surface. The consequence of this is that the traditional book trade, both Waterstones and independents, has an opportunity to appeal to heavy book buyers through their specialism in books, combined with their knowledge and passion.

Although Waterstones and other traditional bookshops were late to the party with online bookselling, they are now catching up. Waterstones and its various specialist brands such as Blackwell's, Hatchards and Foyle's are now building sales and loyalty through websites and online activities, targeting specific customer bases with relevant, curated emails. The human selection is bearing fruit and book buyers are recognising that they prefer this more specific and personal interaction.

Despite the huge convenience of the Amazon business, many regular book buyers seem to have recognised how important bookshops are to them. We all know about the incredible value and convenience of shopping on Amazon, but is that all that book buyers want? We know that Amazon's algorithms can suggest books to us that are similar to the one we have just read, but not only are those suggestions often rather obvious, in reality many readers often don't want to follow the enjoyment of one book with another very similar volume. We like to be surprised, we like difference, and we actively seek new experiences.

A bookshop and a human bookseller can deliver the serendipity of multiple choices. The wonderful appeal of books is the many different journeys they offer, the discovery of the different and the new. We don't know where our reading pathway will lead us next and often the most enjoyable books are the least expected. A bookshop and a bookseller are best placed to offer such inspiration and recommendation. And we revel in the human interaction that a bookshop provides.

Chrissy Ryan, owner of BookBar in north London, a new bookshop that opened in 2021, said in an article in *The Bookseller* magazine, 'Bookshops are the antithesis of the algorithm – we know that reading is an emotive thing and that booksellers use their emotional intelligence to recommend the right book for the right reader. It's our job to create an experience.' Bookshops have to offer something different and really lean into the personal and human interaction offered by buying from a real-life bookseller. Amazon will always win on the size of its range, but even the smallest range in the smallest bookshop has an advantage over this. Book buyers like to browse, they like to touch books, they like to look inside and feel them. These are all the values that Tim Waterstone championed, and they remain a distinct alternative to online shopping. In addition, while Amazon can supply all sorts of information and reviews, most book buyers value talking to a real person about books.

We also appreciate and value the bricks-and-mortar bookshop's contribution to and involvement in the local community. Bookshops offer author events, book groups, storytimes for children and organise author talks in schools, alongside other connections to the local community. Bookshops and libraries are often involved in initiatives to get more children reading and are a force for good, not just a business taking our money.

BookBar is one of a wave of great new independent bookshops that have breathed new life into this centuries-old trade. The newest bookshops are looking for interesting ways to entice customers into their shops, including running a café or, as in this case, a bar, alongside selling books. The shops are defined by their vibrant and welcoming culture, a lively events programme and well-supported book groups, all creating a real sense of a place to be. The trade has brushed off the dustiness of years gone by and now feels fresh and exciting, offering customers better social interaction. Spaces like Bookbar encourage customers to discuss books and share their passions.

And many of these new shops are run by women, overturning the previous male dominance. Among these pioneering female booksellers are the aforementioned Chrissy Ryan at BookBar; Olivia Rosenthall at Maldon Books in Essex; Amanda Truman at Truman Books in Leeds; Diane Park at Wave of Nostalgia in Haworth; Emma Corfield-Walters at Book-Ish in Crickhowell in Wales; Helen Stanton at Forum Books in Corbridge; and Amber Harrison and Karen Brazier at Folde in Dorset. There are many more.

And the newest bookshops embrace a world of diversity, champion regional specialities and promote specific causes, often political, proclaiming how much the book trade has changed since the 1980s. There has been a rich history of gay and lesbian bookshops in Britain for decades, particularly dating back to the 1970s and 1980s, as well as black interest, political and radical bookshops. This sector has suffered the same fate as general independent bookshops, with many forced to close due to the abolition of the NBA, increased rates and rents and competition from online booksellers. But recent years have seen a flowering of radical booksellers once more. There are many new LGBTQIA+ bookshops across the country, offering books that are often not stocked by general bookshops, as well as connecting customers to a whole range of events, assistance and services within their communities. Among these are Category Is Books in Glasgow; The Bookish Type in Leeds; Juno Books in Sheffield; and Queer Lit in Manchester.

We also have Afrori Books in Brighton, specialising in books from black authors; New Beacon Books in Finsbury Park, promoting African and Caribbean literature; and Round Table Books in Brixton, a black-owned children's bookshop which promotes 'books with diverse characters, be that race, sexuality, gender or disability'. The Alliance of Radical Booksellers now boasts over fifty members in the UK, including long-established stalwarts such as Gay's the Word, set up in 1979, and the wonderful Five Leaves Bookshop in Nottingham, launched by Ross Bradshaw in 2013.

Most 'general' independent bookshops also now stock a much-improved range of books, including LGBTQIA+, black interest, political and radical writing. While I wouldn't pretend that Britain is entirely a nation of tolerance, I feel that there is a better acceptance of a wider range of viewpoints today, enriching our culture. The trade has matured and come of age and now better reflects our modern country. These passionate booksellers continue to raise awareness of key issues and champion books that are underrepresented in the chains and not promoted by most major online booksellers.

This wide range of new booksellers is working hard to bring new ideas to the business and offering exciting alternatives to the very routine ordering of books from an online retailer. Meryl Halls from the BA states, 'Bookshops bring social and cultural capital to every town, village, suburb or city centre they are part of, and punch way above their weight in terms of impact and engagement locally, and nationally.'

Among today's great independent bookshops, there are several significant and important mini-chains that are marked out by their quality, many run by ex-chain booksellers. Probably the best example is the Topping chain of bookshops, started by Robert Topping, previously manager of Waterstones Deansgate in Manchester, back in that chain's glory days. Topping fell out with the new management at Waterstones in the early 2000s, refusing to reduce his stockholding, holding on to Tim Waterstone's original idea of a large, well-stocked bookshop.

Going his own way, Topping responded by opening a beautiful bookshop in Ely in Cambridgeshire with his wife Louise, which is notable both for being crammed full of books and its lively and well-attended events programme. Topping's confidence in this model paid off and he subsequently opened a second shop in Bath in 2007, a third in St Andrews in 2014 and a larger shop in Edinburgh in 2019. In 2021, he relocated the Bath shop to much larger new premises in the old Georgian Friends Meeting House in York Street. He proclaimed that the shop has more shelf space than any other British independent bookshop, stocking over 75,000 titles. Topping's will open a new shop in York in 2025.

Topping & Company have demonstrated that, in the right area, the traditional independent bookshop can thrive and succeed, despite the existence of Amazon and supermarkets. Husband-and-wife team Andy and Victoria Rossiter now boast a six-shop mini-chain with Rossiter Books branches in Ross-on-Wye, Monmouth, Leominster, Cheltenham,

Malvern and Hereford. While Victoria is an experienced ex-secondary school teacher, Andy was a manager for both Waterstones and Ottakar's.

Another ex-Waterstones and Ottakar's manager, Wayne Winstone, now has three branches of Winstone Books in Sherborne, Sidmouth and Frome. And Helen Stanton, also ex-Waterstones, owns three bookshops in the north-east, Forum Books, The Bound and The Accidental Bookshop. And Adam Hewson, who worked for Waterstones and Books Etc, now has three branches of Hewson Books in Kew, Sheen and Brentford.

These shops reflect the best traditions of strong, local, independent bookshops, that are embedded in their local communities and run by passionate and enthusiastic booksellers. Adam Hewson believes that one of Tim Waterstone's greatest legacies are his experienced alumni now running some of the UK's best independent bookshops.

While discussing Topping's enlarged new shop in Bath, it's certainly worth mentioning the city's other great independent bookshop, Mr B's Emporium in John Street. Founded by husband-and-wife team Nic and Juliette Bottomley, Mr B's has twice been named as the UK's best independent bookshop and appeared in a 2015 *Guardian* list of the ten best bookshops in the world. The shop is a labyrinth of discovery, with multiple rooms, each with a different feel to the last. The bookshop hosts many events but is also well known for how it relates to its customers. It boasts a large team of incredibly passionate readers who share opinions on the books they love and seem determined to find the right books for every customer, championing what they call 'opiniated bookselling'. The shop offers reading spas and personalised subscriptions, alongside seemingly limitless lists of recommendations, excelling at traditional bookselling with a modern twist.

To enter these or many of the other great independent bookshops around the UK today will restore your faith in physical bookshops and give you hope for the future of the book trade. There are too many brilliant independents in business today to name them all, but it should be mentioned that a good number of existing bookshops have weathered all the problems of the past few decades and are still thriving. Among these are the Sevenoaks Bookshop, originally opened in 1948 and now owned by Fleur Sinclair, another inspirational female bookseller who has enlarged and updated the shop to create one of the most attractive independents in Britain that runs a busy events programme. Others include Davids Bookshop in Letchworth, founded in 1963, and the Red Lion Bookshop, which was opened in Colchester in 1978 by Sarah and Peter Donaldson.

There is a very strong, positive feeling in the current book trade, which was lacking just a few years ago, a quite remarkable turnaround after all that the trade has been through in those recent decades. Presenting the Bookseller of the Year Award in 2022, Tom Tivnan, *The Bookseller*'s managing editor, said:

> We just may be in the golden age of independent bookselling. The last 10 or 15 years have been the most testing of times for indies as they have battled against online competition, supermarket deep discounting, rising business rates and, of course recently, a global pandemic. But they have met the challenges; indies are thriving and the number of shops is rising.

As a postscript to this, it can certainly be argued that selling books through Amazon and supermarkets and in digital and audio formats has widened the book market, reached more customers and made books more affordable. This was the aim of Caxton, de Worde, Lackington, Allen Lane, Paul Hamlyn and Terry Maher – to make books accessible to as wide an audience as possible and, by keeping prices low, make reading and the wonderful world of books available to everyone, not just a privileged elite who can afford the higher prices. My only caveat to that would be that, while online retailers and supermarkets can reach readers that bookshops cannot, bookshops and libraries play a very important role in supporting writing, bringing books to all parts of the community and constantly seeking to push the boundaries of what literature can be and who can read it.

For potential readers today, there is plenty of choice as to how to access books, and bookshops earn their market share by offering something very different to their competitors. As an industry, we need to find a healthy balance between those multiple channels. We need to strive to protect the physical booksellers and ensure that the playing field is made more level, to continue to grow the book market even further. But recent years have certainly proved that the British book trade has not only weathered the stormy seas of the past few decades, but it is thriving once more.

PART THREE

The Shape of Things to Come

13

The Road Ahead
for Bookselling

Maldon Books in Essex. (Author's collection)

This book's title has several meanings. The term generally refers to the length of time that a product is stocked by a shop before it becomes unsellable. This usually relates to food, but most books also have a 'shelf life', often of only a few months. A select few books are fortunate enough to last longer, but most of the books published are released, attract a bit of attention (if they are lucky), then disappear from bookshop shelves. Such is the nature of the book trade and the retail business more generally. Authors, publishers and booksellers must navigate this ongoing process, trying to create books that will hold the public's attention for more than just a moment, books that will make their mark.

If we widen that definition slightly in the context of this narrative, our bookshop in Chelmsford had a certain 'shelf life' before it was no longer needed. Bookshops and publishers come and go – such is the nature of things. In a tough, modern economic climate and up against fierce online competition, the 'shelf life' of a bookshop today can often be all too brief or, at minimum, under constant threat of being curtailed.

'Shelf Life' can also refer to a career working in books, such as the many lives we have described in this narrative. Throughout this book, I have used some of my own experience, my 'shelf life', to help tell the story of the book trade's history and to look at some of the key issues the trade has faced and is still navigating. But I'm keen to make the point that I am just one cog in this great machine that we call the book trade. This book is not just about me, but really about thousands and thousands of people like me, all equally important cogs in this machine that delivers books to readers.

To explore a few more ideas about the changes of recent years, the state of the book trade now and its future direction, I've enlisted the help of other voices within the book trade, people I have met over the past few decades. They offer disparate views on many of the issues and themes discussed in this book. Their experience also shines a light on different roles within the book trade and on the lives of some of those other 'cogs'. Each of them has their own story to tell, their own career and their own personal book-trade journey – their 'shelf life'.

With the help of these other voices, this section of the book seeks to identify the legacy of the changes that the book trade has undergone in the past four or five decades. Despite all the turmoil, the trade has undoubtedly improved because of these changes and is now a very different beast to what it was back in the early 1980s. And, arguably, it is better equipped to face the challenges of a modern global business.

The Waterstones Effect

It is hard to underestimate the long-term impact of the creation of the Waterstones chain. We have examined in depth how Tim Waterstone transformed the state of bookshops in the UK, not only by introducing larger and better-stocked stores to our high streets, but also by forcing other competitors to up their game and improve, or face closure.

Adam Hewson is company director of Hewson Books and an ex-Waterstones employee. He identifies a fascinating point about the legacy of Waterstones. Not only did they transform bookselling in Britain in the 1980s and 1990s with much better bookshops, setting the standard for all others to follow, but they trained and developed a wealth of bookselling talent, many of whom continue to contribute to the strength of today's book trade beyond Waterstones, as leading independent booksellers, publishers and, in some cases, authors.

Adam is one of those who benefitted from his Waterstones years and is now the proud owner of three independent bookshops in Kew, Sheen and Brentford. His bookselling career started in the late 1980s, working for Bilbo's, an independent bookshop in Bath, before he joined Waterstones in the 1990s. Adam speaks highly of the Waterstones shop management training schemes: 'These were done by booksellers going to other shops to train and share ideas, organised through regional managers.' It produced a cohort of experienced managers who went on to open their own bookshops later, including Patrick Neale, Andy Rossiter, Hereward Corbett, Hazel Broadfoot, Helen Stanton, Alex and Emma Milne-White and Robert Topping. These are some of the leading independent booksellers in Britain today:

We learned what books to stock to make money. We learned what books were needed to give our shops kudos, even though they may not make a lot of money. We learned about new titles, and how long to keep them. We became people who didn't just love books, but people who love selling books.

Paul Baggaley, now editor-in-chief at Bloomsbury Publishing, also started his career at Waterstones and owes a debt of gratitude to the chain. As a booklover, Paul had always known that he wanted to work in publishing so, in his last year at Oxford, he bought a copy of the *Writer's & Artist's Yearbook* and made a list of all the publishers who produced the sort of books he loved. He duly wrote to them all asking about work and several even offered him jobs, but only as unpaid internships.

As Paul was in the process of moving to London, he needed a job that paid. A friend had just started working at a new bookshop chain called Waterstones and suggested Paul apply there too. He did so, and very soon after:

> … was interviewed by Tim Waterstone and offered a job working at the High Street Kensington branch. After combining this with studying for a further degree for three years, Tim Waterstone intimated that if I worked full-time and stayed a year, I would undoubtedly be promoted to Assistant Manager, then Manager.

These were the very early days of Waterstones. The chain was opening new stores on a regular basis, and that meant lots of opportunities.

Paul told me about this exciting time at the growing chain. He worked at several branches before becoming manager of the Charing Cross Road bookshop, next door to Foyles. Robert Topping and Andy Rossiter were working for the chain at that time, both of whom went on to open their own bookshops, and Will Atkinson, who went on to be publisher at Faber and Atlantic Books.

The Charing Cross Road branch was a huge success. The service from Foyles was terrible, so a well-run and well-stocked new bookshop next door was bound to profit from this. Waterstones held events on several nights each week and was a magnet for a whole host of big-name authors. As manager, Paul had a fridge in his office that was always full of wine left over from these events, paid for by the publishers. Paul got to know most of the writers from the events, who would often pop in to share the leftover wine in the fridge. They were all useful connections for Paul's later career in publishing.

These were the glory days of Waterstones, as it expanded across the country and transformed bookselling in Britain. Paul managed two further branches for Waterstones, in Dublin and Hampstead, before being promoted to a head-office marketing role, visiting stores across the country to advise them how to compete against the threats from other expanding chains.

Next, Paul moved into publishing with a job at Harvill Press, which was newly independent after its buy-out from HarperCollins and where I first met him. Paul was publicity and marketing manager, but also responsible for developing Harvill's paperback list, which included many great authors. Haruki Murakami and Henning Mankell were just starting to break through, and the backlist included Richard Ford, James Salter and W.G. Sebald, among many other illustrious names. From his previous experience, Paul knew how well these books would do in Waterstones stores.

Unfortunately, the list was too small to be viable and Harvill Press was eventually sold to Random House. After working at Random House and then HarperCollins for a few years, Paul became publisher at Picador, where he stayed for over twelve years. More recently, Paul joined Bloomsbury as editor-in-chief, where he works today, holding one of the more prestigious jobs in publishing. The important experience gained at Waterstones has underpinned Paul's career.

Kate Gunning, now head of membership development at the BA, also started her book-trade career at Waterstones. Kate had always loved books, like so many involved in this business. She had a Saturday job in the late 1970s and early 1980s as a library assistant in Chippenham, Wiltshire, and worked there during her gap year too. Despite graduating with a good degree in Russian and French, Kate had no big career plan. She had moved to Bristol and was working at the BBC in the archives department. But, deep down, she knew she wanted to work with books.

One day, she walked into Waterstones in Bath and was bowled over by this amazing new bookshop. In that instant, she knew that she wanted to work there. By chance, an old school friend happened to be working on the till and, because of their conversation, Kate got a temp job with Waterstones that Christmas.

The experience was transformational. Kate loved working for Waterstones and eventually secured a full-time job working for the Cheltenham branch in early 1988. At the time, the deputy manager there was Martin Latham, later renowned as long-time manager of Waterstones in Canterbury (and, coincidentally, author of another book about the book trade).

Kate was in awe of Tim Waterstone's creation and remains 'grateful for and appreciative of her time working for Waterstones during the chain's heyday'. She even worked for W.H. Smith in Paris for a while (under the same management), before going on to manage the Waterstones Covent Garden and High Street Kensington shops. 'It was a brilliant time working with a unique cohort of talented booksellers, many of whom are now independent booksellers', she commented, echoing Adam Hewson.

Katharine Fry, content manager at Ingram, was for many years the head of trade buying at Blackwell's before its sale to Waterstones. She also gained important experience at Waterstones early in her career. Katharine seemed destined to work in bookselling. Her parents met each other while working in the Norrington Room at Blackwell's in Broad Street, Oxford and, growing up in Oxford, Katharine was in and out of the shop as a child. Her dad managed to get work experience jobs for her and her brother Richard, after which both were offered part-time jobs.

While at university in Hull, Katharine got a job with Waterstones and then stayed for five years. It was a culture shock moving from the academic and traditional atmosphere of Blackwell's to a general bookshop selling to a variety of customers seeking a wide range of books. But Katharine feels that she learned so much at Waterstones, despite her dad's disapproval of this big-chain bookshop, one of the key discounters following the collapse of the NBA.

Her time in Hull was a real education in all aspects of bookselling, working in goods-in, opening and closing the shop and cashing up. She enjoyed serving all types of customers, particularly those coming in at Christmas looking slightly intimidated, who were clearly not regular bookshop visitors – the book buyers who pioneers like Terry Maher were trying to attract.

So many people now working in bookselling and publishing started their careers at Waterstones and that legacy lives on through their many roles. In recent years, Waterstones has changed and adapted to the new trading environment and is a hugely important part of the British bookselling landscape, particularly after its purchases of Foyles and Blackwell's. Kate Gunning, like many others I spoke to, is 'full of praise for how James Daunt has turned the chain around and made it fit for purpose for the twenty-first century'. Likewise, Paul Baggaley talked to me about how Waterstones has done well to survive the impact of the abolition of the NBA and the subsequent growth in book sales through supermarkets and Amazon. Waterstones obviously played an important role in Paul's career and still means a great deal to him, as it does to many in publishing. He is really pleased to see Waterstones thriving and opening new stores again.

Most of those I spoke to were optimistic for the future of Waterstones. Right now, both Waterstones and the independents seem to be in a good place and the book-buying public is appreciating their offer. But at some point, Waterstones will be sold. The chain is owned by private equity company Elliott, which will eventually want a return on its investment. What happens then is difficult to guess, but currently, under Elliott's backing and the stewardship of James Daunt and Kate Skipper, it offers stability and strong leadership to the bricks-and-mortar book trade. One must hope that those foundations will be strong enough to withstand a change of ownership, to continue the growth into the next decades. But predicting too far ahead in retail is never a good idea, as this narrative has amply proved.

The Transformation of
Independent Bookshops

It is twenty-five years now since our bookshop closed, so I've had plenty of time to reflect on its short lifespan. Although we were successful and much loved by our customers during our two decades of existence, we were typical of the more traditional independent bookshops that were swept away as the bigger and better bookshop chains spread across the country.

Neil Green, now fields sales manager for Dorling Kindersley, became a Penguin hardback rep in the mid-1980s, reflecting the company's expansion after the recent purchase of lists such as Michael Joseph, Ebury and Hamish Hamilton. Some of the titles Neil remembers selling at that time were new hardback novels from best-selling author Dick Francis, the perennial *Pears Cyclopedia* and the *Fellwalking with Wainwright* TV tie-ins.

It was around this time that Neil started calling on our bookshop in Chelmsford, and his memories are testament to the fact that, in that time and place, we were a good bookshop. Neil remembers us being quite a modern shop and very on top of our stock control. We were one of his first customers to combine new title subscriptions via a rep with reordering stock from wholesalers for greater efficiency, something that more bookshops adopted in future years, and which is very much the norm today. This was a speedier method of bookselling and didn't rely on monthly stock checks from a rep to restock backlist.

We still really valued that relationship with the publishers' reps, though, and I remember us promoting many titles that Neil sold to us. We always did exceptionally well with every new Dick Francis hardback novel and would regularly take a large display bin from Neil to promote these. Both those and the Wainwright titles featured in our window displays and Neil would supply us with the necessary point-of-sale material (posters, showcards and so on).

Kieron Smith, now digital director at Blackwell's and Waterstones, was manager of the Ottakar's store in Chelmsford whose opening in 1988 played a huge part in the closure of our family bookshop. Kathleen and I had been impressed by Ottakar's stores but, nonetheless, at that time we very much viewed Ottakar's as the enemy. What I learned in subsequent years, particularly as a sales rep visiting other bookshops, was that there were many working much harder and doing a much better job than us to attract and retain customers.

Kieron had worked for several years for W.H. Smith before joining Ottakar's, so came with a wealth of experience in store management. He was also involved in setting up a website for Ottakar's at a time when we weren't even aware of such things.

We were very guilty of considering both Ottakar's and Waterstones (who opened in Chelmsford just a few months later) as faceless chains. But they were not faceless. They were staffed by enthusiastic and passionate booksellers, brimming with great ideas to bring better bookshops to our town – and we failed to recognise this. They didn't put us out of business simply by being so much bigger than us; they did it by being good at their jobs as well. Kieron was very much at the forefront of this and only as I got to know him later in his career did I appreciate what a good bookseller he has been throughout the years and what a great advocate for our trade generally.

Kieron told me recently that when he opened the Chelmsford store he 'was aware of the independent offers in the town', but:

> My focus was on making my shop a success as quickly as possible, prior to the Waterstones opening 1–2 months later. We focused on events which would engage large sections of the local community. Getting Harry Redknapp and Terry Pratchett to sign was a fantastic coup, but we also ran facepainting every Saturday, business breakfasts, political debates and even a singles night. We were the upstarts to the incumbents of Waterstones and WH Smith. Ottakar's focus on smaller regional towns, its more personal ethos and delegated buying power, made it a less corporate and more nimble entrant, certainly as far as I was concerned.

Adam Hewson, like Kieron, also played a role in the closure of our family bookshop. In the late 1990s, he was working at Waterstones as part of the market town expansion programme, targeting Ilford, Altrincham, Bury, Warrington, Chelmsford, Kettering, Chichester and Telford, among others, for new Waterstones stores. 'Waterstones in the mid to late 1990s was the bee's knees', he told me. 'We knew that as soon as we opened up, Past Times would follow, then the Body

Shop, if lucky a Thorntons. Councils all over the country wanted a Waterstones!' As part of this, he was responsible for setting up and staffing the Waterstones branch that opened in Chelmsford in 1998, just a few months after Ottakar's.

I don't bear Adam or Kieron any ill will. This was just business, and I was to learn in the years ahead how good these chain bookshops were, and how much they improved the standard of bookselling in the UK.

When we had opened our bookshop in Chelmsford in 1984, there were many other independent bookshops across Essex. Sadly, just like our shop, most of these no longer exist – collateral damage from the multiple changes of recent decades. But Red Lion Books in Colchester, just 20 miles up the road from our shop, is an exception. It was set up by Sarah and Peter Donaldson back in 1978, predating our bookshop, and still thrives today, some forty-six years later – an example of an independent bookshop that survived the upheaval. Sarah and Peter still own the shop, but these days are less involved in the day-to-day running, passing much of that responsibility into the capable hands of their manager, Jo Coldwell.

Red Lion Books quickly established specialisms in several key areas, which were to underpin their success. One of these was children's books and school supply, which has always been a large part of the shop and a particular passion of Sarah's. They also focused initially on self-sufficiency, which was very much in vogue at that time, represented most memorably by the BBC TV series *The Good Life*. But perhaps the most important specialism for Red Lion Books was science fiction and fantasy (SFF), a personal interest of Peter's. This was a huge mainstay of the shop for many years and, until recently, it accounted for almost half of all their fiction sales. The shop was a destination for SFF readers from far and wide and Red Lion imported US books that were otherwise unavailable in the UK to feed this demand. The shop also hosted signings by many big names within the field, including *Game of Thrones* author George R.R. Martin. As Peter says, 'I remember George Martin telling us that his books were just about to be filmed, so we got him just at the right time'. The shop built up a very close relationship with best-selling *Discworld* author Terry Pratchett and hosted four signings with him over the years. These would be so popular that there was always a very long queue stretching down Colchester High Street. On one occasion, Terry was at the shop for four hours and signed over 700 copies for customers.

Other events included several midnight openings to celebrate each new Harry Potter title's release. For the final book, *Harry Potter and the Deathly Hallows*, Red Lion hired out the whole of Colchester Castle and sold 300 tickets to fans, who received their book at midnight, but beforehand were organised into houses (by the Sorting Hat, of course) and joined in multiple Potter-themed activities. The shop had to draft in friends and family to help run this huge event.

These specialisms and related events not only put Red Lion firmly on the map but provided a steady income and an important edge when faced with competition. Several chain bookshops opened in Colchester in the 1980s and 1990s – first Hatchards, then Dillons and Waterstones, although today there is just the one branch of Waterstones. Unlike our bookshop's experience, Red Lion were strong enough to survive this wave of newcomers. Peter and Sarah, though, did have a tough time during the late 1990s and early 2000s following the abolition of the NBA, when first supermarkets and then Amazon discounted many bestsellers and key business was lost to them. But they came through those challenges, too.

Red Lion today believes strongly in the importance of connecting with customers. Manager Jo loves books and people and runs hugely popular book club evenings in a local restaurant, as well as hosting multiple events within the shop. Sarah is still involved in the children's and school supply part of the business, while Peter runs the company accounts and payroll. They have created and maintained a Colchester institution and remain optimistic for the immediate future, heartened by the number of new independent bookshops opening across the UK. They are a fine example of the unique character, devotion, passion and enthusiasm displayed by so many of our independent booksellers.

Red Lion surviving and continuing to thrive is one positive good-news story about independent booksellers. The recent wave of new independent bookshop openings is also something to restore faith in the bricks-and-mortar trade – especially good news after the turmoil of preceding decades. Maldon Books is situated in the small Essex town of

Maldon, on the Blackwater Estuary, just 10 miles from Chelmsford and close to where we now live. It only opened in 2019, but it has become our local bookshop. The shop is owned by Olivia Rosenthall and is a great example of the new wave of independent bookshops that have opened in recent years, many of which are run by women.

Olivia has not only always loved books but has also had a long-held ambition to be a writer. She has had several short stories published and is currently working on a novel. She tries to write at least two or three times a week but finds it difficult to carve out time alongside running her bookshop.

Olivia's bookselling journey began when she was doing an MA in creative writing at the University of Kent in Canterbury, with half of the course being taught in Paris. While there, she had an amazing opportunity to work for a month at the legendary Shakespeare & Co. bookshop on the Left Bank. For Olivia, working there was a dream job, one she describes as 'such a fantastic experience that cemented my career path'. She was incredibly impressed by the knowledgeable and professional booksellers that she was working alongside.

Duly inspired, on her return to Kent she went to work at Waterstones in Canterbury, under the management of Martin Latham. It was while she was there that she met Howard, now her husband, who was also working for Waterstones. She then worked at Harbour Books in Whitstable before moving back to Essex.

Walking around the town of Maldon one afternoon with her mother, she saw a shop available to rent and, egged on by her mother, Olivia decided to enquire about this as a possible site for her own bookshop. At that point, Olivia had no funds and very little idea how to start a new business. However, with a start-up loan, some shelving from Ikea and help from the BA, Maldon Books was astonishingly opened just six weeks later in December 2019. Obviously, with her bookselling background, Olivia wasn't clueless. In fact, her industry experience stood her in good stead, and she knew who to turn to, 'Publishers' reps, the BA and the wholesaler Gardners were all really helpful'.

From the very first day, the people of Maldon welcomed the shop with open arms. Olivia also talks about the strong community of independent shops in the town, who all work closely together, which has helped the bookshop's success. However, after a few successful months' trading, the Covid pandemic hit and Maldon Books, like all independent bookshops, was forced to close its doors. But the town rallied round and Maldon Books' website activity increased dramatically, and the shop processed hundreds of customer orders, which helped them survive. Working together through adversity strengthened the bond between the bookshop and its customers.

Now in more normal times, the shop continues to grow its events programme. Some have been held in the shop itself but, for big-name authors, Olivia has hired out the local church or space at the neighbouring Blue Boar Hotel. Olivia believes that her customers really appreciate having a physical bookshop in the town and she has 'the Amazon conversation' much less these days. There is a strong feeling of a renaissance in this appreciation of independent bookshops. Olivia told me that 'customers really value hand-selling' and the human contact that a good independent bookshop supplies.

I visited the shop on a busy afternoon and our discussion was constantly interrupted (in a good way) by customers coming to the counter either to buy books or order something, most of which would be supplied the next day, thanks to the service of the wholesaler Gardners. It was wonderful watching Olivia interact with her customers, most of whom she knew by name, and talking about books with them. She was clearly in her element. What a wonderful job and how great to watch a good bookseller in action.

In early 2024, the shop expanded by taking over the shop next door, doubling its floor space and adding a vinyl record shop run by Howard (whose dad also runs a record shop, in Kent). Having such a lively and active new bookshop on our doorstep is a great addition to the area and it is good to see them doing so well. It is wonderful to see how much the local customers want their own bookshop and are willing to support it. It is also heartening to see things coming full circle. After all the upheavals of recent decades, causing the closure of many independent bookshops including my own, to witness the opening of a new bookshop is a real pleasure.

Experiential Bookselling

One of the major factors in the recent revival and flourishing of the bookshop sector is the development of experiential bookselling. No longer is it enough for a bookshop to just be a transactional location where books are sold. To be a success today, with the multitude of other pressures vying for customers' attentions, a bookshop has to offer its customers an experience – a reason to come through its doors. There are more diversions for our leisure time than ever before and, should we choose to invest our time in reading a book, for many of us buying online or digitally is a very simple, time-saving option.

Booksellers must work harder than ever to attract customers. This includes constantly updating website and social media offerings; holding regular events – and these need to be many and varied (fiction authors talking about their latest novels, chefs demonstrating recipes from their latest cookbook, travel writers recounting fascinating escapades from their journeys); running a café – possibly serving wine in the early evenings too; running at least one book group, maybe several; hosting debates and discussions on a variety of topics; being a venue for other groups to meet (art groups, knit and natter, and so on); holding children's storytimes; bringing in children's authors to talk to young readers about their latest book and offering tailored or themed subscription services and specialist recommendations. This is all in addition to working with local schools, theatres, cinemas and other arts organisations.

If that sounds like a lot, then you are starting to understand how challenging a modern bookseller's job is and how the role demands not only a wide book knowledge but a bottomless pit of energy and enthusiasm. Underpinning this is a closer relationship between publishers and booksellers. In the past decade, publishers have woken up to the importance of bookshops and are offering them an increased number of authors for events and unique editions of some of the biggest titles for independents (and they offer different exclusives to Waterstones stores, too). There is plenty more that publishers can do to work more closely with their bookselling partners, though. In an interview with online platform The Flip, BA president and owner of

Sevenoaks Bookshop, Fleur Sinclair, said she'd 'like to see bookshops and booksellers recognized as equal partners with publishers [...] invited to the table on an equal footing'.

Before working for the BA, Kate Gunning joined Random House as independent bookshops manager. Kate's job involved building relationships with indie bookshops, working alongside the reps. She was very involved with the movement to develop the value-added side of bookselling, commissioning special editions, exclusives and signed editions for the indies. In-person events became much more important for bookshops after the advent of online bookselling and e-books, offering something against which those channels cannot compete. Publishers were forced to recognise that, if they wanted bricks-and-mortar bookshops to survive, they needed to get involved. Kate's job involved persuading publishers and authors to take indie bookshops more seriously. This has now become the norm.

Neil Green is a big fan of independent bookshops and their work ethic and has been really pleased to witness this recent revival in bricks-and-mortar bookselling, both from Waterstones and the independents. Neil believes 'the independents are once again the drivers of the industry'. While there will always be obvious big-name celebrity bestsellers (Neil has sold the likes of Jamie Oliver and Richard Osman for many years), it is the indies who have championed, hand-sold and delivered surprise bestsellers time and again. This is, at heart, where the book trade is at its best – people talking about and sharing their love of books. Publishers, authors, booksellers and readers increasingly recognise the importance of this and how you can't get this from an algorithm.

Kate Gunning is even more closely involved with indie bookshops through her current role at the BA, where she is head of membership development, one of eleven permanent staff at the BA. This role includes 'helping those who are looking to set up a bookshop as well as those who have just opened and are still in need of guidance and a helping hand'. Kate organises courses for those considering taking up bookselling as a career as well as work placements, so that they get to spend a day working in a bookshop. Kate also regularly talks to students at universities around the UK who are studying for an MA in publishing, showing them that bookselling is a profession worthy of consideration. It's important to note that the BA works on behalf of Waterstones and W.H. Smith as well as independent bookshops.

The past five years have seen a real growth in the number of new bookshops opening. However, in the past couple of years, economic conditions on our high streets have become very tough. Margins in this business are always tight and the added pressure of the rise in the cost of living has forced several bookshops to close. Kate remains sanguine about the future of physical books and bookshops, commenting, 'Authors and publishers still need good booksellers to sell and champion their books to readers; and bookshops play an invaluable role in their local communities and have shown, time and time again, how resilient and innovative they can be in the face of multiple challenges.' She very much believes in the good work undertaken by the BA, especially its role in supporting potential, new and experienced booksellers alike.

The BA remains integral to the survival and growth of the book trade and, arguably, today it is more important than ever. It also runs a Shopfloor Publishers Scheme, encouraging senior people working within publishing to spend a day working on the shopfloor of a bookshop. Meryl Halls, managing director at the BA, says, 'The feedback from booksellers and publishers who have taken part in the scheme previously has been overwhelmingly positive, with the initiative leading to greater understanding on both sides, and opportunities for collaboration.'

The experiential offer may indeed be the answer for a wide range of high-street shops, not just bookshops. Our lives are increasingly dominated by online activity, yet most of us still crave human interaction in some form. The way we use our town centres may be transformed in the future from an emphasis on shopping into destinations more focused on leisure, meeting others and attending the sorts of activities now being offered by bookshops. It certainly demands a lot more from our booksellers, but that hard work bring rewards and creates something exciting, personal and enriching for both booksellers and customers. If we want our bookshops to exist ten years from now, we need to actively support such activities.

The Changing Role of the Rep

Along with this closer relationship between bookseller and publisher, we should not forget the importance of the publishers' sales rep. Their modern role now includes a huge amount of relationship management, as they are not only salespeople but an important link between the publisher producing the book and the bookshop selling it. Many booksellers will wax lyrical about their reps and the incredibly important work they do, but this is often undervalued by publishers. Indeed, many publishers have reduced their sales forces repeatedly over past decades.

Adam Hewson makes some very good points about the importance of sales reps:

> There is passion in bookselling. A writer has a passion and puts pen to paper. That author gets an agent, or engages a publisher, moving the passion to the next person. That passion has to go via the publisher's editorial, marketing, publicity and design teams to make the book work, that team has to pass the passion to the sales team, whose reps visit bookshops to get the bookshops passionate about the author's book so that we can get the passion to the reader. At any stage, if the passion fails, the book fails. The journey is only important if the passion of the author gets to the reader. The best tool for a publisher isn't a link to Amazon, which has no passion for books at all, but to ensure that booksellers get excited about books. I believe that the sales rep is the single most important link in the chain from publisher to customer, but alas it is often the most neglected.
>
> Many publishers don't send reps out because they feel the small orders they get don't justify the costs involved. Often publishers don't understand that bookshops are also (begrudgingly) the shop windows for Amazon. If I put a book in my shop windows, it certainly increases sales for me. However, books in our windows are also seen by thousands of people who walk past the shop and go home and purchase online. Our windows can generate considerably more sales for rival online retailers than for us. For a publisher (especially a small publisher), having books in an independent shop window is gold.

Publishers with a sales team are much more likely to get that (free) window space, and the sale of a couple of copies to the bookshop may mean dozens of copies bought online.

Adam's experience comes from several decades of bookselling for some of the key players during those years. Now, his insights echo those of many independent bookshops. While we do see more publishers working more closely with bookshops, there is clearly more that can be done to connect books to readers. Indie bookshop managers like Adam are at the heart of a strong revival in their sector. Maybe publishers should consider increasing the number of reps they have out in the field, too, to underpin this strengthening of relationships between publisher and bookseller.

Bookshops Online

One other area where our bricks-and-mortar bookshops can continue to improve is through their online offer. Kieron Smith has long believed that the key to success online for bookshops is not to try to replicate what Amazon does. Bookshops have a massive advantage with their physical shops, their individuality and their human booksellers. They should play to these strengths. 'Booksellers have failed to grasp the real potential of the online revolution,' says Kieron. 'It's all to do with integration with traditional retailing skills.'

After leaving Ottakar's, Kieron honed his skills in the e-commerce sector with roles at Waterstones, The Book Depository (subsequently purchased by Amazon and now defunct) and, more recently, Blackwell's (now owned by Waterstones). In this current role, Kieron has succeeded in linking the online offer to the strengths of the physical bookshops and its booksellers.

Today, Blackwell's web offer is targeted and personalised. It feels like the online equivalent of walking into a bookshop and talking to a bookseller. The Waterstones/Blackwell's offer, which can also be seen in separate and unique iterations with Foyles and Hatchards, is a very different proposition to Amazon's. 'We manage the site end-to-end in-house, including our own development team, content, marketing, customer service and distribution', says Kieron. He believes that the secret is to have the physical and online offers working in tandem:

> Bookshops are great, they offer a tactile and social space that is perfect for serendipity. Online provides sheer scale of titles, search, etc. Bringing both together is just perfect. This allows shops to use online's wider range, offering online pick-up points in stores and more than that, the opportunity for booksellers across the estate to shout from the online rooftops about the books they love, the lists they can put together.

And he is optimistic about bookshops harnessing advances in technology to get even better at this:

> Good booksellers are representing where a great deal of retail would like to go, we're seeing more bookshops open and greater sales of physical copies – but based on a mix of broad availability, experiences in shops that really connect with customers (we run thousands of events a year), with knowledgeable people across the business who are thinking cross-channels.

Bookshop.org also operates in this space, providing a unique online offer but at the same time supporting independent bookshops. Improving the online offer does mean more hard work for our booksellers, but this is another area ripe for improvement. The more effectively a bricks-and-mortar bookshop can link its online presence to its activities in the shop itself, the more successful it will be in retaining customers and stealing custom from Amazon and other purely online competitors. As Kieron explains, the bookshop has unique advantages both in its physical space (for all those 'experiential' offerings) but also in the expertise of its booksellers. Utilising that to best effect online is a vital piece of a bookshop's offer and significant in its ability to future-proof the business.

No one doubts that the years ahead will be tough for bookshops. But the recent revival in bricks-and-mortar bookselling, both through Waterstones and the independent sector, is a hugely positive development and something to be built upon. Booksellers cannot afford to rest on their laurels. They must continue to explore more ways to attract customers and tie them in to their bookshops. Publishers, booksellers and customers all have a part to play in this and a shared responsibility for the future of our wonderful bookshops.

14

The Road Ahead
for Publishing

Hatchards bookshop in Piccadilly, London. (Alamy)

The Changing Publishing Landscape

The British publishing sector seems to be in fine fettle and perhaps enjoying a period of relative stability after the multiple upheavals of recent decades. We seem to be enjoying a golden era of great fiction, non-fiction and children's publishing. However, there are, as always, plenty of problems on the road ahead and we shall deal with some of those in this chapter.

Richard Charkin, an industry stalwart who has held key roles at Oxford University Press, Reed, Macmillan and Bloomsbury and now owns Mensch Publishing, praises the fact that publishing today has 'better systems and better management', while Francis Bennett, MD of Marble Hill Publishing, identifies the extra workload involved in being a publisher today, saying, 'Publishers used to have to sell physical books to bookshops and libraries. Now they have to sell digital and audio rights as well, they have to use social media etc. Marketing books has become a complex and very involved process.'

Hugh Andrew, MD at Birlinn, presents a positive outlook on the current state of the trade, believing that the main change over recent decades has been 'managing a vastly increasing number of channels beyond print'. Birlinn is a fine example of a small independent publisher, set up by Hugh in 1992 in his back bedroom, which has grown magnificently to be one of Scotland's leading publishers. Hugh, a former bookshop manager and sales rep, launched the list with just four titles and now produces around 165 books a year.

A sector previously consisting of small family-run or owner-led businesses is today dominated by multinational global publishing conglomerates. The Penguin Books story is the epitome of this transition, journeying from small beginnings to its current position as the world's largest general publisher. Founded by Allen Lane back in the 1930s, it was an immediate success and experienced rapid growth in the following years. Following Lane's death in 1970, however, the company was in financial trouble and was sold to the Pearson group, a newspaper company that was rapidly becoming a big player in book publishing. After a series of acquisitions, including big names such as Pitman and Longman, Pearson developed into a leading academic publisher. As that side of its business grew, it offloaded its general publishing arm (Penguin, DK, Ladybird, Michael Joseph and so on) to the Bertelsmann media group in 2013. There, Penguin joined forces with the huge American publisher Random House (already owned by Bertelsmann) to form Penguin Random House, now the biggest book publisher on this planet.

The 'Big Four' publishers (Penguin Random House, HarperCollins, Macmillan and Hachette) now form the backbone of the British book trade, accounting for nearly half of all book sales. Nielsen reported that in the first half of 2024, 47 per cent of UK book sales were from the 'Big Four'. This includes massive academic business but also general trade sales from most of the big-name authors writing today, such as Richard Osman, John Grisham, Jeffrey Archer, Sophie Kinsella, Stephen King, Jamie Oliver, Jojo Moyes and hundreds more. It's worth noting that Penguin Random House itself has the lion's share of this, accounting for just shy of 20 per cent of all book sales in the UK.

There has always been big business, but today it is so much bigger than it has ever been before. These huge corporations are an integral part of our book trade, supporting most of our biggest-selling titles, and are responsible for a very large number of the books we read. But, despite this trend towards conglomeration, the British book trade still boasts a wealth of brilliant and innovative publishers, accounting for that other 53 per cent of the business. These include hundreds of very small companies but equally the list includes much larger houses such as Profile, Oneworld, Usborne, Oxford University Press and Faber.

And then there is Bloomsbury, now so big that it rivals the 'Big Four' corporates in terms of turnover. Its success echoes Penguin's story: a small independent that has itself grown into a virtual conglomerate. Bloomsbury currently delivers over 4 per cent of UK book sales, not far behind Macmillan – and it continues to grow.

The trade needs the innovation and competition from the independents, who are more likely to take risks on new authors and offer something new. Although many of the smaller independents often live a precarious financial existence (akin to many independent bookshops), they play a vibrant role in the book business and are as necessary in their way as the big corporates to the trade's future.

But what are we likely to see in the years ahead? Will these massive publishers just grow bigger and bigger? Will we continue to see the flourishing of smaller houses? Francis Bennett, now MD and owner of Marble Hill Publishing, has worked in the book trade for over fifty years, including extensive experience at some of the bigger publishers, Collins, Hutchinson, Sphere and Thomson. After a lifetime in corporate publishing, Francis launched the tiny, independent Marble Hill in 2019. 'Why start my own publishing company after fifty years in the book trade?' he commented. 'Because it's what I know and what I love. The opportunity to publish two or three worthwhile books a year, without worrying about budgets, is too good to miss.' He believes in the importance of independent publishers as a counterweight to the big corporates. 'The problem is, the bigger the corporates become, the more they resemble distributors. Great support for major authors – but what else? Smaller publishers can support authors with valuable books but less earning power, essential for the role the publisher plays in society.'

Hugh Andrew, while admitting that the big publishers offer 'money, credibility with authors and trade, market access and supplier prices', believes that smaller independent publishers (and Birlinn is not exactly tiny these days) can compete 'by publishing quicker and smarter, and by personal service, treating authors as human beings'.

A healthy balance between corporates and smaller independent publishers seems to be essential for the trade's well-being, although Richard Charkin believes 'the balance is simply a question of economics'. That may well be true, but luckily there seems to be a constant supply of bookish types keen to set up small publishing houses, bringing new ideas into the market. As Richard went on to say, in all likelihood 'the bigger publishers will continue to grow by acquisition whereas the start-ups and smaller ones will generate true organic growth'.

There are always more people ready to set up publishing houses, just as there are always more people keen to open bookshops. Not all of these will succeed, but some will not only succeed but grow to play an important role in our publishing future. Just as the bookselling sector needs its chains as well as the independents, so the publishing sector needs both the mighty corporates and the constant flood of new houses to bring original ideas into the arena.

Bloomsbury is a fine example of a small independent that has grown to challenge the 'Big Four'. In his memoir, *My Back Pages*, Richard Charkin talks about the challenges he faced in 2007 when he joined Bloomsbury Publishing. The company was 'in a highly unusual position and facing a fascinating challenge'. *Harry Potter and the Deathly Hallows*, the final instalment in J.K. Rowling's bestselling series, was released that year and, driven by that title, Bloomsbury's income for 2007 was £150 million. The company had benefitted enormously from J.K. Rowling's astonishing success, but 'the rollercoaster ride was coming to an end'.

A significant part of Richard's role was to find new future revenue streams to replace the Harry Potter 'rollercoaster'. While the boy wizard would continue to bring in considerable revenue, it could never hope to match the sales of those initial glory years, and the company needed more growth, not less. Bloomsbury CEO Nigel Newton had already set things in motion by acquiring A&C Black and the Methuen drama list, and Richard continued this by acquiring Continuum (which was brought into the newly created Bloomsbury Academic division), along with Bristol Classical Press, military specialist Osprey, the Arden Shakespeare and Wisden.

The company also ventured into legal publishing by acquiring Hart Publishing, Tottel Publishing and the Family Law division of Jordan's. This spree of acquisitions has continued, most recently adding Head of Zeus and Rowman & Littlefield. Bloomsbury also now has a very profitable digital resources division, selling to US libraries. To top that, the Harry Potter books are still selling, there is more new material being released and there is a forthcoming TV series to keep fuelling those sales.

Bloomsbury, which was only launched in 1987, is a great example of an independent publisher that has successfully grown to compete with the corporate giants in a very short timescale (with a little help from a certain Master Potter!). Paul Baggaley's role as editor-in-chief at Bloomsbury Publishing (he joined in 2020) has also involved continuing to increase the range of what the company publishes to improve profitability.

Bloomsbury is still a specialist in serious fiction and non-fiction, on which it built its reputation, but Paul has also increased the commercial side of the general trade list. This has involved developing Raven Books, specialising in crime and thrillers. And he has achieved huge success with the romantasy list, now boasting the bestselling author in that genre, Sarah J. Maas. Her sales are so big that Paul believes 'Sarah J Maas is in danger of becoming the next J.K. Rowling'!

Huge conglomerates, large independents, medium-sized independents and tiny one-man bands are all part of the mix of the modern publishing landscape. Each has a role to play and is a necessary part of the trade. The competition between them can be fierce but is also essential. Sometimes, you need large financial muscle to succeed, and the most successful authors need the support that a large multinational company can bring. But, in other circumstances, it pays to be small and nimble, able to publish new and exciting authors in smaller print runs to dip their toes into the market.

Wider Access to Books

A big theme throughout this book has been widening the book market to reach potential readers who don't usually visit bookshops. Selling books through supermarkets, Amazon and other online retailers, and through discounters like The Book People or The Works or selling books in digital or audio format have all played a significant role in expanding readership. They have given a much wider range of readers access to books, often at more affordable prices. As a caveat, it should be said there is much more that still needs to be done to bring books to the more deprived sections of our population, particularly children.

But this hugely beneficial widening of the market has created problems for publishers. A book publisher ideally wants to sell its books through as many outlets as possible but must walk a tightrope to do so, as the big online retailers, supermarkets and discounters all demand much bigger discounts than do the bricks-and-mortar retailers. Yet, as detailed in the previous chapter, publishers are now working more closely with physical bookshops, both chains and independents, as they recognise the importance of this sector. Keeping all parts of the trade happy is a challenge to publishers.

Neil Green told me that publishers must balance what he calls the 'trinity' – that is, the independents, high-street book chains and online retailers (and other discounters). They all have a role to play in bringing books to readers and getting the right balance between them, and not being seen to offer preferential terms to any one sector is an ongoing task for publishers. Ideally, the book trade needs all of these channels working effectively but that is not always easy.

Sarah Walden has spent most of her career working for the discounters, predominantly The Book People, where she was head of buying. The Book People was set up by Ted Smart and Seni Glaister to offer cheaper books to a wider range of customers than the traditional book trade. Ted Smart was proud that The Book People had been involved with the abolition of the NBA. As Sarah told me, 'It always seemed as if they really did want to get books into the hands of people who couldn't afford full price books. They both had a passion for accessibility and reaching customers who wouldn't normally go into a Waterstones, Dillons or Borders.'

Sarah believes that the book trade is better without fixed pricing:

> I think it supports literacy. However, I totally accept that if we had a better funded free-access model, i.e. libraries that flourished and were supported, then we could better sustain a full price model in retail, but while there is nowhere for people on low incomes to go for books, it is better that the likes of The Works, The Book People and World of Books exist than not.

I put the counter-argument that, on heavily discounted books, publishers and authors earn less money but Sarah isn't worried for the publishers: 'Their models work on these sales and often they use the larger firm sale volumes to improve the cost of their trade stock.' She does see the argument about authors, 'but there is also value in getting their books out there in larger numbers and they do still receive some royalties'.

Playing devil's advocate, I suggested that offering books at low prices takes business away from bricks-and-mortar bookshops. Bookshops are surely a good thing, for promoting literature, getting children reading, and so on, so how can we square this circle and help bookshops survive while trying to widen the book market for even the most disadvantaged potential readers? Sarah believes 'indies have their own value, hand-selling and offering personal recommendation. They have very different book selections to those of discount stores. I think there is room for everyone.' This remains one of the challenges in the book trade, this ongoing desire to widen the book market while trying to ensure that bookshops can survive and thrive.

Sarah is now a publisher herself, setting up the children's house Noodle Juice in 2020. She is navigating the difficulties for publishers to make money in a competitive market:

> I'll sell my books to anyone who will buy them. Publishing non-brand non-fiction is really hard work. It doesn't matter how good the books are, if you can't afford huge marketing budgets then it's a hard road to plough. Right now, I make more money packaging books for other publishers than I do my own.

Sarah's career path presents a very enlightening look at an important sector in this business and her desire to supply books to the widest possible market is admirable. The book trade is a complex and multifaceted beast that must work through all these points of view in the years ahead to deliver the best possible outcomes for the end user – the reader.

Robert Snuggs, managing director of Bounce Sales & Marketing, has had a long career in publishing. In the late 1980s, after some years working in export sales, Robert moved over to UK sales working at Reed for Richard Charkin, who had just launched a major new paperback list, Mandarin. Robert had to set up a UK sales force to sell this list alongside other titles from the huge Reed stable. Robert describes Charkin, a key figure in the book trade at that time, as 'the most interesting boss I've ever had'. He was 'deliberately provocative but really very interesting, always fizzing with ideas'.

Robert and his team did some big business. This was the period when the existence of the NBA was under threat and Reed was one of the main publishers pushing for its abolition. Robert remembers selling more than 1,000 dumpbins for the paperback edition of Michael Jackson's *Moonwalk*. And he recalled the excitement surrounding Madonna's book *Sex*, which sold out on publication day.

Robert, like Richard Charkin, believed that the NBA was out of date and some discounting promotions would be good for the trade. He claims to have done one of the first supermarket discount deals, selling books to Tesco. However, Robert also thinks that much of the discounting went too far, particularly when discounting guaranteed bestsellers, such as the Harry Potter books and, more recently, Prince Harry's *Spare* – books that didn't need any help in selling. He does believe that the excessive heavy discounting has settled down now.

The trade is still working through these issues, on the one hand trying to offer books to readers through as many routes as possible, on the other trying to protect margins so that authors and publishers can make money from this business. It remains an area that will trouble the trade in the years ahead, but the overriding aim will be to continue selling to as many customers as possible.

Richard Charkin believes that a 'publisher's job is partly to maximise authors' income, not to try to intervene in retail competition'. Hugh Andrew puts it very simply, saying, 'If anyone will buy profitably from us we will sell to them!' There remains, however, the issue of trying not to be seen to be offering preferential treatment to one customer over another, keeping 'the trinity' in balance, as Neil Green suggests.

Multiple Channels

As we have touched upon, the modern publisher must be adept at selling its books through multiple channels. These include all the different physical retailers, online sellers and the digital market (both e-book and audio). The digital sector is currently experiencing growth through a variety of subscription models now vying for customers – the digital equivalent of Charles Mudie's circulating libraries. Everand (previously known as Scribd) is the market leader for e-book subscription libraries, but others are snapping at their heels. Audible dominates the audio subscription market, but Spotify (which has obviously been hugely successful in the digital music subscription market) and Libro are also growing. All of these channels not only offer a wide variety of ways to access books, but a dizzying array of pricing options too. Somehow, the modern publisher must get the best out of all routes to market.

It is worth taking a moment to look at the impact of self-publishing too. We have seen that this has mushroomed dramatically following the e-book revolution when Amazon waded into this market. Jonathan White, who has had a long career in publishing and started out as a bookseller for Dillons, now works as sales and marketing manager at Troubador Publishing, which delivers a wider self-publishing service than Amazon for would-be authors. It offers a variety of packages, which authors pay for to publish their books in print, e-book or audio format. The company offers design, production, distribution, marketing and publicity for the books and has succeeded in selling such titles into Waterstones, independent bookshops and other retailers, offering a bespoke service for each book.

Jonathan's career has covered many different parts of the trade, and this is another fascinating area that has grown massively since the advent of digital books. He now uses his extensive experience from many parts of the business to help authors opting to follow the self-publishing route. He 'absolutely believes that self-publishing should exist' and should be a part of the variety and mix of the modern book trade. Some successful self-published authors go on to be published by traditional publishers; others prefer to remain in control, as we have seen. The trade can embrace all options and is now much more varied in its routes to market than in any previous iterations.

Self-publishing now delivers an interesting extra route to market for authors, mainly because of digital and print-on-demand options. And this is an option where the author feels more in control of their destiny. The effects of this on the existing book trade have been very minor so far, but this could well grow in the years ahead. Although it is difficult to see the self-publishing model affecting the traditional publishers any time soon, there is no room for complacency. There has been massive growth in this sector in the past fifteen years and every sign that this will continue.

Environmental Impact

Another important issue that is repeatedly raised in discussions with publishers is the environmental impact of publishing and bookselling. Francis Bennett rightly points out:

> We cannot continue to ship vast quantities of books around the world, it's unsustainable. Printers must (a) adapt to print on demand; (b) they must form active trading partnerships with printers in many other countries (to replace shipping printed books around the world); and (c) all printers must be able to distribute on demand titles from their warehouses. A huge change which will benefit the book trade in so many ways and mean vastly reduced stock write-off against profits etc.

This makes sound sense and certainly there are those within the trade working on these issues. Ingram and many others offer print-on-demand facilities and both Francis Bennett and Richard Charkin (with Marble Hill and Mensch respectively) now publish their books using print-on-demand technology in a bid to avoid huge overstocks of titles, reduce wastage and cut costs.

Penguin Random House UK reported a 3 per cent decrease in carbon emissions in 2024 due to making 'sustainable decisions at every stage of the book design process and phasing out papers with a high-carbon footprint in favour of paper from mills that have a lower-carbon footprint'. And a 2024 survey from the Independent Publishers Guild (IPG) reported that '21% of independent publishers now have a formal sustainability policy, while 49% have some guidelines and 30% have no established guidance'.

While these numbers suggest the trade is starting to address these issues, there is clearly much more to be achieved. We need to see publishers looking into this in greater depth and finding new ways to make it work. This is an issue that we will undoubtedly hear more about in the years ahead.

In these discussions, we should recognise that digital publishing is currently much more environmentally friendly than print publishing. If we want the print medium to continue (and, for now, it would seem that we do), we must look at better ways of producing our books. Too many books (particularly illustrated titles) are produced in the Far East because it is so much cheaper, and then have to be shipped halfway round the world to be sold. This seems unsustainable in the long term. And printing large quantities books on the old 'speculative publishing' model, in the hope that they will sell, doesn't seem to chime with environmental goals.

The positive developments we have witnessed so far are dwarfed by existing practices that have excessive environmental impact, are wasteful of resources and barely cost-effective. The trade needs to take a long, hard look at itself and agree that the report card currently says quite loudly, 'Could do better'.

The Future of Diversity

One of the most fascinating transformations in the book trade over recent decades has been the changes to personnel. The trade is no longer dominated by white males, as it was four decades ago, and is now more diverse and representative of our modern society. The three most significant changes have been the increase in roles for women, a greater regional diversity in books and authors published, and more people of colour working in the industry.

At the time of writing, two of the biggest publishers in Britain, Macmillan and Bonnier, are led by women (Joanna Prior and Perminda Mann respectively) and the presidents of both the BA and PA are women (both, in fact, women of colour). Three of the largest independent publishers are also now led by women – Rebecca Gray at Profile, Mary Cannam at Faber and Nicola Usborne at Usborne. In addition, Kate Skipper is COO of Waterstones, Meryl Halls is CEO of the BA, Bridget Shine is chief executive of the IPG and Anna Ganley is chief executive of the Society of Authors. I could list many more and, in most companies, there is now a preponderance of women in senior roles. Publishing generally is now dominated by women across the board and while equal pay across the sexes is not yet the norm, it is becoming more commonplace.

In 2024, the IPG reported that 64 per cent of independent publishing staff is now female. Hachette UK has been listed as one of the *Times'* Top 50 Employers for Gender Equality 2024 for the fifth consecutive year, but it should be noted that no other publisher makes the list. So, while there has been a real sea-change in attitudes within the trade, this trend needs to go further in the years ahead. In many companies, women are still facing barriers to career progression and pay parity with male colleagues. While publishing has come a long way in recent decades, this is another area where more work is required. Publishing should be a gold standard against which other industries are measured, but the lack of pay parity between the sexes is inexcusable in the twenty-first century.

UK publishing has also been aware for centuries that it has been London-centric. Many publishers and trade organisations are now taking action to change this. Hachette has set up regional offices to encourage a wider pool of talent from across the country and most of the big publishers are involved in similar initiatives to widen their reach beyond the capital. Regional publishing is in a better place than it has ever been, which is regularly showcased by *The Bookseller* magazine and trade organisations. The personnel working in publishing are now being drawn from a much wider net across the regions, which means that the voices being published and sold in our bookshops are less London, south-east and Oxbridge-focussed and better reflect the wider diverse range of lives in the UK. In the past, those wanting to work in publishing often had to move to London to do so, but too often this is not economically viable due to high living costs and low salaries. Offering more opportunities through publishing jobs in the regions is a step forward.

The Northern Fiction Alliance is a group of small publishers aiming to increase opportunities for their lists and regional talent. It started in 2016 with just four publishers working together to promote their books at key international book fairs to 'showcase and sell the work of their exciting and diverse authors in order to help build a strong cultural identity of British writing, as well as publishing based in the North of England'. The Alliance now boasts more than twenty publishers, and its work continues to grow.

New Writing North, a charity based in Newcastle, set up to empower writing and reading in the north of England, is another exemplary example of the players working to improve our understanding and appreciation of literature from every corner of our country. It is leading a coalition, which includes publishers Hachette UK, Faber and Simon & Schuster UK among its number, to create a new Centre for Writing in Newcastle through government funding. The charity and publishers are working together to challenge and 'reposition the southern and London bias of the writing industries'.

Linked to the drive to attract more regional voices into publishing, bookselling and writing are initiatives like the Working-Class Writers Festival. This aims to encourage and 'increase the representation of working-class writers across the country, whilst also connecting audiences, authors, readers, agents and editors'. The festival's artistic director is Natasha Carthew, an award-winning working-class writer and poet and a passionate campaigner for working-class representation in the arts. The festival is supported by Arts Council England, but also Policy Press, Hachette and Penguin Random House.

It is great to see publishers involved in initiatives like this. Change is happening, but there needs to be much more like this in the years ahead to continue the trade's transformation and realignment. It can only be beneficial for the books that the industry produces.

Likewise, there is an increase in people of colour working in the bigger publishing houses, but there is plenty of room here for further improvement. The cultural mix of those working in publishing and bookselling is changing, as is that of the writers they are promoting and the subjects of the books being championed. In its first Environmental, Social, Governance (ESG) Report in 2024, Penguin Random House UK reported that, while 'it met or exceeded the UK benchmark for ethnicity, disability, sexual orientation and gender, it failed to meet the socio-economic level. Socio-economic diversity of new hires, colleagues and senior leaders is our most significant area for improvement.'

The IPG's 2024 Independent Publishing Report demonstrated that 13 per cent of independent publishing personnel are now 'non-white'. This shows improvement from the previous survey in 2022, but is still below the national average, emphasising, that as a trade, we still have more work to do. Changes are happening gradually in bookselling too, and not just through specialist black bookshops. Fleur Sinclair, owner of Sevenaoks Bookshop in Kent since 2015, is now the first black female president of the BA, representing a slowly emerging trend in general bookselling. In a recent interview with The Flip, she said, 'Just my visibility as a black woman in this position is enough to instigate some change.'

In similar fashion, Perminda Mann, CEO of Bonnier Books and president of the PA, is of Indian descent. Not only has she demonstrated that women and people of colour can achieve major roles within the industry, but she is keen to use her position to improve access to books for the disadvantaged in society. On taking up the role at the PA, she emphasised the need for government to:

> ensure that every child has the chance to access books. Give them books to read purely for pleasure. Because according to research reported by World Book Day, children who read for pleasure are more likely to succeed. I wouldn't be here today if I didn't have access to books in my local library, my parents certainly couldn't afford them.

There are many such positive news stories that we can use to demonstrate how the trade has changed, and these stories give us hope for its future direction. But everyone involved in these areas would stress that there is further work on the road ahead. All of us in bookselling, writing and publishing must redouble our efforts to ensure we maintain this momentum and improve further in the years ahead.

15

Two Big Issues for the Book Trade

The annual London Book Fair at Olympia London. (Author's collection)

In the preceding chapters, we have touched upon many of the issues currently concerning those working in bookselling and publishing. This chapter seeks to deal with two big themes that will define the future of the book trade for many years to come – the future impact of technology and the future of reading. Both issues, while very different, are fundamental to the future of this business. Many within the trade are currently working hard in these areas, but all of us (booksellers, publishers, writers and readers) need to get more involved to help define the future path of this industry.

The Future Impact of Technology

Forty years ago, when I joined the book trade at the start of the 1980s, I didn't foresee the rapid expansion of chain bookshops, the growth of the big publishing conglomerates or the abolition of the NBA but, like most of the book trade, I was even less prepared for the growth of the internet, the creation of books in digital format and the ubiquity of mobile phones and tablets, all of which would completely transform how books were created and sold. Now, a quarter of the way into this new century, we cannot hope to envisage what developments await us in the next forty years.

Technological change since the 1970s and 1980s has been massive and is ongoing, so we can only assume that more developments are to be expected in the years ahead. But it is virtually impossible to guess what these might be. There are those experimenting with further human and machine interface – implants through which we could access the internet direct into our brain and communication through the virtual world, perhaps holding office meetings in alternative reality (AR) through our avatars? Much of this sounds far-fetched now, but all these ideas are currently being advanced.

There could be many upcoming developments that will radically change how we live our lives and interact with each other. Any or all of these could have an impact on whether or how much people need books in their lives. To date, I believe that the book trade has successfully navigated the threats posed by such technological developments to help preserve and promote the print book rather than replace it. But that doesn't mean that things will remain that way.

Most worrying, perhaps, are developments that are already happening. The younger generation are now very used to discovering content digitally, through a phone or tablet. And, equally, they are used to buying online via their phones. All of this represents a danger to the future of the print book and the physical bookshop. In addition to this, there are so many other distractions for potential readers, not least social media, online gaming, online videos and reels through YouTube, TikTok and other platforms.

We must redouble efforts to get young people to engage with print books, such as recent TikTok campaigns that have indeed created a love of the book as a physical object in readers of young adult fiction, romantasy and other genre titles. There has also been a recent trend for Gen Zs to extol the virtues of an escape from the digital world. The physical book has become part of that, featured in dreamy pictures of bookshelves or booklovers reading in 'Instagrammable' locations or photographing their 'TBR' ('to-be-read') pile of books. Instagram is awash with 'book-grammers', as TikTok is with 'book-tokkers'.

Whatever we may think of the performative nature of this, there is no denying that it is getting young people reading and valuing print books, and surely that can only be a positive thing. This audience has so many alternative forms of media vying for its attention, just a scroll and a click away, so publishers, booksellers and authors need to be constantly inventive to attract and retain them as readers. The plethora of great literature and non-fiction that we are currently experiencing is certainly helping in this, but we cannot afford to be complacent.

Perhaps the most urgent technological developments to deal with right now are the possibilities and threats created by the use of artificial intelligence (AI). AI is the current buzz subject in the book trade, as it is in so many industries. Underpinning this is the question of how much we want machines taking over tasks that are currently undertaken by humans. Although this has been happening since the Industrial Revolution, there is little doubt that AI offers the ability to rapidly speed up this process and transfer an increasingly large number of tasks over to machines.

There are many in the book trade who are urging a calm appraisal of the possibilities, rather than an immediate plunge into using AI for everything. Equally, there are others proclaiming loudly about the wonderful things AI can do and how transformative it could be for the industry.

Sarah Walden is one concerned about the impact of technology:

> I think we have to be very nervous about the impact GAI/AI will have on the creative space. We all thought that AI would be about taking the grunt work out so we can work in more interesting roles, yet what seems to be happening is that it's the creative that's being replaced. As costs rise, and our desire to be sustainable drives those costs, I think we also have to reflect that volumes will contract as market pricing increases.

There are many suggestions also to use AI on the creative side of publishing – to write advertising or promotional copy, 'voice' audiobooks, edit texts, translate books from another language, even to help authors write their books or assist in their research. I don't want to rule any of these out, but these are certainly areas where I think we need to tread more cautiously. These are processes that benefit from human input and creativity, first and foremost. Most of us would be reluctant to cede these functions to a machine.

Kieron Smith remains unconvinced and unexcited about the attractions of AI. He proudly proclaims that Blackwell's online recommendations are generated by human booksellers, not algorithm or AI:

> When asking Chat-GPT to make some book recommendations recently, it made up several of the titles and authors it suggested (they literally did not exist!) I am sure this type of obvious faux pas will be overcome soon, however the access to data which it could have, is a challenge to human bookselling.

There may well be jobs gathering metadata, proofreading or editing that could be done by well-programmed AI, but we are not there yet. For most parts of the book trade, though, the human touch is surely its core attraction. 'Fundamentally, people add the creative value to the book trade,' says Kieron:

> Whether in roles as authors, publishers, editors, illustrators, translators, in production or as booksellers. To quickly dismiss all this human energy and imagination would be a mistake. As AI makes its way over the top of the hype cycle it is good to reflect on how we can celebrate our human talent even more, and make sure it is front and centre.

Discussions are underway about what AI can do for bookselling and publishing, and most would agree that handing over the 'grunt work' to machines makes sense. We just need to define what that 'grunt work' actually is. It could involve stock forecasting and estimating demand, improving sustainability, sales analysis, automated customer service, compilation of data and proofreading.

As a small publisher, Francis Bennett told me that he has 'used AI for audiobooks and it works brilliantly and saves money. I am also soon to use it to translate a book into a foreign language before I offer a few (roughly translated) chapters to a foreign publisher!' Similarly, Richard Charkin is currently using AI for marketing and metadata work, but also thinks in the future that it can be used for 'voicing' audiobooks and translations. While this is all cost-cutting and time-saving, particularly for smaller publishers, it is also taking the jobs of those currently involved in these roles. Such is always the way with new technological advancements, but these are still important considerations.

Nadim Sadek, founder and CEO at Shimmer AI, believes that AI can be used to revolutionise the way books are marketed to readers, drilling down to find the exact right book for each potential customer, especially the marketing of deep backlist titles. Using AI creates the capacity to do this in much greater depth. Shimmer AI's website says:

> Authors often feel frustrated with the limited promotion of their books by traditional publishers. Marketing departments struggle to effectively connect with readers due to limited resources and the strain of managing exasperated authors. On the other hand, readers yearn

for a more effective way to find books that suit their tastes. There is a vast untapped potential for matching willing audiences with suitable books, written by talented authors who seek greater reach.

There are authors experimenting with writing in co-operation with AI, who see interesting possibilities from a human–machine collaboration. There are multiple opportunities in all of this, but also inherent danger, too. When interviewed by *The Guardian*, author Bernadine Evaristo said that AI is 'an impressive beast, but one that needs to be tamed'. She argues for human creativity, 'Writers like stretching our imaginations, coming up with ideas … Most of us write our books ourselves and while we are influenced by other writers, we're not a chatbot that has been trained on hundreds of thousands of novels for the sole purpose of mimicking human creativity.'

As an industry, we need to keep talking about what we want to use technology for, where our red lines are and what strictures we need to put in place if so required. If we are not careful, the trade could be taken over by new practices before we are aware of what is happening. Already, there are thousands of AI-created books available online, including fake and cheaper versions of books by human authors, most of zero value or interest. But machines learn and they will get better at this unless we put regulations and restrictions in place.

Perhaps the biggest danger at the moment is the threat to copyright. ChatGPT and other large language models were developed using the texts of thousands of existing books, all without the permission of authors, agents or publishers. This is a fundamental problem for the trade going forward.

Let us consider as a hypothetical example that ChatGPT has downloaded all the crime novels of Richard Osman in the Thursday Murder Club series. Richard Osman may only write one title in this series per year, or indeed may not write any more at all. A fan of the series could feasibly ask ChatGPT to create a new novel in this series. Based on the other novels that it has ingested and countless other similar books, characters and plots, ChatGPT can then have a pretty good stab at creating a new book in the series. Richard Osman, his agent and his publisher receive no compensation for this new work.

This could happen to any famous writer – John Grisham, Margaret Atwood, Jeffrey Archer, Maggie O'Farrell or whoever. The possibility is quite alarming. The use of existing authors' works to create 'new' works is a huge threat to the existing status quo and the copyright laws that underpin it. As Caroline Cummins from the PA recently said in an article in *The Bookseller*, 'AI growth cannot come at the expense of intellectual property rights. That puts the creative industries, and the value of human creativity itself, at risk.'

The argument around copyright and the correct remuneration to publishers and authors goes back centuries. Dickens famously upset audiences on his first American trip in the nineteenth century by bemoaning the fact that he earned nothing from US sales of his books, whereas the locals believed in the free market and their 'right' to sell his books without his (or his publisher's) agreement. There are better laws in place today, but the huge multinational online and digital marketplace is difficult to police.

Anna Ganley, chief executive of the Society of Authors, reported in May 2024:

> 97% of voting Society of Authors' members collectively asserted that they do not consent to their works being used to develop generative artificial intelligence (GAI) systems without their permission, credit, or remuneration. It is a foundational principle of copyright law that before using a copyright-protected work, the user should agree terms with the rightsholder.

The Society of Authors is working together with the Authors' Licensing and Collecting Society (ALCS) in action against this.

Barbara Hayes, chief executive of ALCS, is trying to navigate through this technological minefield. 'At ALCS, we believe writers should have a choice regarding the use of their works', she said in a recent statement. 'The development of generative artificial intelligence (AI) technologies envisages the use of writers' works and so ALCS believes that writers should exercise choice around permissions and compensation for such uses.' The ALCS is working on a collective agreement of authors, agents and publishers to create a new industry standard with new rules for these serious developments.

At the time of this book going to press, several publishers were in the process of agreeing deals with tech companies to licence limited use of their authors' work for training AI models. Both publisher and author would be remunerated for this and authors could choose to be part of such an arrangement or not. This is a step forward but, as Philip Jones, editor of *The Bookseller*, commented, 'As to what happens when the (AI) brain is trained, that's a question we all must face together.' We are only at the start of this difficult discussion.

These are huge issues facing the book trade, which could alter its very foundations once more. The IPG's 2024 Report found that only 18 per cent of independent publishers think they are ready for the challenges and opportunities that AI brings. The trade is in danger of burying its head in the sand and hoping the storm will blow over. It won't. There will need to be many more seminars and many more discussions on this subject to find a way forward, and then joint action. This cannot be brushed under the carpet.

Juxtaposed to all the future challenges that technology will pose, we should remember just how enduring print books and physical bookshops have been down the centuries. We are social beings and crave connection, so it seems unlikely that we will turn our backs on human authors, the serendipitous joy of visits to bookshops, author events, book festivals and book clubs and choose the soulless digital world instead. We should remember how customers feel that a bookshop is 'theirs' as much as it belongs to its owners, that in many ways it is a public and community space. And we should remember that print books and physical bookshops supply a connection that the digital, machine and online worlds cannot compete with. However, the trade needs to be constantly working to protect these advantages to ensure that we can enjoy all of this into the future.

The Future of Reading

In its latest annual survey in 2024, the National Literacy Trust reported 'that just one in three children and young people aged 8 to 18 said they enjoyed reading in their free time'. This is the lowest level since they started asking this question in 2005. Perhaps more worryingly, reading for enjoyment was weakest for children from disadvantaged backgrounds. Francesca Simon, author of the Horrid Henry books and an ambassador for the National Literacy Trust, is one of many raising the alarm, 'We cannot let a generation of children lose out on the benefits that reading can bring: inspiring the imagination, the comfort and escape of another world, and the very real and impactful literacy skills it supports.' Another report from the Reading Agency in July 2024 reported that half of UK adults don't regularly read and almost one in four young people aged 16 to 24 say they've never been readers.

In a recent article for the *New Statesman*, bestselling children's author Katharine Rundell wrote about the importance of getting children reading and giving children access to books:

> The National Literacy Trust estimates that nearly a million children in the UK do not own a book of their own. Between 2010 and 2020, almost 800 libraries were closed [...] the UK's spending on libraries is far lower than most European countries', and steadily dropping: from £18 per capita annually in 2010 down to around £12 now, compared to around £25 per capita in Europe. Finland spends £50. We need children to have access to a cornucopia of books, a huge variety.

In our modern twenty-first-century society, there are more reasons than ever not to pick up a book. Multiple radio shows, podcasts, hundreds of TV channels, online streaming services, cinema, the infinite internet, social media sites, gaming – the list goes on. If the book trade is to have a future, it needs readers first and foremost. Books must continue to be relevant in our modern world.

The book business has never simply been about making money. Most of those involved in bookselling and publishing – from Caxton, Lackington, Mudie, W.H. Smith, John Murray, Allen Lane and Tim Waterstone, right through to booksellers and publishers today – have been united in their goal, first and foremost, to altruistically share their love of books with others. Most of us in the book trade work in this business because we are passionate about books and understand the good that they can deliver to readers and the knock-on effects for society as a whole.

Not only are basic reading skills essential for success at work and in society generally, but reading books enlarges our knowledge, increases our understanding, makes us more empathetic. Books underpin a more cohesive society, make us better human beings – and better workers. Books help us experience a multitude of emotions. Their stories and learning underpin our lives and culture and make us more rounded and interesting people.

Books are essential to the well-being of our society. And, because we know all this, it is our duty – not just those of us working in the book trade, but all of us who love books – to ensure that books are available to the widest cross-section of society. Books are for everyone and this needs to begin at birth. There are many threats to the future of the book, but the biggest threat will be a reduction in readers.

Two things that urgently need to be addressed by central government and local councils are, first, access to books for babies and pre-school children, no matter their background, and second, better access to books in school. We need to revive government schemes to get free books into the hands of new parents to encourage them to read to their children. In 2024, the National Literacy Trust announced a new three-year strategy to promote early years literacy. It will work with parents, schools, teachers and librarians to ensure that literacy is a priority. Charities such as the Book Trust are also constantly working to get more children reading, with a particular emphasis on low-income households.

And, as part of these efforts, we need to improve school library provision. During the past fifteen years, under the banner of 'austerity', the UK government has overseen a shocking decline in public libraries and school libraries. With ongoing cuts to local council budgets, there is concern about further closures. Over 800 public libraries have closed since 2010 and there has been a 30 per cent decline in library spend during that period. At the time of writing, 14 per cent of primary schools do not have a dedicated library area.

Working to rectify this, the Great School Libraries campaign is a joint initiative of the School Library Association, the Chartered Institute of Library & Information Professionals (CILIP) and the CILIP School Libraries Group. Its aim is 'to bring back libraries and access to librarians in every school in the UK'. Its guiding principle is 'a firm belief that every child deserves a great school library'. It is supported by children's authors such as Julia Donaldson, who describes school libraries as 'beneficial to education and to society as a whole, narrowing the gap in aspiration and ability in children'. Other writers campaigning on this issue and arguing for it to be a legal requirement that schools have libraries include Philip Pullman and Michael Morpurgo.

The PA is also supporting this campaign. On becoming PA president in 2024, Bonnier CEO Perminda Mann called on governments to back libraries:

> We should have one in every school. We should have one in every town. We must reverse budget cuts that have paralysed public libraries across the nation. It's high time to recognise their value. Restore them to their rightful place at the beating heart of communities up and down the country. These should be shared assets where anybody can reach for the shelves and alter the course of their lives forever.

Penguin Random House is playing a major role in this campaign, too. Through its World of Stories programme, it has supplied hundreds of schools with 400 Puffin Books and 100 books from other publishers completely free of charge to improve or instigate their library provision. This is a brilliant and welcome move from the UK's leading publisher and demonstrates the altruistic motives behind many participants in this industry. A cynic might suggest that, by promoting a love of books in the early years, this also secures the book buyers of the future, but the book trade is a business – it needs to make money to survive, but if, in doing so, it is also delivering something positive to society, then surely that is no bad thing.

Alongside these charities and campaigning organisations, we should remind ourselves of the brilliant work that booksellers do for schools. Most independent bookshops are involved in some measure of school supply and, for some, it is a huge part of their business. They not only supply books to schools but offer recommendations and take authors into schools to talk to children, bringing authors face to face with potential readers, whatever their background.

And many independents run storytimes, children's book clubs and other events for youngsters to ensure they have access to books. The best bookshops work closely with children's book publishers to ensure that books are available to all and that authors can engage with young readers in shops or in schools. Most independent bookshops are very embedded in their local community, providing a unique resource for parents and children.

Waterstones also plays a big role in encouraging children's reading. It sponsors the Waterstones Children's Laureate programme in association with the Book Trust, through which a key children's author (in the role for two years) acts as an ambassador for books, promoting their value to educators and to government, as well as through the media. Accepting the role in 2024, Frank Cottrell Boyce said, 'I write children's books because I think they help build the apparatus of happiness inside us. I'm going to do everything in my power to get reading as a right for all into the national conversation.' Waterstones also champions the best in new children's writing with the Waterstones Children's Book Prize, as well as hosting regular free online school author events that reach thousands of pupils.

This is a hugely important issue that needs ongoing work from a wide range of stakeholders within the book trade, alongside those working in education and in government. Encouraging new readers, giving everyone access to books and promoting the good that books can deliver are all vital to the future of this industry and the future existence of books. This is more important than any other issue facing the book trade today.

Epilogue

The Last Word

A busy day at Robbs Bookshop, with Peter Robb, the author's father.

The bookselling and publishing landscape has witnessed continuous change over the centuries. From scrolls to manuscripts and print books, right through to today's e-book and audio versions, the format of the book itself has undergone successive changes. The book trade as we know it grew steadily from the fifteenth century when William Caxton introduced the printing press into Britain. From that point, a nascent book industry developed as others set up their own presses and started printing books, widening the range of books on offer. From the eighteenth century, the country experienced both a huge expansion in printed publications and a growth in bookshops to sell them.

Bookshop growth stalled momentarily in the nineteenth century, as readers obtained their books from Mudie's and other circulating libraries. However, the twentieth century saw the biggest growth yet, with Allen Lane's paperback revolution making books more easily affordable to all classes. The bookshop sector expanded on the back of this, and bestselling books regularly sold in excess of a million copies.

From the earliest scrolls to the present day has been a long and fascinating journey, driven by those passionate to share their love of books with others. Having weathered the storms of the past four or five decades, there is much to celebrate in today's book trade. Despite bigger and bigger publishing conglomerates, we are also in the midst of a hugely encouraging revival of the independent sector. Across both big and small companies, there has been a sea-change in personnel and the industry is now better represented by women, people of colour and people from all regions of the UK. This is being reflected in the books being published and the authorial voices we are now reading, as well as in the personnel of our bookshops. Much progress has been made but, in all these areas, there is more work to do.

We are also seeing signs of rebirth with more new bookshops opening. The UK's bookshops face multiple challenges, but across Waterstones, W.H. Smith and the independents, there is a general feeling that, having survived the many changes that the trade has undergone, they are now flourishing once more.

The ending of the Net Book Agreement has confused the public's perception of book pricing, and this continues to be an issue. Undoubtedly, the availability of cheaper books from online retailers, supermarkets and other discounters has widened the book market and made it possible for more would-be readers to afford books. But this has made it difficult for bricks-and-mortar bookshops to compete in selling the biggest-selling titles – book sales that should underpin their businesses. The trade has not yet found a happy medium to satisfy all sides and needs to keep looking at ideas to solve this conundrum.

The explosion of digital versions of books (e-book and audio) and the accompanying growth in self-publishing has transformed how readers engage with books. This wide variety of media used to access books has also contributed to growth in the book market and made books available to a much larger audience.

But what about the future? Will this cautious optimism prevail? Or should we be wary of reading too much into this short period of rude health? Perhaps more importantly, what can we do, both as a trade and more widely as a nation, to protect the future of books and bookshops against threats to their existence in the coming decades. What does the future hold for the future of reading, the print book and physical book-shops? And what impact will new developments in technology have on the long-term future of bookselling and publishing?

I don't believe that print books or physical bookshops are in danger of disappearing in the next five to ten years. But, in the current climate, margins to make money from publishing and selling books are incredibly tight. If this persists, many booksellers could go out of business in the years ahead and, likewise, many publishers could fold or be sold. And we cannot predict what other technological developments the trade may have to confront further down the road.

So, how can we better protect the future of booksellers and publishers?

Fundamental to all of this is giving more children access to books by supporting the campaign for better library provision in our schools and towns however we can. We need to get books to all babies and young children – particularly those families who are struggling financially or where parents don't read themselves – and foster a love of reading.

I believe that government should also support new independent bookshops with a start-up grant and some form of ongoing funding for the first three to five years. All bookshops should be supported with a reduction in business rates in recognition of their importance to local communities and their educational value. I have discussed how other European countries, such as France and Germany, support their bookshops better and we need to petition for something similar in the UK.

The BA does campaign on these issues, but there needs to be wider trade recognition of the importance of this, not only to the book trade, but also for our country's cultural health. In a recent interview with *The Bookseller*, author Isabella Hamad argued that 'the UK should follow the example of other European countries that have a stronger governmental funding model for festivals and cultural infrastructure, instead of forcing such a heavy reliance on corporate sponsorship'. Alongside this, and I'm aware this is a big issue, online retailers should be taxed equitably with their bricks-and-mortar counterparts to provide a more level playing field.

I would also suggest that the UK needs to reintroduce some form of price control, perhaps a maximum discount off the RRP of 10 per cent? Or perhaps we should investigate bringing in something like the US Robinson-Patman Act, which dictates that a publisher has to offer the same terms to all customers, thereby not disadvantaging the independent bookshop against the chain bookshop or the likes of Amazon.

In abolishing the NBA, the UK book trade did away with any controls and there remains an element of chaos in the market. I would argue that this needs some modicum of regulation. This seems unlikely at the moment, and I'm not sure there is much appetite for it, but it would provide a more level playing field to enable physical bookshops to compete fairly with their online rivals and supermarkets. In tandem with this, perhaps publishers and booksellers together could investigate ways to keep RRPs as low as possible as part of making books accessible to all, one of the main themes running through this book.

The trade must persist in its efforts to make publishing and bookselling better reflect modern Britain, with all its diversity, differing perspectives and multiple issues. This can be demonstrated by the personnel involved in the trade but also in the priorities exhibited by the companies working within it. Authors, publishers, booksellers, librarians, sales reps, editors – all have a duty to produce and sell books that reflect all parts of the community. Children should be able to find characters that they identify with in books, as well as exploring characters and worlds that they don't have access to.

We have witnessed massive progress in the last ten years with publishers and authors working much more closely with physical bookshops, both the chains and the independents. This has been evidenced by the development in experiential bookselling, providing more incentive for customers to visit the physical bookshops to buy a unique edition or hear an author talk, come to a supper club, wine-tasting, political debate or book club. As a trade, we must keep looking for new ideas for how we can use bookshops to connect with readers. Further inventive utilisation of social media platforms, such as TikTok, to promote authors, books and bookshops needs to be pursued to reach new readers.

And, as readers, if we value the print book and physical bookshops, we need to get involved in helping preserve their future. This means pausing before we press the 'Buy' button from an online retailer and reminding ourselves how much better our experience will be if we visit our local bookshop to obtain the required book. It will require more effort, and it might cost a little bit more, but our life will be improved by that visit and by talking to a bookseller. We will enjoy the book all the more for buying it from a real person. And we need to make more effort to support the wonderful events hosted by our bookshops. Not only will this support that shop, but it will enrich our lives too.

I have confidence that the book trade is now a much better, more diverse and more mature entity than it was forty years ago. Its current cohort of publishers, writers, booksellers and trade organisations are much better placed and much better informed than their predecessors to deal with the issues facing them. We cannot deny that the book trade faces many ongoing issues, but today's trade has learned lessons from the upheavals of the recent past and seems better prepared to cope with the challenges on the road ahead.

It is worth taking a step back from the rollercoaster of new technologies and new developments to focus on the importance of the book itself, the foundation of the entire book trade. In my own case, falling in love with books through the first book I ever owned, *Ginger's Adventures*, then through Enid Blyton, Narnia and so many other wonderful childhood gems, has not only led to a lifelong love of books, but to a life working with books and promoting their joys to others. Every booklover has their own reading pathway full of memorable books – those read to us by parents or recommended by friends, or ones we discovered in bookshops.

In her memoir *A Bite of the Apple*, Lennie Goodings, chair of Virago Books, says:

> What I love about publishing is that no matter how sophisticated, how technological, how digital our industry becomes, one fact remains: publishing still comes down to one person telling another, you must read this book. Publishing is driven by that passion, conviction and excitement.

We are so lucky to have access to so many brilliant books to shout about, both the classics of previous eras and the wonderful new writing of today – books from across the globe and from multiple cultures. We should celebrate this and, as booksellers, publishers and readers have done for generations, continue our efforts to introduce books to the widest possible audience so that everyone can gain from the benefits that books deliver.

Useful Information

To Find Your Local Independent Bookshop

It is easy these days to find details for the many current bookshops listed in this book from Google, but you can search via the BA too. I would recommend following relevant local bookshops on social media, with Instagram probably being the favoured platform, to keep updated on events and new book releases. I would also recommend referring to these sources whenever you are travelling within the UK so you can discover bookshops across the regions: www.booksellers.org.uk/bookshopsearch.

Waterstones

You can easily find your local branch of Waterstones, Blackwells, Foyles or Hatchards through their websites and social media. All will supply plentiful information on forthcoming books and you can sign up for newsletters:

www.waterstones.com
blackwells.co.uk/bookshop/home
www.foyles.co.uk
www.hatchards.co.uk

NB When first launched by Tim Waterstone, 'Waterstone's' was spelt with an apostrophe before the 's'. However, since James Daunt took over management of the chain, the apostrophe was dropped. Throughout this narrative we have used the current 'Waterstones' styling.

Bookshop.org

Bookshop.org is an online bookshop with a mission to financially support local, independent bookshops: uk.bookshop.org

Book Prizes

The Booker Prize – thebookerprizes.com
The Women's Prize – womensprize.com
Nero Book Awards – nerobookawards.com

Charities and Campaigning Groups

The Book Trust – www.booktrust.org.uk
The Literacy Trust – literacytrust.org.uk
Great School Libraries – www.greatschoollibraries.org.uk
World of Stories – www.worldofstories.co.uk

Acknowledgements

The writing of this book started very much as a solo endeavour but, at a certain point, I of course needed the involvement of others to progress the project. I am incredibly grateful to Andrew Franklin at Profile, Paul Baggaley at Bloomsbury and Stephanie Duncan at Penguin Random House, who were the first readers a couple of years ago of a vastly different manuscript. Their comments helped steer me in a new direction and significantly improve the book's structure. Likewise, the agent Andrew Lownie gave me very good advice about how to pitch the book to agents and publishers.

Tom Cull becoming my agent was a game-changer. I will be eternally grateful to Tom for taking me on and then helping to shape the manuscript and the proposal to secure a publisher.

I am also indebted to Claire Hartley at The History Press for bidding to buy the book. This was another significant leap forward and I am so grateful to Claire for putting her faith in me and this book. To add to that, for her work on the manuscript, her incredibly insightful suggestions and the general overseeing of this book to publication, I cannot thank her enough. I would also like to thank everyone else at The History Press for their support and hard work to get this book from idea to physical reality, in particular Cynthia Hamilton, Laura Hunt, Rebecca Newton and Ian Pearson. Working in the industry as I do, I am very aware how important the whole team is to a book's publication.

I also want to thank the team of friends, colleagues and acquaintances within the trade who have read all or part of the manuscript at various stages and offered advice. These include Philip Downer, Maria Vassilopoulos, Alan Staton, James Raven, Suzanne Collier, Juliet Mabey, Kate Skipper, Eva Von Reuss and Greg Evaristo. Several of these also took the time to speak by phone or Zoom and, not only gave me advice, but also recounted anecdotes and information that supplied more crucial background for the text. I would also like to thank the many others who have read the text, offered advice and supplied endorsements, including Adam Smyth, Simon Heffer, James Daunt, Sarah Harkness, D.J. Taylor and Martin Latham.

Huge thanks must go to those who were involved in the third section of the book, who not only gave up their time to talk to me but also read the manuscript and offered extensive feedback. This group gave me so much of their time very willingly and enthusiastically and really helped me to mould the book into the form you are holding in your hands. The book industry is full of wonderful people, but I cannot get over how generous and helpful this group have been. So, thank you to Adam Hewson, Kate Gunning, Paul Baggaley, Richard Charkin, Francis Bennett, Sarah Walden, Jonathan White, Kieron Smith, Peter and Sarah Donaldson, Robert Snuggs, Olivia Rosenthall, Neil Green, Hugh Andrew and Katharine Fry.

I have dedicated this book to my mum and dad, Joyce and Peter Robb, for introducing me to books in the first place and filling my childhood with stories, but I am also very grateful that they funded the setting up of our family bookshop that began my book-trade journey. Throughout that journey, and throughout the writing of this book, my wife Kathleen has been a huge support, reader of the text and positive critic, helping me get to the finishing line and working with me to complete and then promote this book. Well over thirty years ago, I told her that I was writing a book, but that one (and a few others) never quite came to fruition. Now, I have finally repaid her faith in me! And I am very grateful for the support of our children, Emily and Edward, who also read parts of the manuscript along the way and gave me very positive encouragement. Writing a book, it turns out, is really *not* a solo endeavour!

Bibliography

This book has grown over several years from an initial idea into something much wider than its original intention and much of this has come from reading. Most of the background reading for this book has been a labour of love, leading me down numerous rabbit holes, as I delved ever deeper into book-trade history. This is a huge subject – there is always so much more I could learn – and inevitably this book can only present a slice of the whole subject. But the books I've read have not only furnished me with factual content for this book, but have also helped form my opinions and, in some cases, change them.

I have read numerous general histories of Britain and England that have supplied background (Ackroyd and Tombs for general history, Kynaston and Sandbrook more recent) as well as multiple biographies of key authors, most of which have plentiful information about publishing. I have used more specific book-trade histories (especially those from Raven and Thompson), which have drilled down into the minutiae of the industry. A range of biographies and autobiographies of those involved in bookselling and publishing over the years have helped supply a much wider perspective on the events covered in this book and the issues discussed.

But there are so many other sources I have drawn upon as well, not least the weekly issues and archives of *The Bookseller* magazine (which I have been reading for forty years) and other trade newsletters, as well as reports and articles from the BA and PA, among others. I have also referred to a multitude of relevant articles from the archives of *The Guardian*, *Independent* and *New Statesman*. And I have found information from radio programmes, podcasts (of which there are now several focussing on the book trade), publisher and bookseller websites, social media and YouTube videos.

To add to all this, I have used a lot of information from my personal experience of working in this business for forty years and that of the many others I have spoken to and discussed issues with. It has been very informative to weigh other views against mine, either from these discussions or from my reading.

Ackroyd, Peter, *Dickens* (London: Sinclair-Stevenson, 1990).

Ackroyd, Peter, *Chaucer: Brief Lives* (London: Chatto & Windus, 2004).

Ackroyd, Peter, *The History of England Volume I: Foundation* (London: Macmillan, 2011).

Ackroyd, Peter, *The History of England Volume III: Civil War* (London: Macmillan, 2014).

Ackroyd, Peter, *The History of England Volume IV: Revolution* (London: Macmillan, 2016).

Ackroyd, Peter, *The History of England Volume V: Dominion* (London: Macmillan, 2018).

Athill, Diana, *Stet: A Memoir* (London: Granta Books, 2000).

Baines, Phil, *Penguin by Design: A Cover Story* (London: Allen Lane, 2005).

Baines, Phil, *Puffin by Design: 70 Years of Imagination 1940–2010* (London: Allen Lane, 2010).

Barber, Michael, *Anthony Powell: A Life* (London: Duckworth Overlook, 2004).

Barker, Juliet, *The Brontës: Wild Genius on the Moors: The Story of a Literary Family* (New York: Pegasus Books, 2010).

Blake, N.F., *Caxton: England's First Publisher* (London: Osprey, 1976).

Blythell, Shaun, *The Diary of a Bookseller* (London: Profile Books, 2017).

Bounford, Julie E., *This Book is About Heffers: The Bookshop That is Known All Over the World* (Cambridge: GottaHaveBooks, 2016).

Bowen, Elizabeth, *Mulberry Tree & Other Writings* (London: Virago Press, 1986).

Bradley, Sue (ed.), *The British Book Trade: An Oral History* (London: British Library, 2008).

Briggs, Asa, *A History of Longmans and Their Books 1724–1990* (London: British Library, 2008).

Buford, Bill (ed.), *Granta 7: Best of Young British Novelists* (London: Penguin, 1983).

Butler, Dorothy, *Babies Need Books* (London: The Bodley Head, 1980).

Buzbee, Lewis, *The Yellow-Lighted Bookshop: A Memoir, A History* (Minnesota: Graywolf Press, 2006).

Caine, Danny, *How to Resist Amazon and Why* (Portland: Microcosm Publishing, 2019).

Carpenter, Humphrey, *The Seven Lives of John Murray: The Story of a Publishing Dynasty* (London: John Murray, 2008).

Charkin, Richard, & Tom Campbell, *His Back Pages: An Undeniably Personal History of Publishing 1972–2022* (London: Marble Hill Publishers, 2023).

Cholmeley, Jane, *A Bookshop of One's Own: How a Group of Women Set Out to Change the World* (London: Mudlark, 2024).

Corfield, Penelope J., *The Georgians: The Deeds & Misdeeds of 18th Century Britain* (London: Yale, 2022).

Crick, Bernard, *George Orwell: A Life* (London: Secker & Warburg, 1980).

Curwen, Henry, *A History of Booksellers: The Old and the New* (London: Cambridge University Press, 1874[?]).

Faber, Toby, *Faber & Faber: The Untold Story* (London: Faber, 2019).

Fitzgerald, Penelope, *The Bookshop* (London: Gerald Duckworth, 1978).

Fowles, John, *The Journals: Volume 1* (London: Cape, 2003).

Fowles, John, *The Journals: Volume 2* (London: Cape, 2006).

Gissing, George, *New Grub Street* (Oxford: Oxford University Press, 1993).

Gissing, George, *The Odd Women* (Oxford: Oxford University Press, 2000).

Goodings, Lennie, *A Bite of the Apple: A Life with Books, Writers and Virago* (Oxford: Oxford University Press, 2020).

Goring, Paul, *Eighteenth Century Literature and Culture* (London: Continuum, 2008).

Griest, Guinevere L., *Mudie's Circulating Library & The Victorian Novel* (Newton Abbot: David & Charles, 1970).

Grove, Valerie, *Kaye Webb: So Much to Tell* (London: Viking, 2010).

Gyasi, Yaa, *Transcendent Kingdom* (New York: Alfred A. Knopf, 2020).

Halperin, John, *Gissing: A Life in Books* (Oxford: Oxford University Press, 1982).

Hanff, Helene, *84 Charing Cross Road* (London: Andre Deutsch, 1971).

Harding, Thomas, *The Maverick: George Weidenfeld and the Golden Age of Publishing* (London: Weidenfeld & Nicolson, 2023).

Harkness, Sarah, *Literature for the People: How the Pioneering Macmillan Brothers Built a Publishing Powerhouse* (London: Macmillan, 2024).

Harman, Claire, *Charlotte Brontë: A Life* (London: Viking, 2015).

Hay, Daisy, *Dinner with Joseph Johnson: Books & Friendship in a Revolutionary Age* (London: Chatto & Windus, 2022).

Jarvis, Stephen, *Death and Mr Pickwick* (London: Jonathan Cape, 2014).

Keay, Anna, *The Restless Republic: Britain Without a Crown* (London: William Collins, 2022).

Kropp, Paul, & Wendy Cooling, *The Reading Solution: Making Your Child a Reader for Life* (Canada: Random House, 1993).

Kynaston, David, *Austerity Britain 1945–51* (London: Bloomsbury, 2007).

Kynaston, David, *Family Britain 1951–57* (London: Bloomsbury, 2009).

Kynaston, David, *Modernity Britain Book One: Opening the Box 1957–59* (London: Bloomsbury, 2013).

Kynaston, David, *Modernity Britain Book Two: A Shake of the Dice 1959–62* (London: Bloomsbury, 2014).

Kynaston, David, *On the Cusp: Days of '62* (London: Bloomsbury, 2021).

Kynaston, David, *A Northern Wind: Britain 1962–65* (London: Bloomsbury, 2023).

Lackington, James, *Confessions of James Lackington* (London [?]).

Lackington, James, *Memoirs of the First Forty-Five Years of the Life of James Lackington* (London: 1794[?]).

Latham, Martin, *The Bookseller's Tale* (London: Particular Books, 2020).

Lewis, Jeremy, *Penguin Special: The Life and Times of Allen Lane* (London: Viking, 2005).

Loxton, Alice, *Uproar! Satire, Scandal and Printmakers in Georgian London* (London: Icon Books, 2023).

McKitterick, David, *Print, Manuscript and the Search for Order 1450–1830* (Cambridge: Cambrige University Press, 2003).

MacMillan, Frederick, *The Net Book Agreement 1899 and the Book War 1906–1908* (Glasgow: Robert Maclehose & Co. Ltd, 1924).

Maher, Terry, *Against His Better Judgement: Adventures in the City and in the Book Trade* (London: Sinclair-Stevenson, 1994).

Mangan, Lucy, *Bookworm: A Memoir of Childhood Reading* (London: Square Peg, 2018).

Manguel, Alberto, *A History of Reading* (London: HarperCollins, 1996).

Marston, Edward, *Sketches of Booksellers of Other Days* (New York: Charles Scribner's Sons, 1901).

Maschler, Tom, *Publisher* (London: Picador, 2005).

Moran, James, *Wynkyn de Worde: Father of Fleet Street* (London: Wynkyn de Worde Society, 1960).

Nokes, David, *Jane Austen* (London: Fourth Estate, 1997).

Nokes, David, *Samuel Johnson: A Life* (London: Faber & Faber, 2009).

Norrie, Ian, *Mumby's Publishing and Bookselling in the Twentieth Century* (Sixth Edition, London: Bell & Hyman, 1982).

Norrie, Ian, *Mentors & Friends: Short Lives of Prominent Publishers and Booksellers He has Known* (London: Elliot & Thompson, 2006).

Norrie, Ian, *The Business of Lunch: A Bookman's Life and Travels* (London: Quartet, 2009).

Ogilvie, Sarah, *The Dictionary People: The Unsung Heroes Who Created the Oxford English Dictionary* (London: Chatto & Windus, 2023).

Painter, George D., *William Caxton: A Quincentenary Biography of England's First Printer* (London: Chatto & Windus, 1976).

Pettegree, Andrew, & Arthur der Weduwen, *The Library: A Fragile History* (London: Profile Books, 2021).

Rausing, Sigrid, *Granta 163: Best of Young British Novelists* (London: Granta, 2023).

Raven, James, *The Business of Books: Booksellers and the English Book Trade 1450–1850* (London: Yale University Press, 2007).

Raven, James (ed.), *The Oxford Illustrated History of the Book* (Oxford: Oxford University Press, 2020).

Rentzenbrink, Cathy, *Dear Reader: The Comfort and Joy of Books* (London: Picador, 2020).

Roberts, Colin H., & T.C. Skeat, *The Birth of the Codex* (New York: Oxford University Press/British Academy, 1983).

Rooney, Paul Raphael, & Anna Gasperini, *New Directions in Book History: Media and Print Culture Consumption in Nineteenth-Century Britain* (London: Palgrave Macmillan, 2016).

Sadek, Nadim, *Shimmer, Don't Shake: How Publishing Can Embrace AI* (London: Forbes Books/Mensch Publishing, 2023).

Samuel, Bill, *An Accidental Bookseller: A Personal Memoir of Foyles* (London: Puxley Productions Ltd, 2019).

Sandbrook, Dominic, *Never Had It So Good: A History of Britain from Suez to the Beatles* (London: Little, Brown, 2005).

Sandbrook, Dominic, *White Heat: A History of Britain in the Swinging Sixties* (London: Little Brown, 2006).

Sandbrook, Dominic, *State of Emergency: The Way We Were: Britain 1970–1974* (London: Allen Lane, 2010).

Sandbrook, Dominic, *Seasons in the Sun: The Battle for Britain, 1974–1979* (London: Allen Lane, 2012).

Sandbrook, Dominic, *Who Dares Wins: Britain, 1979–1982* (London: Allen Lane, 2019).

Slater, Michael, *Charles Dickens* (London: Yale University Press, 2009).

Smith, Emma, *Portable Magic: A History of Books and their Readers* (London: Allen Lane, 2022).

Smyth, Adam, *The Book Makers: A History of the Book in 18 Remarkable Lives* (London: The Bodley Head, 2024).

Solnit, Rebecca, *Orwell's Roses* (London: Granta Books, 2021).

Spurling, Hilary, *Anthony Powell: Dancing to the Music of Time* (London: Hamish Hamilton 2017).

Stevenson, Iain, *Book Makers* (London: British Library, 2010).

Stone, Brad, *The Everything Store: Jeff Bezos and the Age of Amazon* (London: Bantam Press, 2013).

Stone, Brad, *Amazon Unbound: Jeff Bezos and the Invention of a Global Empire* (London: Simon & Schuster, 2021).

Taylor, D.J., *A Vain Conceit: British Fiction in the 1980s* (London: Bloomsbury, 1989).

Taylor, D.J., *Orwell: The Life* (London: Chatto & Windus, 2003).

Taylor, D.J., *The Prose Factory: Literary Life in England Since 1918* (London: Chatto & Windus, 2016).

Taylor, D.J., *Orwell: The New Life* (London: Constable, 2023).

Thompson, John B., *Merchants of Culture: The Publishing Business in the Twenty-First Century* (Cambridge: Polity Press, 2012).

Thompson, John B., *Book Wars: The Digital Revolution in Publishing* (Cambridge: Polity Press, 2021).

Tolentino, Jia, *Trick Mirror: Reflections on Self-Delusion* (London: Fourth Estate, 2019).

Tomalin, Claire, *Jane Austen: A Life* (London: Viking, 1997).

Tomalin, Claire, *Charles Dickens: A Life* (London: Viking, 2011).

Tombs, Robert, *The English and their History* (London: Allen Lane, 2014).

Walsh, John, *Circus of Dreams: Adventures in the 1980s Literary World* (London: Constable, 2022).

Waterstone, Tim, *The Face Pressed Against a Window: The Bookseller Who Built Waterstones* (London: Atlantic Books, 2019).

Watt, Ian, *The Rise of the Novel: Studies in Defoe, Richardson and Fielding* (London, Chatto & Windus, 1957).

Williams, Abigail, *The Social Life of Books: Reading Together in the Eighteenth Century Home* (London: Yale University Press, 2017).

Wilson, Charles, *First With the News: The History of W.H. Smith 1792–1972* (London: Jonathan Cape, 1985).

Winterson, Jeanette, *12 Bytes: How Artificial Intelligence Will Change the Way we Live and Love* (London: Jonathan Cape, 2021).

Other Sources

Biblio File (podcast) – thebibliofile.ca

Book Brunch – www.bookbrunch.co.uk

The Bookseller – www.thebookseller.com

The Bookshop (podcast) – thebookshoppodcast.buzzsprout.com

The Flip: www.the-flip.co.uk

In Our Time: Caxton and the Printing Press (BBC Radio 4): www.bbc.co.uk/sounds/play/b01nbqz3

Ladybird – ladybirdflyawayhome.com

The New Yorker

The New Statesman/*The New Statesman* Podcast

Publishing Perspectives – publishingperspectives.com

Retail Craft (podcast): internetretailing.net/media/retailcraft-podcast

Timeshift: The Ladybird Books Story – The Bugs That Got Britain Reading (BBC4): www.dailymotion.com/video/x66pkmy

Index

Note: italicised page references indicate illustrations